SHETLAND

Dedicated to the Ratter family, especially Lizzie, who left us too soon.

JAMES & TOM MORTON

SHETLAND
COOKING ON THE EDGE OF THE WORLD

Photography by Andy Sewell

quadrille

Publishing Director and Editor: Sarah Lavelle
Designer: Will Webb
Photographer: Andy Sewell
Recipes and Food Styling: James Morton
Additional Recipes: Tom Morton
Copy Editor: Samantha Stanley
Editorial Assistant: Harriet Webster
Production Director: Vincent Smith
Production Controller: Nikolaus Ginelli

First published in 2018 by Quadrille,
an imprint of Hardie Grant Publishing

Quadrille
52–54 Southwark Street
London SE1 1UN
quadrille.com

Cataloguing in Publication Data: a catalogue record for this book is available from
the British Library.

ISBN: 978 1 84949 967 5

Printed in China

Contents

Hello and welcome.

My name's James. I live in Scotland, but I grew up in a place called
Shetland. The Shetland Isles.

Shetland is like another country but isn't one. To find it, jump on the
boat from Aberdeen; you'll arc around Orkney and 12 or 14 hours later
arrive in Lerwick, the capital. Drive out of the ferry terminal and turn
right, take the main road north for 35 miles. At the end of the road my
family home is on your left. If you don't mind dogs, pop in and say hullo.

The person who answers that door is the person with whom I share
these rationed pages – my father, Tom. I apologise if it gets confusing; we
write in a similar way. Perhaps unsurprisingly, after we've both annotated
and amended each other's words.

This might be my fourth hefty book, but it is my father's... tenth?
Eleventh? Anyway, it's his first one about food, so I've been allowed to
stamp my foot. If you've any problems with the recipes, that's my
responsibility; angrily tweet me, not him. The split infinitives?
Controversial views on fishermen? Take that up with him.

Co-authorships in food books are not unheard of and they are not
even unusual. Fathers and sons working together in harmony on the same
subject, however, is a little odd. It was the brainchild of my friend and our
editor Sarah Lavelle, mostly because we both kept insinuating we were
about to write the same book. It made sense to write it together, in harmony.
It also follows that this is not a cookbook in the traditional sense.

This book is about place. It's about a culture and a community spirit
that has been all but lost in the rest of the UK. It is about how isolation has
caused evolutions and intricacies to develop that are very special and need
further appreciation. And it is about that which needs saving; about a
culture that with the onset of oil and the internet has faded into obscurity.

This book and its recipes are about Shetland, and what makes it the most
contented place in the world.

INTRODUCTION

A brief word about Shetland

Where is it?

It's in the sea, up from Scotland. No, further up than that: beyond Orkney, which is only a hop, skip and a jump off Caithness. Keep going right a bit. There you are – that long scattering of over 100 different islands and islets, only 15 of which are inhabited by humans or their approximate relatives. You are in Shetland. On a map you'll usually find us in the little box, near the oil.

The main sea port is Lerwick – the Isles' capital and only town. The historic centre is Scalloway, which is a village about 5 miles down the main road and which becomes more lovely with each passing year. Grey, cluttered, and at first glance very similar to many dreich towns in north-eastern Scotland.

Here we are, more than 100 miles (160 km) from the nearest coast of mainland Scotland, about 210 miles (340 km) north of Aberdeen; 230 miles (370 km) west of Bergen in Norway; 230 miles (370 km) south east of Tórshavn in the Faroe Islands. You'll often hear people who should know better (notably myself, in a past life as a journalist, where inaccuracy is a way of life) saying that the nearest railway station to Lerwick is in Bergen. This is nonsense. The nearest railway station is in Thurso, Scotland.

Don't you mean 'The Shetlands'?

No. It's not, never has been and never is 'The Shetlands'. Despite what it says in your newspaper, magazine, dictionary or that guy you met down the pub who says he used to work in the North Sea oil industry. It's 'Shetland', singular.

It's singular in Norse (Hjaltland) and Faroese (Hetland) – 'Shetland' is simply a phonetic transliteration taken from a drunk Norseman with no teeth by an even drunker Scot with a shaky quill. 'Hjalt' and 'Het' both mean the hilt or cross guard of a sword, which is reminiscent of the archipelago's shape and captures the place's strategical importance in the warlike raiding of the (much more fertile and lucrative) bits of land to the south.

From a Celtic southerner's point of view (that is to say, in Gaelic) the uncivilised lumps of rock north of Orkney were known as Inse Catt: 'Islands of the Cat People'. This is a reference to the nasty, wee hairy Picts who survived in Shetland longer than anywhere else inside their upside-down, stone-built flowerpot redoubts: the ones known as brochs. Until the Vikings got round to wiping them out.

Incidentally, whilst research has proven that the Shetland population contains large quantities of Scandinavian genetic stuff, there is a theory that the Norsemen who stayed in (but not 'on'; never 'on'...) Shetland were rubbish Vikings. They were the ones who whinged, the ones who got seasick, the ones who got ill, the ones nobody liked. The fearties who wanted off at the first landfall, or were unceremoniously dumped so the brave, fully sea-legged lads could go on their merry way, pillaging. The ones who stayed in Orkney were the farmers who saw all that fertile greensward and thought, "Och aye, this'll do. We shall establish a bourgeoisie!"

But, as I say, that's only a theory.

Does Shetland have any proper history?

Shetland's got more going on than you can shake a tushkar at. (Tushkar, similar to *tuisgear* in Gaelic: a tool used to cut peat.) But, basically, it comes down to this: Picts (wee hairy cat-like creatures), wiped out by Vikings, mostly. One or two are thought to have survived at the tundra round the back of Ronas Hill, the highest point in Shetland.

Up until the ninth century, the Vikings are content to plunder. Then, as more and more of the weak, seasick and feartie Vikings get left behind (one view), or big, strong, well-balanced and quite brave Vikings fall for the undoubtedly attractive local women and decide to stay, they decide they might as well just take over (the other view).

Fine. Shetland, and indeed, much of Scotland, including the Western Isles, is overrun by big hairy Vikings with axes, magic mushrooms and a tendency to decapitate monks. Then the barons fall out and there are around 300 years of general mayhem and malarkey between the kings and princes of Norway and various sulky lords based in Orkney and Shetland.

And so to the thirteenth century, an all-out war between Alexander of Scotland and Haakon of Norway for control of Scotland. Haakon is over-extended at the Battle of Largs and skulks back to Orkney, giving up Scotland and the Western Isles. Nothing much happens for a couple of hundred years, and then comes the big event, the effects of which still reverberate down to today's Shetland.

It's 1469, and the bankrupt king of Norway, Christian, needs to sort out a bit of a political stand-off by marrying off his daughter to William, King of Scots. There's no money for a dowry so, having already pawned Orkney to raise some gold, he does the same with Shetland. From this point on, Shetland is essentially under Scots control, though the marriage never happens, and there are frequent attempts right up until the nineteenth century to redeem the pledge with large lumps of currency. Still, that's it. Shetland becomes and remains Scottish, despite retaining a land tenure system and legal system based on Norse principles.

Some would like to claim that this means Shetland is not bound by British laws; it is true that Udal law still holds a certain sway on things like foreshore access and rights to driftwood. It was also deployed during a celebrated court case, which came very close to denying the Crown Estate Commissioners authority over the seabed when it came to aquaculture. But not quite.

From the sixteenth century, various Scottish lairdy folk grab Shetland (including an Earl of Morton, a Douglas from the Scottish border). Then there's famine, fishing (loads of herring, then none), more famine, more fishing, two World Wars: Shetland still the hilt of the sword, still strategic, full of soldiers and naval activity. Then the discovery of oil and everyone lives wealthily or not so wealthily, happily and unhappily ever after.

That, my friends, is the history of Shetland. Oh, and some radical socialists get obsessed by the romance of the Vikings just after World War I. They see them as symbolic of revolutionary freedom, and start a festival where everyone dresses up, has a party and burns a galley. That's called Up Helly Aa.

And that's another story altogether (see page 251).

A note about food

As we go through this book, you'll notice it's a recipe book but it's not. From both of us, it's a love story.

There's a lot going on. 23,000 people live here. More fish is landed here than in England, Wales and Northern Ireland combined. We're at the forefront of almost all renewable energies, except solar: the average number of hours of sunshine for December is fifteen. Yes, fifteen.

As you'll come to see, Shetlanders are fiercely proud. And despite the darkness, we are happy. This is perhaps because there are more jobs than people, and partly because we do all the best things in life so well. Music. History. Art. Community. Food. Drink. Jumpers.

There is one aspect of our culture that we do particularly well: celebration. Shetlanders enjoy a bit of revelry. Shetlanders make you feel welcome, like you can only say the right thing and it's never getting late. We call this concept 'foy', an old Scots word that's still in frequent use on the isles today.

Make no mistake: we don't have any Michelin-starred restaurants. We don't have a strong restaurant scene. We don't do dishes – collections of ingredients put together on a plate so that flavours balance off each other. Some attempt has been made to be gastronomic recently and we both hate it.

Shetland's food stems from survival. Even today, the realities of living in a place cut off from the rest of the mainland by a very long and particularly rough sea journey, will hit home. We can provide some things for ourselves, but it pays to be prepared. It pays to make sure there's a way to sustain sustenance until you can get some more.

Welcome to a journey around Shetland food and the people that make it so good.

James and Tom Morton

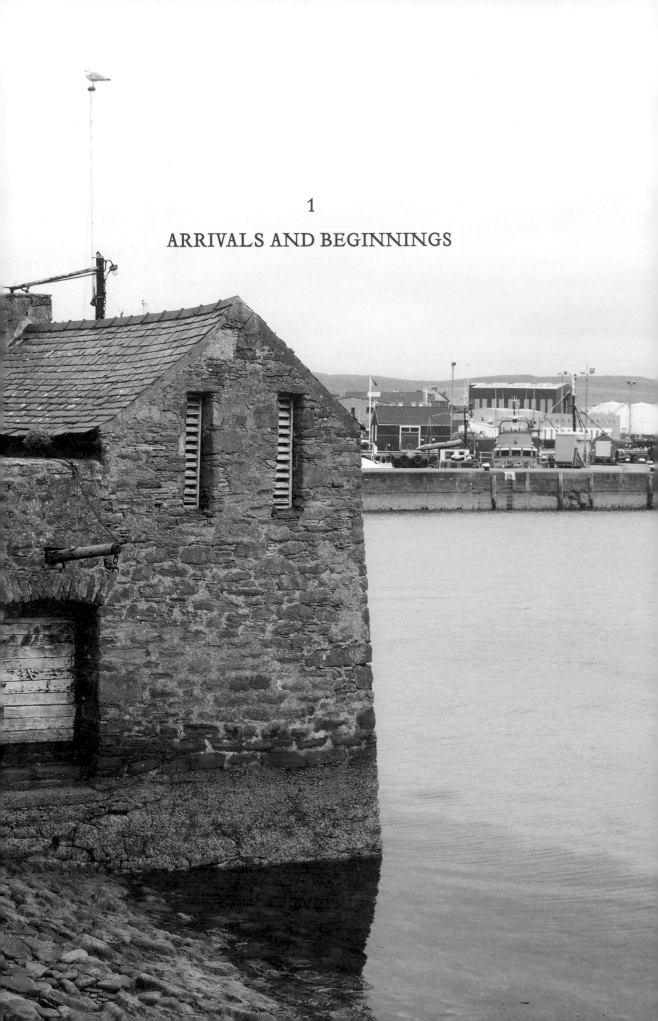

1

ARRIVALS AND BEGINNINGS

Tom

I arrived in Shetland for the first time in the middle of winter, with the island in a frenzy of mud, oil and construction activity. It was 1978, and the biggest oil terminal in Europe was being carved out of peat and rock by some 10,000 travelling workers, housed in two giant camps, at Firth and Toft. It was a black gold klondyke, with fortunes being made and lost, unskilled labourers earning up to £1000 a week, and I was sent to write about it.

The very sociable culture of the island, the reality of its difference from the mainland, hit me first on the ferry north. I had been meant to fly; in fact I'd started out from Glasgow Airport, but the old Viscount hit turbulence on the way north and was forced to make a lumbering landing at Inverness. We were bussed to Aberdeen and told to expect 14 hours on the P&O boat St Clair.

"She's only operating on one engine at the moment," I was told. Really? How long does it take with two engines?

"Fourteen hours. Aye, boy. We'll hae a peerie foy. Whit aboot a dram?"

The man, middle-aged, rosy-nosed, was wearing a Fair Isle sweater (known locally as a gansie, as in 'Guernsey') in an eye-watering electric blue. I never knew his name. Only that he was a fisherman, his boat was in Peterhead, and he was heading home for a wedding. "Three nights, a muckle foy in Whalsay." It would be years before I learned that the tiny island of Whalsay was home to many millionaires, due to the preponderance of gigantic pelagic uber-trawlers. Whalsay is famous for its wonderful golf course, and the best charity shop in the history of the world.

Through a force eight gale we wallowed, plunged and slammed. And ate. And drank. Unified by our dodgy flight and undulating bus trip, we former flyers were given food and drink vouchers, which we spent on enormous North Sea steaks, chips, beer and Stewart's Rum, my first encounter with this strangely settling black spirit.

I don't remember feeling sick. I remember the darkness, and the metallic-taste of bad beer. Drybroughs Heavy – "the heavy that's Scotland's own", according to a popular ad of the time. The smoking indoors, because everyone smoked: Golden Virginia, Samson or Duma roll-ups. And the sweet, comforting fire of that blackest of rums.

"I dis dy first time in da nort isles?"

Yes, I must have replied.

"No dy last, boy, no dy last."

Somebody had a fiddle, and played, I remember thinking, astonishingly well considering the shifting, clanking mountain of tins beside his chained-down chair. I woke to a darkness that over the course of the morning, never quite lifted beyond a murky twilight. Lerwick glowered, stoney, towny, glum. I hired a Mini and drove north into traffic jams of huge Russian earthmoving trucks. Night fell again around 2PM, by which time I was in a quarry near Brae, talking to the Liverpudlian manager, who seemed completely enthused by his exile to a battered portable accommodation unit in the far north of what seemed like nowhere.

"My first week, in the summer, I was asked to a party, and they spit-roasted a sheep, mate, at midnight. Sociable? I've never been anywhere as sociable as this. And I'm from Liverpool, lad. Fancy a beer?"

And so it went on. Cups of strong, sweet, Rayburn-stewed-for-hours tea, my first bannock and the savoury blast of tattie soup. And the sense that visitors were both expected and welcome; that your presence was never an imposition. Shipwreck, fishing and harbour culture, where the sea brings company that may or may not remain forever. Where the return from a voyage is something to be greeted with joy, relief – and a celebration.

Nine years passed. Shetland haunted me, hunted me through citybound dreams, never nightmares. A place of welcome. A place without judgement.

"There's no key," Susan said on the telephone (landline, of course; this was when mobiles were the size of briefcases). "Nobody locks their doors. Just go in and make yourself at home." We had met at a gig in Glasgow; Susan was a doctor visiting from the far-flung Shetland islands.

"Ah, The Shetlands," I said. "I've been there!"

"If you had, you'd know it's never 'The Shetlands'," came the brusque reply. "It's Shetland, singular." By this time a BBC producer in religious affairs, I invented an excuse for a 'recce'. This was early autumn, often the most beautiful of Shetland seasons: hairst, when long, dry, still periods of weather combine with the 'steekit stumba' (heavy mist) to provide a full moon of such surpassing pinkness it could grace a Nick Drake album cover.

And, of course, Susan and I fell in love in Shetland. There were peerie and muckle foys all week long, often at the BBC's expense. The joint of seaweed-fed Foula mutton, procured from some mysterious source on the ultra-bohemian west side of the principal Shetland island (known as the Mainland). Never had I tasted such meat, from the small, hardy, pure Shetland sheep, pungent and herbal with nothing added in the cooking save heat. The long journey to the mysterious outpost known as Burrastow House, where, in an oak-panelled, peat-firelit room, we plucked pearls from local mussels, ate roast hare shot by the owner, Harry Tuckey, served with Shetland black tatties and kale. Gatherings in Susan's gigantic house (rented from the Health Board for £12 a week). A hall dance, somewhere (even now I'd better not say exactly where). Several hundred people, a fleet of Citroën 2CVs outside, with someone bouncing on the canvas roofs. Soup, bannocks, cakes, mutton, cold, now, and if not as magical as the Foula roast, succulent and tender, and perfect for soaking up the rum... Dancing and dancing and dancing. What seemed like the best band in the world. Boston Two-Steps to a rock'n'roll tune; was it Deep Purple's 'Black Night'?

"Is dis dy first time in Shetland? Weel, it'll no be dy last, boy. No dy last."

And it wasn't.

James

Shetland is my escape. I work in Glasgow as a doctor, a lot. As time becomes shorter and I see a more rigid routine stretched ahead, I find solace in returning home. I can go there and claim to be uncontactable, even if I am not, and I can escalate to off-grid if I so choose. When I'm overwhelmed by over-commitment or by my disorganisation, I can step back into a place of peace and family. I can imagine, at least, that I'm back at South House – the little red house with the plastic conservatory and the Singer sewing machine that looks over the beach and across the water of Ronas Voe to the steep slopes of Shetland's highest hill. This is where I grew up.

Marked on crude maps from the sixteenth century, South House is a tiny stone croft that sits on a bed of radon-emitting red granite on the side of a hill above the sea. The house stands at the end of a single track road, about 35 miles north of the main town of Lerwick. Heylor, the collection of about five houses including ours, used to be a vibrant fishing community, the ruins and remnants of which can still be seen. Most of Shetland is an unexcavated archeological treasure-trove, and Heylor is no exception.

Heylor sits above the Blade – a cleaver-shaped beach of sand and pebble that's deserted 99 per cent of the time. As children, this was our playground: the old, mussel-encrusted stone pier with steps from which we could jump into the wet sand at low tide. At high tide, we'd use it to launch the boat, or build dams to block the various crevices that formed as the water rushed in. The beach is home to nesting Tirricks (Arctic Terns) during early summer and therefore off limits: venturing close to their nests of shells meant certain injury, nay death, from the divebombing bastards.

Between the house and the beach lived the pigs. At 5 or 6 years old I remember my bewilderment at Mum and Dad's attempts at self-sufficiency. This might have been down to their general incompetence: the attempts to rear the pigs for pork only ever resulted in a fondness and eventual bond. The pigs were then kept as pets until they died of old age. Not a pork chop nor strip of bacon passed my lips, and my mother still refuses to eat white meat because it reminds her of dear old Derek.

We kept geese, but they just destroyed the garden before escaping using their only partially clipped wings or being killed by the local Bonxie (Great Skua). Another batch actually made it to the dinner table, but they were so tough from their old age and sea-breeze hardening as to be inedible. The chickens were a little more successful – they managed to produce eggs to feed the family. But they, too, were gradually picked off. One by one, they succumbed to our mad St Bernards.

Compared with Heylor, Hillswick is positively urban. It has a shop, with petrol pumps. It has a hotel with a bar and restaurant, and a public hall. Like every pillar of civilisation, it has its own galley shed where the local Viking longship lives and would-be Vikings gather to discuss alcohol and axes. And it has a doctor's surgery, in which my Mum works as the local GP. It has a school, and I was one of only 32 children who attended it. So engrained was the register that I didn't ever have to check any class photographs.

I watched my mum acting as the single-handed GP, accident and emergency, minor-surgeon and emergency retrieval unit for a population of about 800 people over a vast land area. To me, she's just Mum. The doctor, the mother. To everyone else on that island, I know she has been much more. Now I've grown up a little, I'm almost moved to tears when I think of the influence my mother has had. The respect that she garners from locals whose families had lives saved or ended well and the respect passed on to me. The defiance in the face of threats of closure, resulting in year upon year of 24-hour on-call. Growing up, I was troubled by the constant phone calls to our house from the same one or two patients demanding immediate consultations, and who inevitably had nothing wrong with them. I thought this was not the life I wanted to lead. Now, the community and responsibility is something for which I long.

It was a deeply privileged upbringing – short school days with teachers who had few pupils. The bus would drop me at Gran's house about 100 yards down the road. Gran would spoil us with Jaffa Cakes and Dairy Milk. In return I'd make the tea – she liked half tea and half milk, she said, though I could never bring myself to commit. We'd sit and watch old videos about trains. Over and over again.

Gran would bake with me. I'm not sure why it was with me above my siblings – my older brother Magnus never seemed interested, and by the time our younger sister Martha could reach the countertop, Gran's health had started to go downhill. But during those brief, wonderful years, I learned the basics: Scotch pancakes. Crêpes. Apple pie, with pastry made from butter or Stork with lard. Victoria sponge. Lemon meringue pie if I'd been particularly well-behaved.

Thanks to Gran, I grew up with these tools in my arsenal. Whereas Dad came here from afar, and was stunned by its peculiar wondrousness, I grew up encased.

2

FOY ON THE BEACH

foy: how you deal with the darkness and the cold, the isolation and the ever-present threat-and-promise of the sea. In Shetland, you celebrate everything. Survival, being together in ones, threes or hundreds.
Or just being together. Being home.

James

Though the culture of foy permeates the Shetlandic way of life, ask a young Shetlander what 'foy' is, and they would describe an event. Massive, open-air, running across several days. It would be held in a local crofter's field, donated out of good grace or for personal renown. Massive marquees, barbeques and food stalls are essential, as is a beer tent, live folk music and the same hired bouncy castle every time. Camping facilities are evidenced by the empty beer cans that pepper the heather fields the following day.

Spectacular backdrops mark the greatest settings. The Fethaland Foy, held around the uninhabited ruins of an old fishing community. The Mavis Grind Foy, at the metres-wide connection between the peninsula of Northmavine and the rest of the Mainland. And the greatest location: Uyea (pronounced *oi-ah*). Only brief excerpts of the Uyea Foy exist in my memory, and I cannot find any photographic evidence to confirm its occurrence. But I remember travelling slowly down a dirt track for what seemed like hours in a rickety old VW Camper to the sheep-inhabited isle of Uyea. The only link to the mainland is a tombolo – a beach with sea on both sides.

But to limit foy to these single, magnificent events is to misunderstand it. Foy culture is Shetland culture. The number of huge, social events in a given year is limited, and the community is small and tight-knit. Therefore, everyone's going. It'd be rude not to. No-one is ever made to feel unwelcome.

This works on both a large and a small scale. If you're inviting a few friends over, everyone's coming. Equally, you can't just invite friends round for dinner – you should mention it to the four or five other families in the social circle. Which is fine, because there's always enough food to go around.

That food. The food forms the basis of all celebrations and of foy, especially. This is why we are here.

Foys past

We know that foy existed as a concept in the late nineteenth century because there are numerous references to the feasts and festivals of the time in Shetland – the fishing communities at the top of the North Mainland would celebrate the return of their boats with a foy: a feast, a festival.

But 'foy' isn't a word of the Shetland tongue. Like many words and pieces of culture that Shetlanders claim stem from their Scandinavian heritage, it's Scottish through and through. It's a word of the modern Scots and its meaning is subtler than I've made it out to be: although it did once become used solely with respect to fishing, it was originally a feast that marked a farewell, rather than a return.

In the context of Shetlandic culture, I prefer to define foy as a 'coming together' feast. I imagine the return of strong fishermen from their season of dangerous fishing to their humble and homely crofts, the peat fires kept lit by the hardworking women who cooked, cleaned, built, fixed, raised the children and worked the land. The foy was a celebration of that return, necessitated too, by the glut of the fish. But there was also a foy before the beginning of the season, as a goodbye and farewell. After all, each expedition was dangerous, and death was commonplace.

The most famous is the Johnsmas Foy – a huge event in the pre-Victorian Shetland calendar that marked the arrival of the massive Dutch fishing fleet for the beginning of the herring fishery. Johnsmas, or St John's Day, is the celebration of St John the Baptist and falls near midsummer, the Simmer Dim. This feast is still celebrated today, but in a more touristy, plastic and council-organised way, possibly with comedy Viking helmets.

There would have been further foy-ing when the men returned: a goodbye to the sea, you might say; a festival to celebrate the glut and distract from the harsher, harder seasons ahead. It must have marked the severing of the bond with the deep blue, as the easier times of summer ended.

In mainland Scotland, before the word fell out of use, a foy was a feast to mark any end or parting. It could signify the end of an apprenticeship or period of training – a coming-of-age community celebration prior to the hard days of a working life. Most emotively, a foy could be a feast to say farewell to the daughter of the house before she was married. This was quite distinct from the celebrations of the marriage itself, though vital.

I imagine early foys were bittersweet affairs. Close gatherings, filled with stories of seasons past, marking closure before the beginning anew. Intimate, family remembrance of those who were not there – the absences from the imminent wedding. The six crewmen who never returned from a rough sea. The breakage of the bonds formed between men on long nights napping amongst the piles of dead fish on tiny, laden boats. The feast of the closing of the book.

I trawled for references in literature for further confirmation of my musings and found with glee Robert Fergusson's celebrated Scots language poem from 1773: 'The Farmer's Ingle' ('The Farmer's Hearth'). Robert Burns, eat your heart out: it's tremendous reading and worth ploughing through in its entirety, though a Scots dictionary will be an essential pairing.

Across its thirteen stanzas, Fergusson's poem portrays life as is lost in Scotland today. But it could be describing Shetland as it remains: the fireplace is still the heart of the home. The cutting, stacking and gathering of the peats. The chimney filling with the smoke and the steam from the heathery turfs above. The ploughmen fed by their wives around the hearth with hot meals and whisky. 'Wi butter'd bannocks now the girdle reeks' – an image and a scent that takes me and every Shetlander home to the warm wee croft of childhood.

Fergusson depicts a feast from the point of view of the farmer's wife, the protagonist, over a few verses:

> *On some feast-day, the wee-things buskit braw*   (children busked well)
> *Shell heeze her heart up wi'a silent joy*   (hoist)
> *Fu' cadgie that her head was up and saw*   (How cheery)
> *Her ain spin cleething on a darling boy,*   (own spun clothing)
> *Careless tho' death shou'd make the feast her foy*

This was the oldest reference I could find that directly compares feast with foy. It's pretty clear cut – death, whether meaning literal or metaphorical death, would make this her foy. Her farewell feast. The foy to mark what has been before; the wake. The word was even used as an alternative to old-Scots 'fey' - the fate of imminent or looming death.

All associations between foy and the morbid have long since disappeared. Suggest 'having a foy' at a funeral and any Shetlander would stare at you with typically polite confusion. Foy is a celebration, filled with optimism. It may be midsummer, where the light is never-ending, or midwinter, where the cheer and fire more than offset the near-eternal blackness of the sky. A foy still might mark a step onto the next stage in life, amongst family and friends and local people, in good spirits, with good food and good ale, but without having to say farewell.

There's always an excuse to have a foy, any day, for any reason.

Foys present

Much before the eighteenth century, there aren't easily obtainable references to foys, but that doesn't stop the imagination working. These feasts of celebration and farewell and season's end will have existed across the world and at all times of civilisation. The Vikings almost certainly had an equivalent.

My Dad and I were inspired to backdate the concept of foy to Viking times by a very local discovery. If you go out of our house, down to the corner of the road where the single-track bends to the right, and then over the hill, you come to another set of three or four houses and a deep red sandy beach. Just above the beach, next to a stream that seems to carve a crevice in the peat, is a rectangular hole in the ground.

We didn't stumble across (or into) this whilst out walking – it was thanks to this book that we discovered it. During the first round of photography, near midsummer itself, Andy (photographer) and Nat, his partner, were flicking through a great mound of books that sat in our house, as a remnant of Dad's former bookshop. One particular book was on Shetland hikes, and it contained a picture of this pit.

Any baker would recognise it: one foot by three feet, and lined along its sides and floor by large stone slabs. An oven. It was a pit oven, of the most basic design. The idea was that you light a large and roaring fire in it, to heat the slabs at the side and a few more rocks you've placed in the fire itself. Then, you place your food onto the embers, with a ceiling of heated rocks on top, before burying the whole thing. The heat of the rocks and embers slowly roasts your food over the coming hours, and you can dig out your hot meal as the sun sets.

This seemed like the perfect excuse for a Summer Foy. Egged on by Andy, I suggested we cook in the old pit ourselves, but Dad forbade this on the grounds that Historic Scotland might ritually sacrifice us – a not uncommon sanction for defacing historic monuments. Where, then, could we recreate this celebration, without causing harm to the land or upsetting the neighbours?

The beach. The tide would clear away all remnants of our attempt, whether a success or a failure; it would be covered with sand or washed out to sea without a trace. The beach in question was obvious – the West Ayre, one of the most beautiful beaches in Shetland, and a short walk from our house. A swift trip home was simple, lest there be disaster or forgotten utensils. It has a plentiful supply of driftwood for starting fires, hopefully not already claimed by fellow sea foragers. At low tide, West Ayre becomes a white sandy beach, and then with the high tide the sea comes up as far as the smooth granite stones that would be perfect for pit building. And the view… The view that I took for granted growing up. Now I stare with awe.

As enthusiasm amongst us grew at the idea of the pit, so the forecast looked optimistic for the following day. It coincided with the tide times – a high tide in the early afternoon meant we had a good 10 hours of pit building and cooking time. We spent the evening beforehand researching and planning.

For methods, we turned to that reliable source of pit-cooking knowledge: Netflix. We watched an episode of *Chef's Table* that follows Francis Mallman to a private island in Patagonia, where he roasts entire carcasses of meat and vegetables and fish over massive fires. There's no foil, no plastic wrap, just fire and char. Even if we didn't get much practical pit-building information, we got the aesthetic.

Then, all the rest of the internet. We trawled through the pits used across the world: the New Zealand hangis, which can be truly enormous feats of engineering or tiny things built for a lone countryman. Their sandy beaches and big round stones looked almost identical to those a few minutes away, near its antipodes. There are the Neolithic forest pits that were often built throughout the British Isles – these seem to be the fixation of knife-wielding, adenoidal bushcraft obsessives, who provided nearly all the published information available. But they seemed more intent on showing off how well their intricate carving knives open the plastic packets of Tesco chicken.

We found relatively little on the Viking pits, other than evidence that they did indeed use them. We found nothing linking pit ovens and foy, though I hope that in a couple of centuries, some researcher might find this tome (or our buried pit) as evidence of their bond. Better yet, I dream of a day, not too far in the future, where beaches are populated late into the evenings at low tide, somewhere near midsummer, and people are gathering in families and circles of close friends around fires, then embers, and a few hours later they have one of the greatest and most satisfying feasts of their lives. For that is how well ours went.

A Viking pit feast

Step one: preparation

Find a beach that's not too far from the road, because you're going to forget things. Make sure it's got a reasonable tidal range, and it's not too public. I wouldn't do this on Brighton beach – go a bit further afield. You're going to need a good quantity of healthy, non-rotting seaweed, so a bit of rockiness is also essential.

Once your location is secured, think about your packing list. You want to avoid as many trips to the shop as possible. See my list (left).

This will give you enough to get going. Head to the beach and set up camp. Start an hour or two after the tide has begun going out, below the high tide line but not so far down the beach that your pit is at risk of filling with seawater.

Scour the beach for anything you can burn. Driftwood, specifically, and especially dry stuff that's sitting above the high tide line. Avoid tyres. Under ancient Shetlandic law, if someone has turned a piece of driftwood so that it lies perpendicular to the sea, it's claimed. Don't steal other people's wood, but don't use the wet stuff that's just been washed up either. This all does depend on a relatively quiet beach with an abundant dry driftwood supply. If all else fails, you'll have to forage further afield or bring your own.

Whilst you're looking for wood, keep an eye out for seaweed. Pretty much all fresh seaweed is safe to eat, so long as it is indeed fresh. The retreating tide will reveal seaweed that's attached firmly to rocks, and stuff that floats flaccidly, honking. You want the former – taste it raw, and try a few different varieties if the choice is there. Note the ones that taste best.

Step two: the pit

Mark out a rectangle below the high tide line. The size of your cooking area will be smaller than the area you mark because it will be lined with stones, so make it a bit bigger if you're in doubt. I used the edge of my spade, and Andy told me to keep making it bigger.

Dig out your pit – you want it at least as deep as it is wide. We went for a metre deep, with sloping sides so that the sandy walls didn't keep collapsing. We encountered some very heavy stones, which required levering out using the spade and a two-metre long piece of driftwood that had handily washed up on that very tide.

Once the pit is suitably deep, it's time to line it. The choice of stone is crucial – you must use a dense, solid stone without cracks or crevices. It should be dry. Good granite surrounded us, which was an excellent choice.

Selection of British and
  American craft beer
Bottle of Marlborough
  Sauvignon Blanc, chilled
Bottle of good claret
Bottle of gin
Bottle of tonic
Glasses, plastic
Waiter's friend
  (with bottle opener)
Matches
Firelighters
Dry kindling
  (essential driftwood backup)
Dry peat, or some other
  burning material
Axe
Spade
Swimming shorts
Towel
Plates
Cutlery
A sharp knife
Tongs (a stick will do)
Food (see page 33)

You could also use slate or basalt. Do not use limestone or sandstone (non-sedimentary rocks) as the air contained within can expand in the heat of the fire and cause mini-explosions (with potential for injury).

Line your pit with flat pieces of stone until it is completely covered. If you've made the pit that extra bit too big, another layer of rocks will aid in the airflow to the fire.

Next, build the fire. The traditional Shetland way of starting it would be to use red diesel, but I think kindling and dry driftwood (and firelighters) should suffice. Pile them up to cover the entire base of the pit, and light a match underneath. Then add plenty more wood. You'll need enough that you have a roaring flame that fills the pit. And then you'll need some more to build a secondary fire that you'll start once the pit is buried.

Step three: the food

Once you have good-going immolation, bask in its magnificence. When it is at peak-flame, you can add a few more stones. Don't add too many or you'll destroy the flames' air supply; add no more than a quarter of the total number you used to build the pit.

We added some dry peat because that's what we burn in Shetland. Peat itself needs a lot of heat to burn, but produces plenty of heat back, and for a very long time. Once that was on, we had a bit of a wait. When it was burning properly, we added a little more.

When the fire is burning well and the rocks are heating, you've got 30 or 40 minutes to prepare your food.

Our pilot beach-oven foy was constrained by the ingredients we had already or could source locally. Handily, Drew had popped around with 10 lamb shanks a couple of days before. Lamb shanks were the perfect cut, as any bigger joints would have necessitated longer cooking times than the tides allowed. We had tatties from the garden – big, red, floury ones – and a selection of root vegetables from the local shop: neeps (swede), carrots, red onion. Whilst we were there, we picked up some local pork ribs, which were marinated in a sweet barbeque-like sauce.

We'd been mackerel fishing that morning, and the abundance of enormous fish needed eating before their intense freshness subsided. Mercifully, the shop had lemons. For pudding, the second harvest of rhubarb was at peak-size, and would only diminish in flavour as summer wore on. It all came to the beach, along with salt and sugar.

We eschewed the aluminium foil for the most part, for we wanted the flavours of the peat and the seaweed to seep into our ingredients. But the rhubarb's best interests were served elsewhere, so Nat diligently chopped

the rhubarb stalks into chunks and placed them with sugar in tightly wrapped foil parcels. A little bit of dried, or fresh, ginger would have been nice.

The rest of the veg were chopped so they were at least sub-potato size. A few flavour parcels were wrapped so the umami of the onion would not be lost. Everything except the rhubarb was scattered with good sea salt.

We kept the mackerel separate – rather than roast the delicate fish with the hulking meat and the veg for hours, we agreed to smoke it over seaweed and driftwood in a secondary fire by the pit's side. This was started from the embers of the first, just before it was buried.

When the fire is little more than a large pile of burning embers, collect the seaweed you scouted earlier – you're going to need a lot: as much as three people can carry in both hands. Once it's picked, give it a wash in the waves and do not lay it down again on a sandy surface. No-one wants sand in their teeth.

Step four: the burial

Your embers should be glowing and crackling, but no flames should leap from the pit. It's ready

Start by picking out a piece of particularly red peat (if using), and use this to build a second small fire a few feet away. If you haven't got peat to hand, you can use a smouldering piece of charcoal. Don't worry too much about this, there are always firelighters. We'll come back to this in a while.

Back to the pit: use your shovel to fish out the hot rocks that you added once the fire was going, and set them aside. It's easy to forget just how stupendously hot these are once they've been sitting in the sand a while; don't touch.

Spread your embers into a flat pile. Place a couple of layers of fresh seaweed on top – just enough so that the glow and the white of the ash can still be seen. Stand back: be careful to avoid the rush of steam.

Start layering on your food. Put the parcels of rhubarb around the coldest edges of the pit, and spread the meats and largest root vegetables around the hot centre. Just chuck them straight on. Be very careful not to kick sand anywhere near the food.

Once all your food is in, cover with seaweed – lots and lots of seaweed. Imagine an impregnable fortress of seaweed that won't let any sand through. Once you've built that up, use your spade to place your super-hot rocks back on top.

At this point, you have a choice. You can bury the pit with sand, or keep adding more seaweed and big, cold rocks. We went for the former and regretted it. Sand is a nightmare to excavate cleanly. I expected to be able to just lift off the seaweed and the sand would come away too, like peeling the skin off a perfectly cooked piece of fish. That was not the case, and the sand got everywhere. Yes, it will provide near perfect insulation, but it's a pain in the arse in between your teeth.

Once the food is buried, keep your second fire going with more wood over the next couple of hours. We took this time to sit and to wander as a family and as friends. To convince each other to swim in the wonderful water and watch the sun slowly creep sideways above the cliffs. Beer, too.

Step five: a mackerel distraction

After an hour and a half or so of drinking and sunset-watching and keeping the wee second fire topped up, it was time for the prelude to the main event – the mackerel.

As far as dirty cooking goes – by which I mean the act of cooking directly over the heat source – this is relatively clean. Between the sweet flesh of the mackerel and the hot ash are two layers: fish skin and seaweed. Don't worry about it, is what I'm saying. You're not going to be eating ash.

Slice your lemon into gin-and-tonic-sized pieces. Place your slices in the centre of the recently gutted mackerel. If you haven't already salted the mackerel, add loads now.

Lay a single layer of seaweed evenly over the hot fire, and arrange the mackerel on top as soon as possible afterwards. The wet seaweed will prevent the mackerel from burning instantly but will char into its skin. Don't add any more seaweed on top – imagine this is a barbeque and the seaweed is acting as the grill.

Turn the mackerel after a couple of minutes, and check that it is charring adequately. If it isn't, your layer of seaweed might be too thick, in which case lift the fish, remove some seaweed and put the fish back on the glowing flames.

I like my charred, fresh, salty, seaweed-smoked mackerel as 'done' as little as possible – the flesh should still be just-clinging to the spine of the fish. Test for this by trying to pry the flesh from the fish while it continues to cook on the fire. If you can, even with moderate difficulty, it's done.

Plate up. Eat the fish using your hands. Accompanied by nothing.

Step six: excavation

Suitably merry and reeling from the sheer delight of the fish, it's time to tackle the pit.

Gather your family and friends around and arm them with plates and forks. Dust your spade of sand and use the tip to dig out the edge of your pit. Hopefully for you, this is a simple matter of lifting off the layer upon layer of seaweed and rock. For us, it was the undoubtedly more fun experience of digging at random, hoping the spade wouldn't go straight through the foil of the rhubarb parcels.

As you uncover the pit, it's magical; I think because no-one expects it to actually have worked. The first thing we dug up was a single potato – hot and steaming. Too hot to hold, but placed on a plate, the gentle pressure of a fork was enough to tear open the soft skin and reveal the steaming flesh within. This was the best potato I have ever eaten.

Next the meat – again, amazingly, cooked through and succulent. Another half hour and the lamb shanks and pork ribs would have been falling from the bone. A few were quite sandy, admittedly, but a quick rinse in the sea rid them of their teeth-grinding qualities. Besides, it turns out that sitting in the outdoors, tearing the flesh of a shank from the bone by your teeth is one of life's greatest pleasures.

Everything that came out of the pit was cooked and delicious. The carrots and neeps were sweet and soft. The shop-bought pork was smoky and tender. Each needed nothing added, but for a little salt, and each glorified itself. The potatoes needed no butter.

The tide was turning. We mooched as the evening wore on and the chill of the summer evening set in around the still-steaming pit, until the food and wine were gone and the sun was close to setting. When it dipped below the cliff tops for the first time, we buried the stones, sand and seaweed and burned the natural litter. What was left was packed up and the empty bottles clinking against the axe and spade was the sound of a happy crowd returning home.

The practical version

If you decide to attempt it, this will be a once-in-a-few-years event. For most, it will be a once-in-a-lifetime event. And not everyone has access to a suitable beach, or dry peat, or fresh mackerel, or many of the things we had. I'd still implore you to give it a go, one day, in your own time and in your own way. But until then, you can experience the essence of our creation with this practical home version of the mackerel.

Dirty mackerel over seaweed

This is virtually identical to our beach fish, though in urban form.
A barbeque is near essential, though you can do this indoors if you don't
mind a little smoke: just use my hot smoking method (on page 114), and
cover the wood chips with seaweed, fresh or dried, before placing your
mackerel straight on top.

If you choose to barbeque, you still need the wood chips specified here.
Charcoal barbeques give very little flavour, except for pure acrid tarriness,
so the gentle flames from fresh wood are essential.

4 large mackerel, whole
a few handfuls of seaweed,
    such as kelp (preferably fresh,
    dried will do)
1 lemon
good sea salt
a handful of wood chips, for
    smoke (I'd go for oak or beech,
    but any untreated wood will do)

Build your barbeque. People have set ways of doing this, and I don't care
how you do it. The only thing I ask is that you use natural charcoal, where
possible – avoid briquettes. In the spirit of dirty cooking, you could place
some tatties directly onto the flames as the barbeque burns.

Prepare your mackerel – gut them if this has not already been done.
Slice the lemon, and place two or three slices in the middle of each fish.
Coat heavily with salt.

Once your barbeque is at the stage that you'd think it was ready for cooking
– that ashen-white, just-glowing kind of stage – sprinkle on your wood
chips. You want enough to lightly coat the area where you're going to be
cooking your mackerel. Once these have just begun to catch fire (maybe
with the help of a gentle blow), lay your seaweed on top. This should be one
layer thick, no more. Immediately lay your mackerel on top of the seaweed.

Cook for 4–5 minutes on each side. If it's taking longer than this and no
char is developing, you might have too much seaweed. Take some out,
or place the fish directly on the wood chips.

I like my fish just slightly raw, but the longer you have them on the wood
and seaweed the more flavour you'll get.

Serve the mackerel as soon as possible; eat with your hands, with friends,
with no more than a squeeze of lemon to accompany.

3

BANNOCKS AND REEST

This is an entire chapter devoted to two simple foods: bannocks and reestit mutton. Both have been described as Shetland's 'national' fare, but I couldn't decide between them for that title. Though reest is more unique to Shetland, bannocks are taken more seriously here than anywhere else on earth. I'll let you make up your own mind.

The bannock

Bannocks are a Shetlandic staple, claimed in name by many Scots cultures, but owned today by just one.

The bannock is a mixture of flour and liquid. A chemical leavening agent is mainstream and the fluffy texture provided is expected. It has been a staple for generations throughout Scotland, and many hypotheses exist about why the bannock has largely died out but for in Shetland. Certainly, as commercial yeast became widespread across Scotland, sweetened, mass-produced loaves contributed to their demise. But in Shetland, yeasted breads never took off. Perhaps this was due to the lack of a decent artisan (a problem that continues to this day), or perhaps it was due to the poor state in which the yeast arrived after the journey north. Whichever, the quality of the homemade bannock prevailed.

Just a few generations ago, bannocks would have been made from whichever sorts of flour people could get their hands on. Down in Scotland, that'd be ground oats or barley, most likely. Up north, in Orkney and Shetland, it'd be beremeal, an ancient and hardy grain that has a harsh, spelt-like nutty flavour and a low gluten content, making for a dense crumb. Nowadays, refined wheat flour is the primary ingredient of choice, because it's the best. Honestly.

Cooking them over fire is traditional: a flat girdle (griddle) would hang above the hearth on the same smouldering peats that heated the house and water. As peat-fired ovens became mainsteam, so did the 'bottom' (or oven) bannock – a lighter version with a more even texture and greater rise.

I learned from the best: Linda, our babysitter. She taught my sister and me how to make 'girdle' bannocks, and did not hold back if I did it wrongly.

Linda was quite particular on a couple of points. The first was that you must always keep the mixture wet, because you could always add more flour and you might not have any buttermilk spare. Second, she insisted on a strict ratio of two flours – half shop-bought, generic self-raising of any scorned sort, and half 'Voe flour', a bleached, bicarbonate-heavy white flour packaged in the bakery about 17 miles down the road. Renowned for its positive bannock-enriching qualities, Linda insisted Voe flour was 'too strong' to use on its own and gave bannocks a soapy taste. Why that was I didn't know at the time. But I trusted Linda. Her bannocks were and are the best.

Bannock science

The chemistry of bannocks is very interesting. Believe me. It offers a perfect example to explain why chemical leavening works. There are no other factors involved – no egg-white protein complexes or fat-air emulsifications as in cakes, or yeast as in bread. There is only bicarbonate of soda and acid.

Bicarbonate of soda (or sodium bicarbonate or baking soda, or just 'bicarb') is a salt and a mild alkali. When it is heated up, such as in the oven or over a girdle, it breaks down into sodium carbonate, water and carbon dioxide. The last is a gas and is responsible for producing some lift. Bicarb should never be used in isolation, though, as the sodium carbonate (or washing soda) produced tastes just like soap. It might not be noticeable in the first bite, but it will become more unpleasant with time.

If you mix your bicarb with an acid, though, a different chemical reaction occurs. The precise one depends on the acid, but the crux is that you get twice as much carbon dioxide and therefore lift, and you get no soapy taste. Baking powder (baking soda) is therefore a mixture of bicarb and an acid such as cream of tartar.

You've got to be careful with raising agents. Although the reaction occurs more quickly in the oven, it will happen regardless of temperature. This is partly why cakes that are left for ages before baking will have expended all their active ingredients and won't rise, and it is why both self-raising flour and baking powder have an expiry date. The acid and the alkali may be dry, but they are in contact and very slowly reacting.

If you add more ingredients to the situation, bannock chemistry starts to get complicated (or fun, depending on your disposition). Buttermilk, one of the main ingredients of bannocks, is acidic. But it's not very acidic – balancing with bicarbonate alone will give insufficient rise for all but the densest of dense-bannock-lovers. You need to add baking powder on top – and more than you'd expect.

In practice, making sure you have plenty of rise in your bannocks is quite simple. Use the baking powder that's in self-raising flour – any standard sort – and make sure it's in date. Add a touch of bicarb – half a teaspoon for every 200g (7oz) of flour or so in bannocks and buttermilk-enriched muffins. Or, like Linda, you could use a mixture of 'Voe flour' and 'normal' self-raising flour, and forget about any additions.

Girdle bannocks

This is the simplest recipe, as close as I can get on the mainland to Linda's version. If you can find a hold of Voe (Johnson & Woods self-raising) flour, omit half of the bicarb and substitute half the self-raising for it.

550g (4½ scant cups)
  self-raising flour, plus lots extra
  for forming
½ tsp bicarbonate of soda
½ tsp table salt
280ml (1 cup) buttermilk
280ml (1 cup) whole milk

You'll need a girdle (flat griddle pan) or heavy-bottomed frying pan

Makes 12–16 large bannocks, depending on size

Mix your flour, bicarb and salt together in a large bowl with a wooden spoon until evenly distributed.

Add in your buttermilk – this might be a whole carton, in which case you can use the empty tub to measure out the milk. Add this in too, and stir together until you've got a lumpy mixture, but with no dry flour visible. The mix will look a bit like batter – that's OK. If you're too scared, add more flour until it looks like a manageable consistency. But if you want the lightest bannocks, keep it wet. Don't overmix – it should be lumpy and not smooth like a cake mix.

Heat your girdle or heavy frying pan over a medium heat. No oil or butter is necessary.

Spread a generous quantity of flour over a 20cm (8 inch) square area on a clean work surface – you want a lot of flour. Your layer should be 1cm (½ inch) thick, at least. Make a well in the top, then scoop about a quarter of the bannock mixture into the flour. Sprinkle with a generous amount more flour. Using floured hands, work your very floury lump of very wet batter into something resembling a round, approximately 15cm (6 inches) in diameter.

Use a butter knife, scraper or spatula to cut your round into quarters. Pick each up in turn, and transfer to your hot girdle. Keep a close eye on the heat of your girdle as you cook the bannocks – they should take approximately 5 minutes on each side to turn a speckled deep brown colour. Once turned, risen and brown on both sides, place the bannocks on their sides around the edge of the girdle. This gives space to get the next round on. (If making this first batch was too messy, add a bit more flour to the main batter before you form the rest of the bannocks.)

Once all the edges look done, place the bannocks under two folded tea towels to keep warm and continue cooking the rest of the batter. Leave the bannocks to cool to at least lukewarm before you eat them, or you may find them doughy in the middle.

Oven bannocks

When it comes to oven bannocks, there is one name that reigns supreme: Maria Parker. Also famed for her rather blinding, annual Christmas lights display, her name appears in the paper most often as winner of the Oven Bannock category at the Voe Agricultural Show. I'm fortunate enough that she works with my mother, so I'm a regular and grateful recipient.

I have not, however, had the resolve to ask for the recipe, for that, I fear, would be an affront. Therefore, a certain amount of reverse engineering is required. The Maria Parker Bannock is a different beast from the Linda Bannock. They're oven-baked, unbelievably light, fluffy and near crustless. Rather than the deep brown speckle of the girdle bannock, they have a more constant and golden sheen. More cake-like.

That leads me to believe they're enriched. Enriching means to add sugar, butter or eggs to your dough, as it does in bread-making. This can give greater lift, a softer crust and a more even texture. I can just about bring myself to add the first two, but an egg gives such a richness as to render the bannock unpairable with the rich foods for which it is designed, and a stiff dryness that after a day cannot be undone, even by warming. (Much like the dreaded scone.)

I will therefore add sugar – not for sweetness, but for a soft and golden crust – and butter, for adding lightness and cakiness to the texture. I will also substitute some of the whole milk for unsweetened natural yoghurt – this adds greater acidity and therefore you can add even more bicarb for more lift. Its tang counteracts the richness from the other ingredients.

This time, if you have access to Voe flour, you can omit all of the bicarb and substitute the self-raising directly.

550g (4½ scant cups) self-raising flour, plus extra for forming
1 tsp bicarbonate of soda
½ tsp table salt
25g (1oz) caster (superfine) sugar
50g (2oz) butter, unsalted or salted, cold
280ml (1 cup) buttermilk
150ml (⅔ cup) natural yoghurt
150ml (⅔ cup) whole milk

Makes 16 oven bannocks

Preheat your oven to 180°C (350°F)/160°C (320°F) fan/Gas 4. Find a couple of baking trays, and line with baking parchment. Very lightly sprinkle them with flour.

Into a large bowl, weigh your flour, bicarb, salt and sugar. Mix these roughly together with a wooden spoon.

Add the butter and rub this in with your fingers (as you would for pastry) until you've got something that looks like floury breadcrumbs.

Add all the liquid and mix together using a wooden spoon. You want the final mix lumpy and able to hold a little bit of shape, but you'll still need flour to handle it.

Continued overleaf

Heavily flour a work surface, and scrape all the mixture out on top. Add more flour, and pat down your 'splodge' with your hands. You want it roughly 1.5–2cm (¾ inch) thick.

Use a floured square or round cutter to cut out bannocks and place on your prepared trays. Alternatively, for a more rustic finish, use a sharp knife to cut out squares.

Bake your bannocks for just 12–15 minutes, or until light golden all over. Like their girdle equivalent, leave them to at least partially cool before scoffing, though a warm bannock served with melting butter is a sure way to make friends.

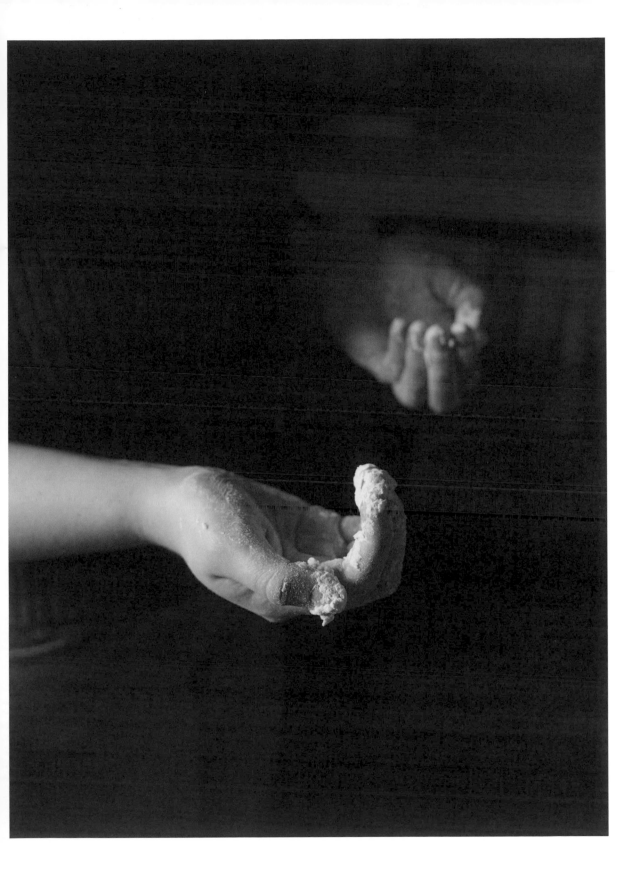

Reestit mutton

Reestit mutton (or just 'reest') is a strange, strange delight that is closer to Shetland's 'national' dish than anything else. It certainly fulfils two of the necessary criteria – its local love is ubiquitous and it isn't really understood by foreigners.

It is mutton – three years or older sheep meat, that is – on the bone, dry cured and then smoke-dried over a peat fire. It is never eaten in its most basic form – raw. I've known a few who attempted it and they are no longer with us. Instead, the preserved meat is boiled and boiled. The idea is to rehydrate the meat and flavour the liquor, which is used as the base for soups.

Reest is the world's greatest stock cube. A wave of umami, one might fashionably state. The density of flavour and salt is so great that many will bring their reest to a boil, then throw away all of the liquor the first or even a second time. They might use the clichéd excuses of inedible salinity, the reeking of rotting lamb and the concentrated carcinogens of a peat fire, but to me that's all good stuff. The first runnings should be saved and stored, at the very least, for dosing into future inferior stocks.

As with bannocks, there are plenty of variations. As mutton has become unfashionable and expensive and even difficult to get hold of in Shetland, lamb or hogget is used. Environmental health might have something to say about packaging meat for sale that has sat above a Rayburn for weeks, so now commercial producers separate the drying and smoking stages. Homemade reest is almost forgotten – I know of no one that does it regularly. So here we go.

Curers long in tooth will scoff and scream at this recipe. A common dry-curing ratio of sugar to salt might be 3 parts sugar to 2 parts salt. For this one, it's skewed slightly, at 1 to 8. That might seem like a lot of salt, but it's fairly standard for reest.

This is a basic recipe. There's no instrumentation for salinity monitoring here; there aren't even any real time frames. And don't worry, there's almost no chance of any infection or illness – let the salt do its work.

Reestit Mutton (top), fresh mutton (bottom)

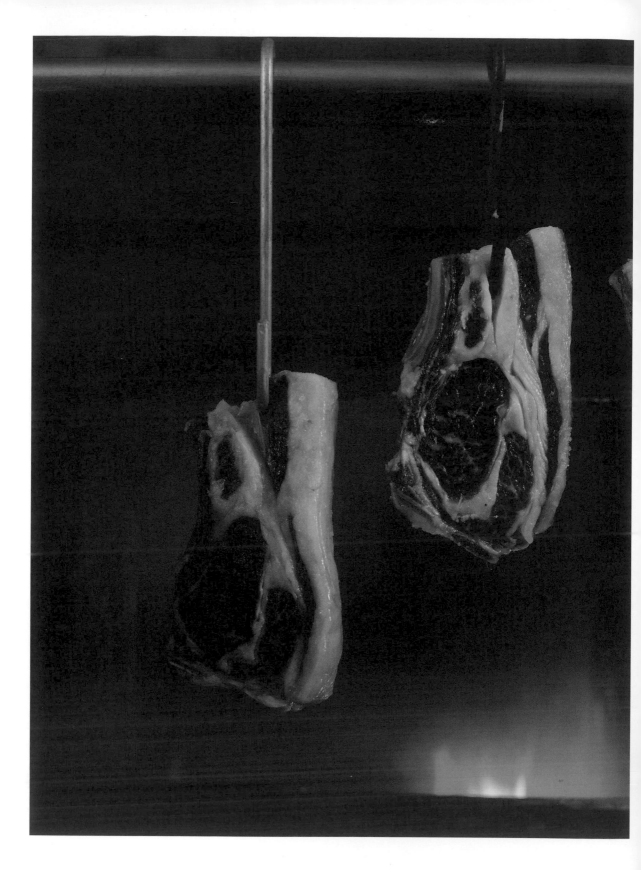

Reest science

Briefly, before we delve into the eating, there are a couple of things to get out of the way. That is, why curing works as a form of preservation and what effects it might have on your health.

This goes back to school-level biology, and I'm not going to patronise you or embarrass myself by going through the complete science of preservation. But I think a little understanding acts as reassurance that you're not going to die. You are not going to die.

Just before making reest, you've got your mutton and your salt. At this point, your meat, as with any fresh meat, has a number of pathogenic bacteria living on it (i.e. those that have the potential to cause you harm). But it will not have enough bacteria to cause any visible change to the meat, nor to make it smell, nor (probably) to cause you any upset if you're healthy. Every bacteria is dose-dependent – you need quite a lot, usually, to cause upset. These will be kept at bay initially by refrigeration and the competitive inhibition of the 'friendly' tenderising bacteria that live alongside.

When you add the salt to the meat, you'll see a film of water form between the two. Osmosis, right? This happens because water will always move from a less concentrated area to a more concentrated one until equalisation approaches. The salt draws the water from the meat. It also draws water from inside the bacterial cells, killing them.

The process of curing can be accelerated with pressure – adding a few heavy books on top will squeeze the water from your meat and the salt into it. As it continues, the meat becomes denser and saltier to the extent that only the hardiest bacteria can survive. Then, following the drying process, there's virtually no water left in the meat at all. Only salt.

By this stage, only a few bacterial spores will remain. Spores are like the lifeboats of bacteria – solid capsules that aren't good at growing, but are very good at staying alive, even in quite unbelievable conditions. The scariest of the spore-formers is *Clostridium botulinum*, which causes botulism, swiftly followed by death. However, so long as conditions remain suitably salty and dry all the way through the meat, spores are unable to turn into bacteria and multiply. Spores will not cause harm in themselves – harm is caused only when they form bacteria proper, and when these bacteria have a suitable environment in which to create their toxins.

Which is almost never in the case of reestit mutton. Not only will the curing and drying processes create such an inhospitable environment, but it is always boiled before eating, for a long period of time. Boiling destroys *botulinum* toxin, end of. And most other toxins, for that matter. You're not going to get food poisoning from reest.

And we've not even got onto the smoking process – the final piece that secures reest's reputation as the world's most preserved food. Smoking, especially dirty smoking from a smouldering peat fire, further impregnates the meat with a host of antibacterial compounds that prevent the spread of badness. Bad for your lungs = bad for bacteria.

Which brings us onto the proverbial elephant. The World Health Organisation says that smoked or preserved foods (as defined by the presence of nitrites) definitely cause cancer. The WHO are hard people to disagree with. When the policy changed, there was predictable furore and those headlines calling for bacon bans.

Let's be absolutely clear. The WHO's enormous collection of data suggested an increased risk of colorectal cancer by 18 per cent from the daily consumption of 50g (2oz) processed meat. Colorectal cancer accounts for 12 per cent of cancers in the UK. The lifetime risk, not taking into account risk factors such as smoking, alcohol, inflammatory bowel disease, fibre intake or inactivity, is approximately 7 per cent for men, 5 per cent for women (Cancer Research UK).

As a healthy non-smoker who eats well, I might reasonably expect my lifetime risk to be lower than average. Let's say it's around the womanly 5 per cent, or thereabouts. By eating bacon every single day, I would be increasing that to 5.9 per cent. A 0.9 per cent absolute, lifetime risk increase of cancer. For bacon? Smoked? Every day? I'll take that.

Reestit mutton from scratch

This is a recipe designed for those who cannot, through geographical or supply issues, get hold of good reest. It is also for those who have a glut of mutton and would like some meat to get them through a harsh winter. Ribs, shanks, legs and chops will all do, but the more bone and fat the better. Smaller pieces are ideal as you want around 500g (1lb 2oz) meat per pot of soup.

1.5–2kg (3lb 5oz–4lb 6oz) mutton pieces (on the bone lamb will do)

1.6kg (3lb 8oz) good sea salt (you might need more – table salt is fine)

200g (scant 1 cup) caster (superfine) sugar

peat – for burning

S-hooks to hang your meat from (mine are from Ikea)

Light your peat fire (see later). This can be done after the four or five days of dry-curing your mutton, but it will add to the ambiance and give your clothes a smokey scent. (If you don't have an open fireplace or Rayburn, follow my guide on page 121 on how to build and use a cold smoker, which you should fuel, or at least supplement, with peat.)

If you've just got one large piece of mutton, cut it into smaller pieces, no bigger than 500g (1lb 2oz) each.

Mix the salt and sugar together in a large bowl. Line a roasting tin with a large sheet of baking parchment (enough to fold over and cover the meat) and generously sprinkle with the salt/sugar mix.

Arrange the meat in the tin – try to pack it tightly – then cover with all the remaining salt and sugar. Make sure every piece of meat is covered.

Fold the baking parchment over the meat to cover it up, then place in the fridge. If your package is flat enough, a heavy weight on top can accelerate the curing process. I tend to just pile on my jam and chutney jars.

After about 24 hours, check on it. Any leaked fluid doesn't need to be drained because it's very salty and will act as a wet cure, but you can drain it off if it is causing a nuisance or getting all over your fridge. Turn the pieces of meat, and make sure you redistribute the salt so that any meaty gaps that have appeared are covered. You might need to add more. Leave for two more days.

Far less water will draw out of the meat over the next couple of days, but the meat will continue to become very salty indeed. On day three, turn it again and redistribute the meat, and maybe drain the liquid off. Remember what it looks like at this point.

Continued overleaf

The next day, if you feel it hasn't changed, slice into the thickest part of the meatiest bit of your mutton, and check it is the same dehydrated colour all the way through. If it is, you're done. If it isn't, give it an extra day.

If you haven't done so already, light your peat fire. If you haven't worked with peat before, first prepare a good fire with wood, and add your peat slabs only when it is very hot.

Don't rinse the meat before hanging it up – take any remaining dry salt and rub it around the meat to dry it slightly. This reduces dripping. Push one half of an S-hook through the meat and hang the meat to dry over your fire. (I use my Rayburn's tea-towel rail.) Leave the door of the Rayburn slightly ajar if your fire isn't open and let your lungs embrace the delicious pollutants. This is where environmental health will have their field day, for the meat should be heated to ideal bacteria-propagating temperature to dry quickly. Trust your salt, and use a probe thermometer to try and judge your ideal distance from the fire: too close and the meat will cook, too far away and it will take a ridiculous amount of time to dry. You want it no more than 20°C (68°F), ideally.

Hang the meat for two weeks. Keep the fire on as much as possible. If you thought the meat started off looking dry, you'll be amazed at how it turns flaky matte. It should really have no moisture left in it at all (any left could conceivably let bacteria thrive).

If you've gone the cold-smoking method, try and emulate the above. I'd suggest a few repeated smokings, each with a gap of at least a day in between. Make sure the meat is equally dry.

Store your reest in a cool, dry place for up to a year. If you're not confident in the bacteria-killing qualities of peat and salt and you want to keep it in the fridge, wrap it tightly in plastic wrap to keep the moisture out. It will store forever and ever in the freezer.

Reest and tattie soup

If this recipe is as far as you get through this wonderful tome then I'll be happy. It is simple and you shall not mess with it – I fear I've gone too far already by frying the onions. To me, reest soup means celebration; it means winter and family and fires and dogs. It means late nights and wild parties and Vikings and bitter, bitter cold. If you taste this soup, you can taste foy.

Thankfully, it couldn't be simpler. If you can't be bothered to make your own reest (see page 59), you might be able to order it online (see page 280). If you can't, you could make this soup using a dry-ish smoked ham instead, but it won't be quite the same.

300–500g (10½oz–1lb 1oz) reest
1 large brown onion
400g (14oz) floury potatoes
300g (10½oz) carrots
300g (10½oz) neeps (swede)
freshly ground black pepper

Makes a big pot with enough soup for 8 people

First, slice off a good sliver of fat from your reest and place this in a small pan.

Place the reest in a large pot, cover with water and bring to the boil. Boil for two hours at least, until the meat is tender. Skim off any smoky scum from the top, as well as unnecessary fat.

After a couple of hours, taste the stock created by the reest. If it is too salty, scoop a quarter of it out (save this – keep in the fridge or freezer) and dilute with more water. Repeat as necessary, to taste.

Melt the fat in the small pan over a low heat. Finely chop the onion and fry it in the wee pan until translucent and starting to turn golden brown. Scrape these into the meaty pot, and use a little stock to rinse out the onion pan.

Chop your tatties, neeps and carrots into large dice – you can leave the skins on to punish your children and bring back memories of my childhood – and add to the pot.

Boil until the vegetables are soft. Taste, and season with black pepper. It's highly unlikely to need salt.

Serve with bannocks (see page 48) and butter.

4
SEA

Come with me, if you will, to Fethaland. It's a strange, beautiful place at the northernmost tip of the Mainland. It takes about an hour to walk there from where you park your car at the very last cemetery.

Nearby are some of Shetland's oldest sites of human activity. A Neolithic axe factory. An ancient monastic settlement on some unclimbable sea stacks. The place a pirate crew buried one of their fellows to watch the Bonxies (Great Skuas) peck his eyes out.

And you reach Fethaland. You see the ruined stone booths of the old ling fishing station. This is where, each summer, the Haaf fishermen would live, going out overnight in their six-oared Sixareen boats: open, unsheltered, sometimes 40 miles out to sea in any and all conditions. Hundreds died here. You can see their names, or their initials at least, and the dates they were here: an outcrop of soapstone has been a place of human memorialisation for 200 years. Leave your own name there if you want. But read those old initials of the people who were, and weep.

Weep for the bravery of these fishermen, often working for landlords who only paid in goods and contempt. Recognise what debt Shetland owes to them, and how important fishing is to these islands.

We have two fish markets in Shetland – Lerwick and Scalloway. In 2015, landings here were of higher volume than those in England, Wales and Northern Ireland combined. More fish is landed in the islands than in any UK port apart from Peterhead, and Shetland fishing boats accounted for more than a fifth (22 per cent) of all landings by UK boats in 2015.

It's a big deal. And there is a lot of money involved. Small inshore creel boats can struggle to make a living and solo operators, especially in winter, can face real danger. Our friend Jim goes out at 3AM on one of Shetland's simmer dim ('midnight sun' – the Shetland twilight in midsummer) mornings, when the sea tends to be calm and the beauty of the ocean is there to be enjoyed. Jim no longer fishes full time; what he does, he does out of love. But some aren't lucky enough to pick and choose. They have to work in tough conditions.

Don't call me a fisherman - James

Cash. That annual quota hit after two weeks.
Fisherman means black fish. International landings onto rigged scales.
Unscrupulous baby seal bludgeoners. 24 hour shifts fuelled by
     what's behind the hidden door.
The destruction of the sea on which they sail.
Don't call me a fisherman, but I like fish. I like to fish.
Not for sport, without challenge. For food, not profit.
For liberty, not stress.

There is still a lot of share fishing in Shetland, particularly on the medium-sized whitefish boats. This is where a boat is family- or communally-owned, and each crew member gets a division of the spoils. Some of the huge pelagic super-trawlers (those that head out to open sea), capable of consuming their limited quotas for mackerel or herring in just a few weeks a year, are owned by multinational companies, but others, notably on the mega-rich island of Whalsay, are still family- or share-owned.*

Sustainability is an issue, and there are strict, warship-enforced quotas as well as voluntary schemes to reduce overfishing. It's fair to say that there has always been, and always will be, a tension between professional fishermen and scientists. The throwing back of dead, undersized fish, too small to legally land, is a perennial issue. And the whole running sore of

---

* To give you an idea of the sums involved, at the time of writing I heard that a new pelagic trawler had just been commissioned by the Whalsay family who owned the Adenia. This handsome, huge boat looked modern and supertrawler-like to me, though she was apparently built in 2003. The Anderson family sold the previous Adenia to a Norwegian firm, and commissioned the new vessel – just under 70 metres long and powered by a 7000 horsepower engine. She will have 10 fish tanks with a capacity of 2050 cubic metres. The boat will be built in Spain. Vessels like these generally come in at somewhere between £70–100 million. And still some of these communities have the cash to pay for such boats.

'black fish' – illegal landings – remains a painful infection in Shetland. Some local crews and the huge Shetland Catch processing plant in Lerwick were caught up in a massive black fish scam which ended with one skipper being fined – wait for it – a total of £47 million. Which they duly paid up. And moved on.

And then we have aquaculture. Shetland mussels – clean, environmentally friendly, healthy as long as you avoid those algal blooms. Shetland scallops – tried and abandoned, as has the industrialisation of sea trout and halibut. But then there's salmon – one of the biggest industries in Shetland. In 2015, the islands produced over 40,000 tonnes of farmed salmon, or 25 per cent of the total for the UK. When I arrived in Shetland, most salmon farms were locally owned. Now, none are. Three huge international companies have taken over the hundreds of cages scattered around the coasts. Shetland's clean, fast-moving coastal waters offer an ideal environment for mass cultivation.

We have to bear in mind some issues. Salmon eat other fish, and commercial feed comes from the industrial fishing of smaller species, like sand-eels. Those industrial fisheries have affected inshore, marginal fishing for human sustenance in developing countries. The current state is not sustainable, and there are projects in place to find alternative, plant-based foods. Supplements affect the colour of the flesh, and the fish are much fattier than the athletic, not to say sometimes emaciated, wild Atlantic salmon. That does make them tastier, mind you.

Salmon in the wild do not crowd together in one place, and therefore they do not dump loads of salmon crap and uneaten feed all over the sea floor as farmed fish do. This can devastate a seabed and cages need fallow periods and to be moved around. Also, there are discharge levels set by a controlling body (in Shetland it's the local council) for pollution.

Parasitic lice are a problem in both wild and farmed fish, as well as other diseases and these are treated with antibiotics. Natural treatments for disease, notably cleaner fish, such as cohabitation with lumpsuckers, which eat lice, are being developed with some success.

And then there are the seals. They will do their damnedest to get at farmed fish at sea. Predator nets stop most of them and there are the dubious 'seal scarers' – underwater speakers that play the sounds of killer whales. Take a trip near a salmon farm in a metal boat and you can hear the clicks and wails amplified through the hull. Despite these measures, seals can be and are sometimes shot. Legally and illegally.

All of which may make you wonder: should I be eating this farmed stuff at all? Despite my protestations, the answer is still a hearty 'yes'. Except this time, you've got fully informed consent. I've been out to the cages, met with and interviewed people at every level of the aquaculture industry in Shetland. They're all more than aware of the problems they face and, in my experience, take great care to overcome them in the cleanest, most environmentally friendly, most kind-to-creatures, healthiest way possible. There's no better place to get your salmon from, for in Shetland we strive towards the goal of true sustainability and balance in the environment.

James even tells me salmon's pretty good for us too. Something about those necessary oils.

There's one other thing. Something I don't like to talk about much because, to be honest, Shetland is almost full in the summer with tourists. Do we need hundreds more, travelling here as brown trout fisher-persons, enjoying some of the best and cheapest loch trout angling in Europe? I mean... do we? Let's shut up and eat salmon.

A note on the recipes

These are recipes we love and make regularly, if the opportunity arises. They are not fancy. They are not difficult. They have been taught to us or contributed by people who are important. Important to us, important to Shetland.

Bare cured salmon

This isn't about preserving – I'm not in the position of having surplus sides of salmon often. It is about deliciousness, as every recipe should be, and frugality. This recipe takes a small half-side of salmon, which might serve 3 or 4 people, and turns it into a centrepiece that will be enough grazing for a small foy-ous gathering.

Besides, I'm not even sure how long salmon that's been mostly cured and not smoked keeps for. It is best eaten within the first couple of days after making it – to be honest, I wouldn't leave it much longer than this. Rotting salmon sounds like the sort of thing I could get into, in an Icelandic sort of way, but not just yet.

approx. 400g (14oz) half a side fresh salmon, skin on
50g (1/3 cup) good sea salt
200g (scant 1 cup) granulated sugar
freshly ground black pepper, to finish

Serve with:
salt water biscuits (see page 204) or oatcakes (see page 233) and pickled beetroot (see page 176)

First, catch your salmon. Or buy it. Dry it using kitchen paper.

Mix the salt and sugar together evenly in a bowl. Place about a third of your mixture into a freezer bag, spread flat on a surface. Place your salmon inside the bag, skin-side down, on top of the salt/sugar mix, and then cover in the remaining salt-sugar mix. Seal the bag.

Place your salmon on a shelf in the fridge and weigh it down using anything flat or heavy – a ceramic roasting dish filled with jam jars is my tool of choice.

After a few hours, check the salmon and pour off the fishy liquid that's accumulated in the bag. Redistribute your curing mixture, trying to leave no piece of flesh uncovered. Add more sugar or salt if necessary. Put the weights back on and leave for a further 24 hours. This will give a fairly heavy cure – you can vary your quantities if you only want a light seasoning.

Rinse your cure off the fish using cold water. Slice with a sharp knife and serve, either on its own or with salt water biscuits or oatcakes and pickled beetroot.

Gravlax with Hovmästarsås

Gravadlax, or gravlax, takes its name from the grave. In the Middle Ages it was made by fishermen burying salmon in the sand above the high tide mark until it fermented – 'burying' in Norse being the 'gravad' part. The Norwegians and the Faroese still ferment through burial: birds (notably puffins) and herring, especially. In Shetland, I've never heard of this happening in modern times.

Gravlax, as it was called when I first tasted it, made by Dave and Debbie Hammond at the sadly now-closed Shetland Smokehouse, was simply cured in salt, Cognac and dill. If made with high-quality fish, it is firm and delicious, with that sweet sharpness you get from really good Matjes herring.

Susan sent me a side of Dave and Debbie's gravlax when I returned to Glasgow after my first trip to Shetland to visit her. It was like a gift from another world. And now I realise that it's remarkably easy to make an equivalent at home, thanks to James. All you need is a fridge and a plastic bag.

The basic recipe here is based on one collected from Kirstin Horngren on the Swedish island of Tistronskär by the excellent Tom Vernon* (*Fat Man on a Bicycle* and its many follow-ups) during his Scandinavian adventure, although I've added the alcohol. The dill sauce (Hovmästarsås) was something I never really worked with, as they say in Shetland, but it is rather lovely.

Gravlax is a real celebration of a dish: Champagne works with it nicely, as does decent sourdough toast. I don't like bannocks with it – you want something crunchy, so oatcakes are a possibility. Try the recipe on page 233. If you don't want to make them, the Oceanic oatcakes from Unst, made with seawater, are exceptional.

*Incidentally, Tom Vernon, who died in 2013 (of a heart attack, and he would have laughed) was an important figure in areas outside of cookery, popularising obesity and cycling. He was communications chief for the British Humanist Association, and it was he who launched a competition for a new logo that procured the so-called 'Happy Human' icon, later adopted by humanist groups throughout the world. He was a significant and tireless campaigner for various causes, most notably the decriminalisation of abortion in Britain.

1kg (2lb 3oz) middle cut
 salmon, preferably in two
 fillets, skin on
4 tbsp table salt
2 tsp white peppercorns, roughly
 crushed
2 tbsp good Cognac (or a peaty
 malt whisky like Lagavulin)
4 tbsp granulated sugar
a large bunch of fresh dill

You'll also need a large and
non-leaky plastic bag

Check the fillets for bones and remove any you see. Leave the skin on.

Mix the salt, pepper, Cognac and sugar together in a bowl.

Place both fillets skin-side down on a chopping board and rub some of this mixture into the flesh of each side. Sandwich a thick pad of dill and plenty of the seasoning mixture between the two fillets, skin side out. Complement the thinner section of one with the thicker of the other.

Slide the salmon into the bag with plenty of dill and seasoning around it, press the air out of the bag and seal it. Place on a tray in the fridge, and then put a flat heavy thing on top, like a breadboard. Weigh down with a stone or equivalent heavy thing. Multiple full jam jars work. Marinate in the fridge for two days, turning once.

Drain the salmon, dry it with kitchen paper and wipe or scrape off the spices. Slice it across, either with a thin, slanting cut for a starter or, for a main course, in thick (about 1cm/½ inch thick) slices.

You can remove the skin before serving, cut it into pieces and fry until crispy to serve with the gravlax, if you like. Serve with or without the dill and mustard sauce or 'hovmästarsås' (see below).

Gravlax is only cured in the mildest sense, and so it doesn't keep. What to do, then, if you've ordered a side of salmon and made yourself a whole heap? I can assure you it's rather lovely fried with bacon and black pudding for breakfast. Just don't get it mixed in with baked beans...

Hovmästarsås

It's like mayonnaise, only not so tricky.

3 tbsp Dijon mustard, or similar
125ml (½ cup) rapeseed oil
1 tbsp red wine vinegar
½ tsp good sea salt
¼ tsp white pepper
1½ tbsp caster (superfine) sugar
handful of dill, finely chopped

Place the mustard in a bowl. Measure out the oil into a jug, and slowly pour into the mustard, while whisking vigorously. (Those wee teardrop-shaped whisks work well.) Keep pouring slowly and whisk until the oil is all added. When it's all in, add the vinegar. Again, slowly, whisking as you go. Add all the other ingredients one by one, in no particular order, checking the taste as you go along. The dill goes in last.

Poached salmon

There are hundreds and thousands of ways you can cook salmon or adapt it into 'generic' family dishes – stick it in some plain carbonara or between a bun to make a burger. I've made salmon sausages, salmon kebabs... It can be fried, roasted, baked and essentially abused.

But here's my favourite salmon recipe. I first tasted this at the old County Hotel in Stornoway, Lewis in the Outer Hebrides. One lunchtime in 1985. As long as the salmon is good, so this dish will be.

1 x 150g (5oz) salmon fillet
  per person
1 orange
1 bay leaf per person

Serve with:
mayonnaise (Hellmann's)
Dijon mustard
fresh dill
Shetland tatties and kale

Place a shallow pan of cold water onto a medium heat. Add a thin slice of orange and a bay leaf per fillet of fish. Bring to a simmer.

Once bubbling, turn off the heat and add the salmon fillet(s). Cover with a lid and leave the water to cool.

After 10 minutes or so, check your salmon. It should be just-about-cooked. Soft and fatty. That's it. Serve on a chipped plate with mayonnaise and mustard, accompanied by tatties and kale. I mix Hellmann's (full-fat) and Dijon mustard with a few sprigs of dill. A classic.

Raw sea trout, burnt butter, charred spring onion

The first time I tasted an iteration of this dish was not in Shetland – it was to the south-east, in Copenhagen. We'd checked into our Airbnb and had wandered into the first restaurant nearby that seemed reasonably priced.

We were seated promptly at the only places left; at a bar overlooking the kitchen. I liked the fact that there were little drawers hidden in the solid oak bar that contained cutlery and napkins; and that the menu had only four options – five courses, with or without wine, and eight courses, with or without wine. The wines were interesting, natural and excellent. The waiters poured themselves a little glass from every bottle to check each was good. And there was unlimited world-class sourdough with whipped butter.

I was impressed. The first course, though, made me want to slap myself. So simple – raw fish, burnt butter, spring's first onions, and prepared by the waiting staff. I tasted this and put down my knife and fork and Googled the place: Michelin star, among the top 50 restaurants in the world. Yeah, yeah. Turns out they're all like that here. This was Relae.

For the rest of that trip, I became irritated by how good the restaurant scene was in Denmark. New Nordic is widespread: little courses of simple ingredients cooked well. And they are charging a lot of money for it – every bit of Scandinavia seems to be a food destination in and of itself.

No one is doing this in Shetland. We have access to stuff that even by Danish or Norwegian standards, is astounding. Nobody has had the courage to stick it on a plate and shout about it. Well, hear me roar.

¼ side of Shetland trout, or farmed salmon, as fresh as possible
8–9 spring onions, preferably harvested directly from perennial spring onions, halved lengthways
olive oil, for frying
50g (1¾oz) good butter
good sea salt
lobster or crab roe, for flavouring the butter (optional)

Serve with:
best-quality sourdough (see page 229), buttered and salted

Makes enough for a small starter for 4

Remove the skin from the fish. Cut it lengthways down the line of the pin bones and then cut thin angled steaks – each about 0.5cm (⅕ inch) thick – from each side. Set aside.

Place a small frying pan over a very high heat, and get it frighteningly hot. Add a little oil, and chuck the spring onions in. You want them to spit and pop and shrivel and slightly char. Keep them moving. When you are happy with them, arrange on four small plates, laid flat and facing the same way.

Arrange your fish slices on top of the onion greens – everyone should get five or six good slices. Any rough or sinuous ones can be discarded for stock.

Return your pan to the high heat and add your butter. Melt, then let spit, then burn just enough so that it goes a deep, dark brown colour. Add a little roe, if using, right at the end for a fishy hit. Don't worry if you don't have any. Spoon two or three teaspoons over each of your portions of raw fish and serve with awesome sourdough and awesome butter and salt.

Tom's Indo-Shetlandic fish 'n' chips

Frankie's is our local fish and chip shop. Named after the family's late dog, Frankie's opened in 2008 in custom-built premises, and serves everything from garlic-grilled scallops to hake, monkfish, halibut and, of course, haddock. Haddock is the fish of choice in these parts, despite its newfound status as less-sustainable-than-cod.

I love Frankie's. Which is not to say that the Lerwick chippies - the Happy Haddock, which does phenomenal chips, and the Fort, whose breaded haddock is superb – aren't wonderful too. But Frankie's is our local. I did eat there at least once a week before a certain heart issue, and it's much more than just a fish and chip shop.

For a start, most of Frankie's menu items are Marine Stewardship Council (MSC)-certified, and all the fish comes from the waters around Shetland, meaning not only that they are sustainably caught or harvested, but that they are very low in food miles.

The shop also runs the Frankie's Fish Course, an educational programme aimed at primary school children. Staff visit schools throughout Shetland to talk about different types of fish and explain why sustainability is vital. They always take along a box of fresh fish and shellfish so that the children can see and touch for themselves, scales, eyes, fins and all.

The shop (well, restaurant) even has an outdoor terrace which is used at least two days a year. It has entered and won a whole heap of awards, even voted best in the UK in 2015 at the National Fish & Chip Awards.

Fish 'n' chips is my favourite fish dish. Basic tastes, me, but this is a mildly spiced recipe. Its batter is not like that from the legendary Frankie's but is modified from that of the late Leslie Forbes and her book *Recipes from the Indian Spice Trail*, now sadly out of print. Think of this as fish pakora.

This recipe is also a compromise, on the insistence of my son. I actually prefer my breaded fish to be bread-free. Not because of an irrational fear of gluten – I'm a fan of the Baltasound Bakery's seawater-made Oceanic Oatcakes, blended or bashed until they are Ruskoline-like. Substitute for breadcrumbs entirely, if you will, using as you would the former, following plain (all-purpose) flour and egg. Oatcake schnitzel, anyone?

4 x 200g (7oz) fresh haddock
  fillets (skinless)

1 egg, beaten
75g (²⁄₃ cup) chickpea (gram)
  flour
¼ tsp ground turmeric
pinch of ground ginger
100g (1 cup) breadcrumbs (or
  stale bread, blitzed)
at least 100g (1 cup) leftover or
  stale oatcakes, crumbled
pinch of chilli powder
table salt
vegetable oil, for frying

For the chips:
2–3 large sweet potatoes,
  washed
2–3 tsp vegetable oil
good sea salt, for seasoning

Makes enough for 4

Preheat your oven to 200°C (400°F)/180°C (350°F) fan/Gas 6. Slice the sweet potatoes into thin lengths somewhat resembling chips, keeping their skins on. Toss these in a roasting tin with the oil and don't add any salt at this point. Stick them in the oven for 20 minutes.

Prepare three plates: in the first, add your gram flour; in the second, beat your egg with a little salt; in the third, mix the turmeric, ginger, breadcrumbs and crumbled oatcakes. Add the chilli powder, if using, and make sure you season your 'oatcrumbs' well.

Dip each piece of fish in turn into the flour, patting off the excess, then into the egg, letting the excess drip, and then into the spicy oatcrumbs.

Preheat a heavy-based frying pan, the base just-coated with vegetable oil, over a medium heat. Fry your fish until golden on each side. A couple of minutes, max.

Try to serve as quickly as possible after cooking, with the chips straight from the oven, sprinkled with plenty of good sea salt.

Mackerel fishing

I have many reasons to visit home. The family, first and foremost. The dog. The house I grew up in and the people I used to know.

These are the obligations I use to get on that long ferry or terrifying plane, but I also crave the solitude. And as soon as I'm home, my mind turns to the water. I want to get out onto the sea. I'm not much of a 'boaty' person – that's far too sociable. My vehicle of choice is the sit-on kayak: cheap, stable and lonely. We have two, and one of them even takes two people sitting in tandem, for when we feel sociable enough to show other people how satisfying solitude can be.

You'd be amazed at the things you can discover. Kayaks need only a couple of feet of width and a few centimetres of depth of water for access, meaning that you can get yourself through some pretty tiny waterways and stuck beneath very low ceilings. Paddle out from the beach next to my house and you're fewer than five minutes from a complex of caves and natural stone arches completely invisible from land. Stuck to these are mussels and sea urchins, which on a calm day you can knock onto your lap.

Leisure aside, the kayak is my choice of fishing vessel, wetsuit-clad in case of an unintended swim. A handline with some mackerel feathers and a weight is all you need – that's the plastic handle around which you wrap some fishing line. A rod would only provide leverage with which to capsize. A stick of driftwood is handy for the coups de grace.

We keep the kayaks at the bottom of the garden above the beach. They're a durable plastic that can last year-round, so they can be dragged down to the sea at any hint of a calm day. On a calm day, you can paddle for hours, with the horizon-filling Atlantic on your left and 200-foot cliffs within touching distance to your right. How far I venture is a decision led by my father's anxiety.

Here, in solitude, is zen. The crisp air and the true scent of the sea; a kind of indescribable minerality like the flintiness of a white wine, soon to be tainted by the ferric reek of flesh.

As familiar things become far away, your perspective changes. The view becomes more map-like, as the land stretches before you. Houses that seemed huge are dwarfed by cliffs previously obscured by little hills; long distances look compressed.

I don't know much about fishing, but I follow the birds, so I have something nice to watch as I wait for the bite. Maybe the seabirds and mackerel are after the same prey. And, as you paddle out, the seals will join you. They're curious and friendly. On a lucky trip, you might have four or five sets of orb-like eyes staring.

Mackerel love a moving target, and so I drop my line to the sea floor, pull it up few metres, and then gently lift the line up and down as the wind and the tide push me one way or another. How long this takes is variable. The feathers lure the mackerel by diffraction, so a calm and bright day is always going to reap more rewards. Sometimes after thirty seconds, your line is full of mackerel. If not, there's the zen.

Mackerel are strong fish. As soon as they bite, you know. A meagre pollack might be mistaken for catching your hook on a reed. As you reel them in you'll catch a glimpse of the four or five slivers of silver tearing around and around, tangling your line as they try to make their escape.

This is where it gets brutal. The lucky ones will rip the hook through their cheek and escape, probably to die of exhaustion or infection. The rest you wrest from the sea and into the canoe and their solid bodies fight. Gradually, the water between your legs turns a reddish brown, from the blood and shit from the struggling fish. The aim is to kill the fish quicker than their suffocation. Nothing is instant. Even following death, they still flap.

The feeling of slaughtering anything with one's own hands, whether it be a large, long-lived mammal or a 'mere' fish, is profound. Those who follow a pescatarian diet would be hypocritical to do so for moral reasons: of course, fish feel pain. We evolved from them. Go out and kill them for yourself and you will feel their pain. Feeling this pain is necessary, and should be part of anyone's choice to eat meat.

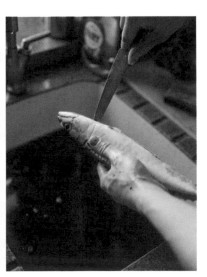  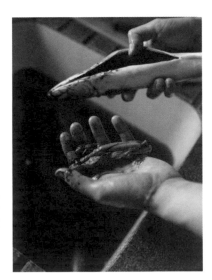

Fish guts and fillets

The best fish you'll ever taste is fried on the bone, as soon as possible after catching and before rigor mortis has had a chance to set in. But before you can fry it, you must gut. This is easy.

Place your fish in the sink. Hold the back of the fish, bottom side pointing up – the tail should be towards you and the head away.

Stick a pointy knife into the fish's arse, with the sharp edge of the blade pointing towards the head-end. In one swift motion, swipe the knife up the belly of the fish, stopping at the fish's neck. You should have made a large opening into the fish's abdominal cavity.

Pull out the guts, making sure to reach forward to grab the heart and to make sure that all of the intestine is removed. Run the open cavity under a cold tap and run a firm finger or thumb down the fish's spine, from the inside. The dense, bloody mess is the fish's kidney and main blood vessels. Put all the innards to one side and repeat with the next fish until they're all done.

Your fish is now ready for cooking. Now, I'm a frugal sort of chap in many ways and I've tried to find a use for mackerel guts but I haven't succeeded. The internet has many bad suggestions. Throw the guts away.

If you want to fillet your fish, there's a bit of a knack to it and it may take you a few goes. I've not included a pictorial step-by-step guide here, because videos are the best way to learn. YouTube it, and make sure you use a sharp, sharp knife. Flat fish (sole, plaice) require a different technique that I will not cover here.

Cut the fish head off – cut behind the pectoral fin, in line with the gills. Use a sharp knife, but save your best for the delicate peeling of the fish's flesh. Good knives should never be used for bone.

Once your fish is headless, place the fish on its side. Make an incision down the spine of the fish, keeping above the dorsal fin.

Extend this incision deeper, always staying just off the spine. Keep extending the incision until you can feel you are clearly into flesh. At this point, angle your knife a little downwards, so as to hug the bones and peel off maximal flesh. You'll know if you're in the right place.

Keep going until you've gone all the way through to the underside of the fish, bearing in mind you'll have to go through some small 'pin' bones that will need to be removed afterwards. Repeat on the other side.

Fresh mackerel pâté

I'd like to claim this recipe is a Shetland original. It's not. Back when I washed dishes at a popular pre-hipsterite café in Glasgow, I was allowed to make the soup and make their mackerel pâté. It was difficult to get wrong, which was why I was allowed to do it. Smoked mackerel, cream, cream cheese, a little lemon to balance, *et voilà*. Something that could be packaged in plastic pots or served with (inevitable) oatcakes as a lunchtime snack before cake.

Mackerel pâté comes into its own, though, when it is made with fresh fish. It's awesome. The key is balance – mackerel is an oily fish, so you need tartness. Lemon, mustard, horseradish, cornichons. All cut through that richness of the fish and the cream cheese. This is sublime, and dangerous, for it is infinitely eatable.

3 whole mackerel, gutted
vegetable oil, for frying
100g (½ cup) full-fat cream
  cheese
juice of 1 lemon
2.5cm (1 inch) fresh
  horseradish, finely grated
1–2 tsp grain mustard
10–15 cornichons
full-fat natural yoghurt, to loosen
good sea salt
freshly ground black pepper

Serve with:
bread or oatcakes and pickled
beetroot (see page 176)

Makes enough for a starter for
6 adults (at least)

I can never bring myself to poach mackerel, so place your gutted fish in a frying pan with a little oil. Fry over a medium heat for 3–4 minutes on each side, until the meat is soft – it should be just cooked through and the meat literally falling off the bone. The skin will peel away.

Remove the meat from the bones and place in a large bowl. Add the cream cheese, half of the lemon juice, half of the horseradish, half of the mustard and a pinch of salt and stir to combine. Taste it, and decide which of these ingredients you want to add more of. For me, it's invariably all of them all, but I like a full-flavoured pâté.

Your cornichons should go in last – chop them finely, then mix in, along with yoghurt, to your desired consistency.

The pâté will keep fresh for a couple of days in the fridge, probably longer. Serve cold, with oatcakes or bread and maybe some pickled beetroot.

Oatmeal-fried mackerel

This is a dish I had often as a child; it's a Scots classic. And I hated it. Not because it wasn't good, but because my economical parents tried to convince me that we were having 'breaded fish'. Which I took to mean fried haddock with mash or chips and beans or peas. You can imagine the emotional scarring.

Now, of course, I cannot believe what my closed mind was missing. There isn't a hint of nostalgia in the enjoyment of this dish. It's wonderful, crisp and buttery oats with melting, oily flesh beneath. The lemon sets it off perfectly. Serve with boiled potatoes soaked in big knobs of butter.

4 mackerel or 8 mackerel fillets
150g (1¼ cups) pinhead
    oatmeal
2 medium eggs
plain (all-purpose) flour, for
    dusting
table salt
1 lemon
at least 100g (3½oz) butter

Serves 4 (2 fillets each)

Catch, gut and fillet the mackerel (see pages 79–82). Pat the flesh dry with kitchen paper.

Prepare four plates: put your flour onto the first and season with a large pinch of salt; onto the next, break your egg, adding another pinch of salt, and beat with a fork; onto the third, place your oatmeal and season this, too, for good measure. Keep the fourth plate clear.

Dunk a fillet into the flour and shake off any excess. Place immediately into the egg and flip over so both sides are covered. Hold it up by the tail end for the excess to drip off. Finally, dunk in the seasoned oatmeal. Once covered, pat off any excess and place on the enigmatic fourth plate.

Preheat a heavy-based frying pan – preferably cast iron – over a medium heat. Once hot, add half the butter. If it spits and turns brown straight away, take it off the heat and let it cool for a minute or two. Fry your prepared mackerel, four at a time if possible, for a couple of minutes on each side, or until light golden brown and crisp. If some of the oats are dry, add more butter. Keep the cooked fish on a baking tray in a low oven while you fry the rest.

Serve with lemon straight away.

Mackerel ceviche

The first time I made this was on television. A few years after appearing on *The Great British Bake Off*, I was asked to come back for a Christmas special (I think someone else must have been busy) and they asked us to make 'Christmas canapés'. Obeying their orders for anecdotes and a connection to home, I came up with these, bites made with mackerel pâté, mackerel ceviche and pickles.

Whilst my puff might have been lacking on that particular occasion, this recipe for a very fishy, very tart canapé has stuck. Served on oatcakes instead of pastry, it's simple and fast, and the meatiness of the mackerel lends itself well to the 'cooking' by acidification. The citric acidity is exquisite with the acetic sweetness of a quick salsa. I'm not one for pairing, but tequila goes very well.

2 fresh mackerel
6 limes
1 mild fresh chilli
1–2 shallots
good sea salt

For the salsa:
150g (7oz) mixed tomatoes
1 lime
good sea salt

Serve with:
Shetland oatcakes (see page 233), or shop-bought, and pickled rhubarb (see page 179)

Makes enough for about 30 canapés, or plenty for picking at at a party

Take your mackerel and fillet it, if this hasn't already been done for you. Don't worry about being precise or extracting the wee bones – they will dissolve.

Grate the lime zest into a shallow dish, then halve the limes and squeeze in the juice.

Finely chop the chilli and shallots and add these to the lime juice, add a large pinch of salt and stir. Taste, if you like, and feel your cheeks adhere.

Pick out your sharpest knife – I have a Yanagiba reserved for only this purpose – and thinly slice your mackerel. You want each piece 2–3mm ($\frac{1}{10}$ inch) thick. You can leave the skin on or take it off; it doesn't matter.

Place your thinly sliced fish into the lime juice and gently mix to make sure as much fish is touching juice as possible and the whole lot is covered. Cover with plastic wrap and pop into the fridge for 1 hour or so, or until your fish has turned the colour of cooked mackerel and started to flake. If it's taking its time, it means your limes aren't very acidic or your fish is too thick. Just leave it a little longer, gently mixing to maximise surface contact.

While the mackerel is in the fridge, make the salsa. Chop the tomatoes, squeeze the lime and mix together in a bowl with plenty of salt.

Serve the fish with the salsa, oatcakes and some pickled rhubarb. Try it.

Clothesline-dried piltock

One of the unfortunate side-effects of mackerel fishing is the piltock – or pollack, as it's known in wider English. You often get these weak, white fish biting on your feathers. And you don't have a choice – once they've struggled against you and you've pulled them aboard, there's no point throwing them back. You've killed them; deal with it.

My favourite way to deal with anything is to eat it. Dry-cured and then air-dried, this fish keeps almost indefinitely. This is still done by layering in salt and sugar before hanging up on the clothesline. I've learned first-hand that this should only be done on a windy day. Try it on a calm summer evening and the flies will have the fish.

To actually use it, you should rehydrate the fish in boiling water to make a wonderful fish stock, or to flavour a pasta sauce in the same way as, or alongside, anchovies. Beyond that, the experimentation is up to you.

4 whole piltock (pollack)
400g (1¾ cups) table salt
300g (1⅓ cup) granulated
   sugar

You'll also need an outdoors
clothesline and clothes pegs

Gut the piltock– save the swim bladder for fining your homebrewed beer (see my previous book, *Brew*) and discard the rest of the guts.

Once gutted, slice the fish heads in half, working from the bottom to the top. This is so you can splay the fish flat, just like how kippers are sold. To do this, simply lie the fish flat on your chopping board with the spine facing directly up. Place the flat of your hand on the dorsum of the fish and press down hard – you'll feel the meat come away and the spine shift to one side.

Sprinkle the fish, on all sides, with a fine layer of salt.

Place half of the salt and sugar in a plastic bag (a large freezer bag) and lay your fish on top in a single layer. Don't stack the fish – both sides should always be in contact with your curing mixture. Cover with the remaining salt and sugar. Seal your bag and place it in the fridge with a baking tray on top weighed down with some large jars. Leave for two days. If it starts leaking water everywhere, drain, redistribute the salt/sugar and re-seal.

Once you have very tough, salty fish, it's time to dry it. Pick a dry, windy day and hang your fish out on the clothesline until it is the texture of leather. This usually takes a few days if it's properly windy. Bring indoors if it starts to rain. You can try this in a cool place indoors, if you have an electric fan you're willing to donate to the cause.

When your fish is dry, wrap it in paper to keep it dry and store. Out of paranoia, I'd keep it in the freezer, but it should last forever if kept cool.

Tom's pickled herring

I could write a whole book about herring. I'm tempted to say I will, but Shetland resident, native Hebridean, Gaelic speaker and all-round good guy Donald S. Murray already has. It's called *Herring Tales: How the Silver Darlings Shaped Human Taste and History*, and I thoroughly recommend it.

I think it's fair to say that my appreciation for the silver darlings began in Shetland, due to my first encounter with Dave and Debbie's incredible picklings. Although preserved herring is often seen as a Scandinavian or Dutch affair – and IKEA should indeed be your first port of call for consistently good jars of matjes or sild – herring is and always has been huge in Russia, and is a major part of Eastern European-rooted Jewish culture, the diaspora throughout the world and specifically of the USA.

Bismarck herring is the salted fillet and roe, pickled in vinegar, white wine and spices. Matjes (or soused) herring is baked or fried in a marinade containing vinegar, spices and sugar, and served in that. But the word 'maatjes' can also refer to (and this is the IKEA version) a mild salt herring, which is made from young fish that have been ripened in brine.

I won't get into the intimidating and horrifically smelly surströmming, made from Baltic herring and fermented until so smelly the tins can never, ever be opened indoors. Mostly, I raid the Swedish Shop when I'm down south or modify the only commercial pickled herring available in Shetland. This is far, far too sweet – I add chilli and balsamic vinegar, but at best this is a half-hearted solution.

The traditional rollmop, which is aggressively acidic and has a tendency to take the roof of your mouth off, should be avoided at all costs. It's only for seriously hungover drunks, or for the medical inducement of migraines for experimental purposes.

You see how herring can waylay you? In relatively recent times - until the early 1990s in fact, hundreds of Russian ships, known as klondikers, would come to Scotland during the herring season to collect the catches of Scottish fishing boats, then salt, pickle and barrel them for export. I once spent a memorable afternoon aboard one of these ships, anchored in the Sound of Bressay, the outer reaches of Lerwick Harbour. The gigantic ex-whaling factory ship was at the time also collecting, on the side, scrapped Lada cars for return to what was then still the Soviet black market. I had brought, on the instructions of a Lerwick shipping agent, a bottle of Smirnoff vodka (made by Diageo near Falkirk) and this was greeted with great joy by the Captain.

"Smirnoff," he said, "best vodka in the world!" Jings, I thought, where's your Stolichnaya, pal? A full-on shipboard foy ensued. We smoked those yellow, lung-ripping Russian cigarettes, the ones with paper filters. The Captain and I finished the bottle whilst eating a feast of pickled herring, vegetables, cheese and black bread. There were many toasts, to political and social structures I doubt any of us truly believed in – the USSR, the Queen, Alex Salmond, Margaret Thatcher, the superior engineering of Lada vehicles, particularly the Niva 4x4. We explored the ship, which I remember had a table tennis room, presumably only for use in port, and then I inched my way drunkenly down a scramble net on the sloping rear slipway which had once seen huge Antarctic whales dragged into the bowels of the ship for flensing. "Smirnoff!" the Captain shouted after me.

2 fresh herring
2 small onions
2 tbsp cider or red wine vinegar
8 tbsp vegetable oil (rapeseed or high-quality neutral vegetable oil; not olive)
1 (or 2) tsp good sea salt
1 (or 2) tsp brown sugar

Serves 2 (makes enough for four fillets – that's two each)

Gut and wash the fish thoroughly (see page 82). Throw away the innards and head. Cut the fish along the spine, and carefully run the knife along the edge of the bones. This is not as easy as it sounds. In fact, it doesn't sound easy, and it isn't. But persist and you'll have mangled things that look a bit like fillets.

Peel and thinly slice the onions and layer them under and over the herring fillets in a shallow dish.

Mix the vinegar and oil together in a small bowl, adding the salt and sugar to taste, then pour this over the fish and onions, cover the dish with plastic wrap and leave to marinate for 3–4 hours.

Chop the fish into chunks, then either pop into a clean jar with the marinade and store in the fridge, or eat straight away. It will keep for a week or so at least, and probably longer. But you'll have eaten it by then.

Mussels

Tom

Our friend Jim was telling us about horse mussels, which are four or five times the size of the farmed mussels you get in your favourite Belgian restaurant-cum-craft-beer bar. In Scotland they're known as clabby doos ('big black mouth') and their reefs are regarded as sensitive habitats by Scottish Natural Heritage. So you don't dredge for them. Jim says they're edible, though you only eat the muscle holding the two shells together.

Jim told me that he was asked by an English engineer working at the oil terminal if he could get him some mussels, of which this chap was inordinately fond. Expecting ordinary ones, when Jim as a joke handed him a bag of giant clabby doos he was astonished.

"I've never seen mussels like these before," he said.

"This is Shetland," replied Jim. "Our mussels are all that size."

The meals Susan and I had in the early stages of our courtship (what an old-fashioned word that is!) in the late 1980s at Burrastow House on Shetland's west side were some of the most memorable of my life. You can still stay and eat at Burrastow, now owned by a man called Pierre and only open in the summer, but it was the winter meals cooked by the Tuckeys and eaten in an oak-panelled, candlelit room before a peat fire that remain with me. The mussels were unfarmed, wild-gathered and full of natural pearls, so that by the time you'd finished, your plate had a treasure of tiny white spheres...

Now Shetland has a thriving mussel-farming business, dominated by two large, locally-owned companies, and it's an environmentally-friendly affair. Mussels don't need to be fed, like salmon. They just grow from spat (early stage mussels) on ropes. They're incredibly good for you. Well, they're incredibly good for you as long as they're not affected by toxic algal bloom or they're rotten. Both of these are extremely rare occurrences but they do happen, so I don't collect from the wild beds at Ronas Voe if there's not an 'R' in the month. The farmed mussels, carefully monitored, checked, purged and tested before sale, are a different matter.

If you're buying mussels in the rest of the UK from a fishmonger, ask where they're from. There's a strong likelihood they'll be from Shetland. The farmed mussels have much thinner, more delicate shells than the heavy ones you collect wild.

James

Collecting and preparing wild mussels

The first step in foraging for mussels is to make sure the water on your particular piece of coastline is clean – no sewage pipes or septic tank outfalls, please. In Shetland, there are known spots for excellent mussel cultivation, and I'm sure this will be the case wherever is your nearest coast. Ronas Voe, where we used to live and home to many commercial mussel farms, is our favourite.

There's a single-track road that runs along the coast, with a steep grassy hill down to a rocky shore. Park in a passing place, and it's a quick scramble to, at low tide, a near limitless supply of mussels – big, thick-shelled mussels, seemingly ancient and encrusted with barnacles and neighboured by whelks and sea urchins.

A bucket is all you need. First, half-fill it with clear seawater, then you can start prying the mussels off the rocks and filling the bucket. Only pick the ones that would have been below sea level at high tide. Or, even better, the ones that are still under water. And pick those that are large, but without too much encrusted on the shells (this makes them easier to prepare). While you're there, take some whelks (winkles) for use in the recipes on pages 96 and 99. Your hands will get cold, but it'll be worth it.

At some stage, you'll get bored or tired. Stop then, or when your bucket is getting too heavy to carry comfortably. Scoop enough seawater in there to cover the mussels completely. Take the bucket home and leave it outside, overnight. This is the 'purge' – it helps the mussels get rid of the sand and grit that might still be inside.

All of your mussels will be locked shut, because they're very much alive. If you do see one gaping a little, that doesn't close when handled, it's dead or stupid. Throw it away.

The next stage is de-bearding and, optionally, de-barnacling. This can take a while as each mussel needs to be handled separately. You can leave the barnacles on, but I find it doesn't add much time to remove a potential source of grittiness. The beard is the wee hairy bit that sticks out from the centre of the mussel; you tore this when you prised the mussel from the rock. It is perfectly edible, but isn't texturally appealing.

The best way is to take a mussel from its purging water and use a pair of pliers to pull off the beard. But you can cut it, too, using a sharp knife, just don't sever any of your own tendons. Use a blunt knife to carefully scrape the shells to remove the barnacles. Rinse in the water, before setting aside.

You can see why it makes most sense to gather only the largest mussels, because it means there are fewer to process to get a decent meal. But, after all that hard work, you'll have a free source of deliciousness and protein that's as ready to cook as any prepacked bag, and far fresher. Watch out for pearls – you might find only one in every 100 mussels, depending on where they're gathered from. We found just one in all the mussels photographed for this book, and that broke Andy the photographer's tooth. He maintains it was worth it.

All mussel preparation can be undertaken outdoors – they are a great beach dinner, served alone or with torn bread, each one scooped from the shells using only another shell. My favourite method of cooking mussels isn't over a fire, but using that wondrous Swedish invention: the Trangia stove. With a little methylated spirits and some wine, a great time can be had.

Scale up the measurements depending on how many people you are cooking for (or when you gave up gathering)

450g (1lb) mussels per person (wild or shop-bought)
a knob of butter
1 garlic clove per person, crushed
25ml (1fl oz) dry white wine per person
1 bay leaf per person

Serve with:
Plenty of best-quality sourdough (see page 229)

Regardless of origin, tap any open mussels on the side of your pan to check that they then lock themselves shut. If they don't, chuck 'em out.

Add your butter and garlic to the pan, and sizzle for a matter of seconds over a high heat.

Add the white wine, mussels and bay leaves. There's no need to season; seawater is good for that.

Place a lid on top and bring to the boil, keeping the heat high. Steam until all shells are open – this should take about 3 minutes from the time you see the first spurts of steam from around the lid until they are done. This will take a little longer with wild mussels because their shells are much thicker – as long as 5 minutes.

Have your bread ready to go and eat straight from the pan. If you don't soak up every last drop of the tasty liquor at the bottom, freeze it to use as the base for a fish stock.

Buckies with kelp beurre blanc and dulse beurre noisette

Buckies, or common whelks to most people in the UK, are utterly abundant in Shetland: lobster creels are full of them. Snail-like, they are surpisingly mobile carnivorous creatures that break into other shellfish for food.

They are rarely eaten in Shetland. I have never seen them for sale, but they are still a source of livelihood for creel fishermen. They are largely exported to France to form part of a *fruits de mer*. It is a sin that barely anyone in Shetland knows about them, because they have a lot of flavour to give. I've used two easily foraged seaweeds in the accompanying butters for this dish: dulse in the noisette (nutty; burnt) for a crispy, sweet hit, and kelp in the blanc (white; emulsified) for mega-umami. Both butters can be used to add depth to any fish dish, with or without any seaweed.

8 live buckies (common whelks)
table salt
2.5cm (1 inch) kelp (or kombu)
50ml (1¾fl oz) sweet sherry,
    plus a little extra
50ml (1¾fl oz) white wine
    vinegar
1 anchovy, from a tin
100g (3½oz) butter, unsalted
    or salted
about 30g (1oz) fresh dulse
vegetable oil, for frying

Makes enough for a starter
for 2–3

Bring a couple of litres of water and a heaped teaspoon of salt to the boil in a large pot. Once boiling, add your buckies in their shells. Boil them for 2 minutes while you fill a bowl with cold water and ice. After 2 minutes, fish them out of the boiling water with a slotted spoon and plunge them into the icy water. Leave them to cool completely.

Use a small fork to pull the buckies out of their shells. Once the flesh is all out, remove the hard discs and the sac-like stomachs. The rest is all edible and pleasant. Keep one shell per person for serving. Place the flesh into a medium pan and cover with 300–400ml (10–14fl oz) water and a dash of sherry. Bring this to a simmer over a medium heat and cook for 30 minutes. Once cooked, remove from the liquor and leave to cool. Reserve the liquor. Once cool, slice the buckies – the thinner the flesh, the crispier they'll be.

To make the beurre blanc, finely chop the kelp and add it to a small pan with the sherry, vinegar, anchovy and approximately 100ml (½ cup) of the original cooking liquor. Reduce this by half, then add about three-quarters of your butter, whisking vigorously to combine. Once emulsified, keep warm over the lowest possible heat you have.

To make the beurre noisette, roughly chop the dulse and place in a frying pan with the rest of your butter. Beware: this will spit as it darkens. Cook over a high heat until the butter is a deep brown and your seaweed is crisp.

To finish, heat a pan or wok to a very high heat. Add a dash of oil and fry the chopped buckies until crisp on all sides. Arrange on a warm plate, fill a clean shell with your beurre blanc and drizzle your burnt butter and dulse around the edge. Serve straight away.

I love whelks

'Whelk' in Shetland means something different from the rest of the UK. While down south it might mean some gargantuan creature (see the previous recipe, page 96), back home it means a 'winkle'. Shetlanders felt that this was such a comical name it was deserving of scorn.

These wee whelks are found everywhere on Shetland. Harvesting them was, until recent price drops, a common way to subsidise one's income; whelk gathering is as easy as wandering down to the shore at low tide and scooping hundreds upon hundreds of handfuls into plastic bags. They were then sold to an exporter for cash, who shipped them to Spain for a very healthy margin. It was win-win, except for the taxman.

If you ask a local if they've actually eaten a whelk, they'll likely answer in the negative. I don't understand what people have against this humble gastropod – they are tender and delicious, if a little fiddly.

My endlessly amusing father even wrote a song about them about 15 years ago. Want proof?

CHORUS:
I love whelks, in the morning
I love whelks, they please my appetite
I love whelks, in the evening,
I love whelks before I go to bed at night

I went down to the shoreline to seek some healthy food
All I found was a stranded whale and he didn't taste too good
I cannot live without them, I love that salty taste
I hear some people sell them, I think that's such a waste

I chased a whelk for miles one day, the length of Ronas Voe
Every time I grabbed at him the faster he would go
I was getting quite exhausted when he turned and looked at me
He said I'm amazed how fast you go on invalidity

Someone told me you could sell a whelk for 50p
I would not consider that they're far too dear to me
I love them with tomato sauce and in my bannocks too
I love the way they wiggle when you begin to chew

good olive oil
4 garlic cloves
2 handfuls of fresh whelks
   (winkles)
large handful of cherry tomatoes
3 anchovies, from a tin (you can
   use the oil from here to drizzle
   over your cooked whelks)
zest of ½ orange
pinch of smoked paprika
juice of 1 lemon

Serve with:
Plenty of best-quality sourdough
(see page 229)

Makes enough for 4 small
appetisers

In a large pan or wok, place a large glug of olive oil. Whilst it heats over a high heat, peel and roughly chop your garlic. When your oil is hot, add the garlic and let it brown, but not burn, to evenly flavour your oil. You've got about 30 seconds until it's burnt.

Add the whelks, tomatoes, anchovies, orange zest and paprika. Keep stirring all the time with a wooden spoon. Crush the tomatoes against the bottom of the pan if they don't burst open themselves. Cook for about 5 minutes.

Squeeze over half the lemon juice and taste the sauce – if it needs more lemon, add the rest. Scoop up your whelks and serve in bowls, finishing with a bit more orange zest and some olive oil on top. Make sure there's plenty of bread around to mop up the sauce, and you have some kind of implement to remove the meat. A toothpick works if you don't have a tiny fork.

Susan's Lobster Thermidor

Jim came round with a lobster for us today. He's a professional, solo creel fisherman who works with a simple open boat. He does it for love, not for profit. He's a local expert in all kinds of shellfish, and that includes things like whelks (winkles, everywhere else) and spoots (razor clams), which he collects and sometimes pickles.

The lobster Jim brought was enormous, ready slaughtered and cooked, and far too much of a treat to eat casually so we'll hang on to it for when guests come round. I always feel a stab of guilt when eating lobster. They can easily be 20 or 30 years old by the time they're caught. And lobsters have been known to live for more than 130 years in captivity. Then there's the question of how to kill them humanely... which, of course, we didn't have to do. The sound of their tissues expanding in boiling water and forcing gas out from their shells sounds like a million tiny screams.

They are, however, absolutely delicious. Trumped.

We're grateful to Jim and the one or two other creel fisherfolk who occasionally pop by with one or two. Lobster thermidor is Susan's speciality. It may seem a bit old-school, but honestly, it is a wonder of flavour. I have a soft spot for this rather retro dish. It's surprisingly simple to make as well, and not too emotionally traumatic if you get a cooked or frozen lobster.

Depending on the size of your lobster you can scale up the other ingredients in accordance.

If you do get one 'fresh', make sure the claws are rubber-banded shut. As for killing it? Well...

I've said that I have a connection to the lobsters in their advanced age. But the real question is: do they feel pain when plunged to their watery demise? There's an evolving consensus that they do; or at least they can. Fishermen might say they are just 'big bugs', and even if they could feel pain that they're dead before they realise they're having a boiling bath. Scientists now disagree – a lobster can feel pain. But that they do in this context is uncertain.

What is for sure is that humans feel awkward. Hence all the ridiculous 'Crustae-stun'-type machines that exist on eBay. They're for appeasing our consciences, not really helping the poor old lobster. Do you really think sheep and cows don't suffer? Face it. They can and, in the processes of supermarket supply, they do. If you want to eat them, they have to be dead first. At least let's kill carefully and with minimum infliction of agony and fuss. Lobsters: stick them in the freezer for 20 minutes to stun, then into the bubbles of doom.

1 cooked lobster, roughly 750g
  (1lb 10oz)
25g (1oz) unsalted butter
at least 1 tbsp olive oil
1 shallot or small onion, finely
  chopped
100ml (½ cup) dry white wine
handful of fresh parsley
handful of fresh tarragon
50ml (1¾fl oz) double cream
1 tsp English mustard
good sea salt
freshly ground black pepper
handful of breadcrumbs (fresh
  or dried)
Parmesan, freshly grated

Serve with:
Plenty of golden chips (see page
78 for sweet potato chips)

Makes enough for a romantic
meal for 2

Remove the lobster's head. Use one of your least favourite knives to slice the shell lengthways, so that you've got two symmetrical tail shells. Get rid of the guts – if there's red roe in there, this can add flavour to stocks and butters. Keep it and freeze it.

Remove the flesh from the body, tail and claws and put to one side. Keep the shells of the body intact, but you can crunch up the claws to get all the meat out.

Chop the meat until it is fine and white and make sure there isn't any shell inside it.

Clean your shell halves, as you'll serve in these.

Melt the butter and oil in a large pan over a medium heat, then add your shallot. Cook until soft, about 5 minutes, or a surprisingly long time.

Add the wine and stir using a wooden spoon to deglaze the pan. Up the heat and cook until the wine has reduced by about half. Turn the heat off.

Chop your herbs finely and add to the pan. Add your lobster meat, cream, mustard, salt and pepper and stir to combine. Taste. It should taste like the best thing you've ever eaten.

To finish, as an optional extra really, preheat your grill (alternatively, use a wood-fired oven, as opposite). Spoon the mixture into your shells and sprinkle with a thin layer of breadcrumbs and some freshly grated parmesan. Grill until golden brown, and serve. With chips! There isn't a better accompaniment.

Brown crab

Crabs are not so popular in this household. Mum once spent a summer in the 1970s working in a crab processing factory. In those days, crab factories were legendarily horrible places to work. Everybody smoked and the cigarette ash got everywhere, including into the crab meat. And Mum and her associates were banned from every pub on the isles due to their stench. Lately, through some rehabilitation, she has begun to enjoy crab claws again, but she took some serious convincing to appreciate the brown meat from inside the shell.

This recipe is so simple because a fresh crab should only be so. It needs almost nothing with it. No mayonnaise. Definitely no pepper. Only bread, bannock or oatcake on which to serve the spreadable brown meat paste followed by a sprinkling of the flaked white meat from the legs and claws.

I don't believe in asking your guests (or indeed, customers) to crack apart the claws and legs to obtain the meat. It may be a novelty but it's a massive faff and done most efficiently in bulk, crab after crab. Factory-like.

The crab pictured was obtained from a creel down the road from our house and cooked within hours. Yes, he was boiled alive (see page 101 for an ethical discussion). He wasn't alive for very long.

1 brown crab, alive
table salt, for the boiling water

Serve with:
white sourdough (or for best-quality sourdough see page 229)

Makes enough for an appetiser for 2–3 people

Bring 3–4 litres (6–8 pints) of water to the boil in a large pot. Add in a tablespoon of salt. You want a proper rolling boil. The more vigorous the boil, the faster the crab will be killed and the less the guilt you'll feel. (You can 'numb' the crabs by placing them in a freezer beforehand, but if I was the crab I think I'd prefer a quick boil to a slow freeze.) Carefully lift the crab by the back of the shell and plunge into the boiling water. Stick a lid on and boil for 15 minutes, then remove the crab using tongs and transfer to a bowl of iced or very cold water.

Once cool, you should prepare a large chopping board or clean work surface and have plenty of kitchen paper or similar to mop up any of the fluid you spill. Start by placing your crab, back-down, onto the board and tear off all the legs and the claws. Set these aside.

Use your thumbs to pry the crab open – the apron (the bit with the legs attached) should easily lever out from the outer shell (carapace). It should take with it the dead man's fingers, or the spongy bitter gills. Discard these.

Continued overleaf

In the carapace, you'll have the mouth at the front, and behind it there's a sac-like stomach. Get rid of this. Everything else in the shell is edible. Use a teaspoon to mix up all the brown meat into a paste and leave it in the shell.

The apron, despite looking like a solid mass of shell, is full of white meat – these were the most proximal and prominent muscles of your crab's powerful legs. Scrape out all the tiny crevices, keeping the white meat together in a bowl. Avoid getting pieces of shell mixed in with the meat.

You don't really need a nutcracker for crab – all the brown meat from the legs and claws can be obtained by dislocating each joint and prying each piece of the limbs apart. Poke the meat through with a knife or drag it out. Once you've got all the meat, serve it on a plate with the shell of brown meat. Enjoy spread onto slices of white sourdough.

5

SMOKE AND FIRE

This book is an honest one. Yes, Shetlanders do indeed wear wool and literally everyone does have a rhubarb patch, but I don't want to paint a picture of a place where every resident lives off the fat of the land, scorning supermarkets for all but the most dire of emergencies. I don't want to insinuate that every house has its own cold smoker, or that we all eat piglet testicles. That would be false.

I do think, though, that it's fun and important to explore the ways of cooking and eating that we often take for granted, or that just aren't done any more. It gives us new ideas and flavour experiences, and an appreciation for subtleties that previously were not known. Whilst many locals will buy local hot-smoked mackerel, very few will attempt to make it themselves. But they should – it's dead easy.

Home hot smoking is an amazing cooking method that has been rediscovered in cheffy circles, but can be used easily by anyone to add flavour to simple dishes. I think everyone should consider it as an everyday way to cook fish and add flavour to meat. Cold smoking, on the other hand, is something everyone who is serious about food should try at least once. If you're into cured meats or cheeses, then you should always consider it. It's a bit more involved, and it takes a long time, but it's worth it. Neither method needs much in the way of special tools or equipment.

The hot smoking process

Hot smoking is when the fire and food are in relatively close proximity. It might be very gentle heat indeed, but the smoking process will also cook your meat or fish. This technique is extremely simple to emulate at home because you need no special equipment; all you need are some wood chips and a grill pan. I might heavily hot smoke a steak with hickory chips before pan frying for a perfect char, or slowly smoke a side of salmon over beech so that it flakes apart as a perfect sharing centrepiece.

A lot of people think of smoking primarily as a way of preserving food – and it is true that bugs do not like the delicious pollutants that coat the meat – but try not to look at it this way. Smoking might slow the growth of stuff that lives on the surface, but it does nothing for the core. It might stop some mould growing on the surface, but it isn't going to protect you against the nasties that are likely to cause serious harm. Smoking is for flavour, as far as this book is concerned.

If you're not already an evangelical smoker, I hope that this method of adding awesome flavour to your fish and meat will change the way you cook. It is so easy, and you don't need anything beyond what you would find in a normal kitchen. To understand why this works, we need to look at the basic principles of cooking with wood.

Wood flames can provide interesting and delicious flavours to fish or meat in three distinct ways. The first is through the direct heating of the meat itself – this creates that classic char. This happens due to the high temperatures causing reactions between the proteins and sugars naturally present on the meat. These are called Maillard reactions, after Louis Camille Maillard, the French physician and chemist who described them in the early 20th century. These give that pleasant umami flavour and contrast in texture that would not be there if the meat was simply poached. There is, however, no difference in the Maillard reactions possible over naked flames or using a hot pan. Cooking bread in a wood oven, for instance, makes no better bread than that cooked in an identical conventional oven.

The second way that hot wood can provide flavour, then, is by the burning of the fat that drips down from the meat or fish onto the high heat. This causes the fat to vaporise or to burn, imparting a pleasantly burnt or 'barbequed' flavour. The combination of these two processes is what makes barbequed food taste really good.

However, traditional barbeques do not impart any wood smoke flavour. If you use charcoal, all of the aromatic compounds from the wood have been incinerated already. In fact, the main reason that you burn the charcoal for so long before beginning to barbeque is to prevent licks of flames causing a thick layer of bitter, black soot on your meat. Some people might mistake this for char, and that is wrong.

The best way to induce beautiful flavour is to use wood – fresh wood, smouldering, before it has the blackness of charcoal. This is where you get the subtleties of the wood carried in the smoke. When I'm barbequing, I do indeed use charcoal and burn to white embers first, but I always have some fresh wood of some kind or another to stick on at the last minute before I add the meat – it transforms the flavour. If I'm in a rush, I might just get a roaring fire going and flash straight on a steak or something that requires high heat and minimal cooking.

Which brings us to examining the best ways of hot smoking at home. The heat involved is nowhere near the same level as when barbequing, so the numbers of Maillard reactions are limited. However, in hot smoking, we sacrifice this for massive fresh smoke flavour. The way we create this is not through direct flames, but heat from smouldering wood.

If you place wood chips or sawdust in a pan and stick them over a low heat on the hob, it will eventually begin to smoulder and smoke in a gentle way, turning the wood into charcoal and no more. This gives us exactly the kind of flavour we are looking for. If you can find a way to suspend your food above this, such as by using a mesh or grill, the heat from the gentle hob will cook your meat as the wood smoulders. Turn that heat too high, though, the wood will burn beyond a charcoal stage and you'll find your meat coated with a bitter, acrid ash. It's not nice on the tongue.

If you are making the wood chips or sawdust yourself, make sure they're from untreated wood. Most woods impart some kind of pleasant flavour, especially that from fruit trees (apple, cherry), as well as oak, beech, maple, ash and walnut. Each has its own set of characteristics, and I encourage you to experiment. If you can get hold of some fresh peat, it's awesome. Soaking everything in whisky or rum beforehand is to be encouraged.

Nota bene

This is an indoor technique. I am obliged to say that you should not leave your smoking wood unsupervised, you should ensure you have good extraction (open a window) and you should have a pail of water to hand to put out any fires you won't cause.

Preparing your food

Marinate, cure or simply season your meat or fish of choice. If I'm trying out a new smoke combination I've never used before, I tend to coat both sides of my raw piece of fish or meat in a thin sprinkling of table salt and a sprinkling of sugar, and leave it to sit on the worktop, uncovered for 15 or 20 minutes. After this time, the flesh will be well seasoned and mildly cured; you'll notice a film of water that can be patted dry with kitchen paper before smoking.

Basic hot smoking method

You will need:
a high-sided roasting tin
  (the older and more battered
  the better)
any kind of wire mesh or grill
  (mine is stolen from a grill pan)
plenty of strong foil
wood chips or sawdust

Place your roasting tin directly onto the hob. Make a small pile of wood chips or sawdust in the middle of it, directly over where your flames or your hob will be in contact. (This can be done with any hob type, including induction.)

Place your grill on top, so that it sits above the wood, but there is plenty of space between the grill and the top of the tin for your meat or fish to sit.

There's no real limit to how much you can smoke at once, but each piece of meat or fish should fit in your tin without touching anything but the grill below. You want maximum contact between the smoke and the meat, so try and leave a good half centimetre between each piece. Place your meat or fish on the grill directly above the wood but not touching it. Fish should go skin side down.

Cover the tin with foil – again, if possible, this should not touch the meat to allow for maximum contact with the smoke. Try to make the tin as 'smoke-tight' as possible.

Turn on your hob and set it to a medium heat. Keep a close eye on it – whenever you hear any signs of sizzling or see any smoke at all coming from around the foil, turn the heat down to as low as it goes. Then you can gently smoke for as long as it takes to cook your meat or fish. 300g (10½oz) fillets of salmon take about 20–25 minutes, but single fillets of mackerel as little as 10 to 15 minutes. A standard 200g (7oz) steak should take no more than 15 minutes to hit medium–rare, but I'd check using a probe thermometer to check.

When you want to check how done your meat or fish is, turn off the heat and let it die down for a minute first. Lift the foil – you'll be surprised how little smoke is released when you peel it back. (If there's loads and loads, your tin is probably too hot.) If you feel your food is cooking too slowly, remove the burnt wood and replace with fresh stuff or transfer the partially cooked and smoked food to a pan and fry it. Don't be precious.

Hot-smoked scallops

Shetland scallops are trawled from the deep raging waters around the islands. They are enormous – like great shellfish-y steaks – and three, maybe four, constitutes a main course. A Shetland scallop supper from Frankie's, the local fish and chip shop, is a favourite of the family.

I shouldn't have ever tried hot-smoked scallops... A trawler had over-trawled with typical voracity, and hadn't sufficient ice to store its glut. Rather than waste, they lightly cured the scallops and then used a rudimentary hot smoker to preserve them. Packaging them as soon as they reached shore, they were sold to locals rather than shipped south with the main batch.

I remember Dad buying these from the wee fish stall in the Toll Clock Shopping Centre in Lerwick, and the conversation with the bearded monger. I remember only being allowed a taste of half of one, hot, in our own dining room, distracted from whatever else I was doing, though these could easily be served cold. They were incredible – soft, sweet, smoky. And the flavour has persisted since. (My memory, as my wife will attest, persists best in foods, rather than places or experiences. Whereas she might remember what plenty of exotic places looked like, I remember each meal we ate. And the things around the meal – the smells, the sights and even topics of conversation or the clothes we were wearing.)

Hot smoking is particularly suited to the huge 'king' scallops of Shetland, for it cooks them gently, allowing a significant smoke flavour to develop and helps prevent you overcooking them, keeping the centre moist and meaty. I've served these with a quick dip made from yoghurt and chives and herbs from the garden, handy for a Shetland summer's day, but they are truly awesome on their own. Feel free to use any variation for the dip – to taste it as you go is important. I think sugar is necessary to balance the yoghurt out, but you might feel differently about sweet and meat going together.

6 very large scallops, roe attached
table salt, for coating
caster (superfine) sugar, for coating
handful of fresh mint leaves
a few chives
200g (scant 1 cup) natural yoghurt
40g (1½oz) caster (superfine) sugar
juice of half a lemon

For the smoke:
smoking wood chips or powder – I'd use oak with a little crumbled peat, if you have it

Allow 1–2 massive scallops each as a starter

Makes enough dip for 4 people

Remove your scallops from the shell (if supplied) and sprinkle them with a light coating of salt – I use the multi-holed bit on a standard tub of table salt – and then sprinkle with sugar. There's no need to leave these to cure. Keep the roe on – it's the best bit.

Prepare your smoker (as described in the basic hot smoking method on page 114) – lay your wood on the bottom of the roasting tin, then place your grill over and your seasoned scallops on top. Cover with foil or a lid and set the tin over a low heat for 15 minutes.

There's no need to turn the scallops, but you can check at this point how they're doing. It's likely they'll need another 5–10 minutes. If you see loads of smoke coming from around the foil, turn the heat right down. You want gentle smoke, not acrid burn.

Check the scallops are done by pushing them with a blunt knife – if they satisfyingly bounce back at you, turn off the heat and leave them to rest (covered) above the wood for about 5–10 minutes or so. Treat them like you'd treat your finest steak. You can also use a kitchen thermometer probe – 55°C (130°F) will mean they're cooked.

Whilst the scallops are resting, whip up your dip. Chop your herbs finely, and add these to your yoghurt, sugar and lemon juice. Mix together thoroughly until there is no sign of your sugar and it doesn't taste grainy. Keep tasting, and adjust lemon and sweetness to your preference. Serve.

Rib steak to share

You can buy all sorts of gadgets and interesting ingredients to add synthetic smoke flavours to your dishes. 'Liquid smoke' is popular, as are various smoke extracts and powders, and a million different barbeque sauces. You can buy smoke guns to blast smoke 'safely' at your food, though I shudder at the efficiency and the expense.

Because you'll be frying your steak anyway, you can partially hot smoke it first so that it remains raw in the middle, but has plenty of flavour imparted. Or you can smoke it until it is perfectly cooked, rest it, and flash it in the pan. Smoking is so much slower that it's harder to ruin your perfectly cooked steak.

As in the previous recipe, the real key here is to be slow and gentle. You want absolutely no bitterness or tannins from the smoke, as that will be the first thing your tongue will touch when the steak eventually makes it into your mouth.

Unless you only want your steak raw (bleu) or cooked (well done), I'd strongly recommend using a thermometer to check the centre of the steak for done-ness. They're cheap to buy and they're very easy to use. It takes any uncertainty out of this cooking method, and you really don't want uncertainty when dealing with such a large and expensive cut of meat. And yes, a rib steak, with the rib in, is pretty much the same as a rib eye, so you could use that too.

500g (roughly 1lb) prime rib steak, the thickness of the rib, bone in
table salt, for sprinkling
sunflower oil (or another high-smoke-point oil), for frying

For the smoke:
wood chips or sawdust – cherry, apple or hickory

Makes enough for 2–3 people to share as a main meal

Remove the steak from the fridge at least an hour before you plan to cook it. Preferably, do it a few hours before, but don't stress. When you take it out, sprinkle a thin layer of salt all over the meat and leave it to come to room temperature.

Place the wood chips or sawdust into the bottom of the smoking/roasting tin, and then your grill on top of that. Place your steak on the grill and cover over with foil (but not touching the meat). Place your tin over a medium heat until you start to hear and see smoke billowing from the sides, then turn your heat right down to low.

Smoke your steak for at least 10 minutes, and then remove from the heat and turn the meat over. Smoke for 10 minutes on the other side. At this point, check with the thermometer. You'll probably have a way to go – you want 50°C (122°F) in the middle for rare, 55°C (130°F) for medium–rare, 60°C (140°F) for medium, and nothing ever above that.

Keep smoking, checking and turning intermittently, until the steak is done to your satisfaction. Unless you've got a monstrous piece of meat, it's not going to take more than another 20 minutes.

Turn off the heat and let the smoked beef sit for 10–15 minutes to rest, still covered, in the tin. As it nears the end, you should set a frying or griddle pan on the highest heat you have. Cast iron is best. Don't season with any oil, yet.

Once your beef is rested and the pan is smoking with anticipatory ferocity, add at least a tablespoon or two of your frying oil. Wait for it to smoke and then add your steak. Flash fry until just golden brown on each side, keeping contact to a minimum. You want 30 seconds to a minute on each side, max. Once golden, remove the steak from the heat and serve, with whatever you normally serve with steak.

Cold smoking

Cold smoking is when smoke is applied to your food without cooking. This is usually done using two chambers connected by a tunnel – in one chamber you light a fire, and the other contains racks or hooks from which you hang your ingredients. The heat should rise from the fire through the roof of the first chamber, and the smoke travels along the tunnel, cooling as it travels, and passing over the food without cooking it.

Or at least, that's the theory. Even the best DIY cold smokers can't eliminate smoke's fundamental property of heat – smoke is only produced from fire, after all. And the longer the smoke is left to warm the tunnel and second chamber, the hotter they get. This means that a poorly designed cold smoker might still cook your food, or worse: many will warm your ingredients up to body temperature and the perfect conditions for bacteria to multiply rapidly, potentially causing harm. Therefore, cold smoking is commonly applied to food that's already been cured or fermented a bit first.

There are a few other ways to impart a smoke flavour using what might technically be regarded as cold smoking. A very simple form is in the production of reestit mutton, or reest (see page 54) – this was probably the most accessible way to both smoke and dry meat in Shetland, and still is. Haunches of meat were hung above the hearth where a peat fire burned. These could and would be hung for up to weeks at a time, giving an extremely intense flavour and causing many soothmoothers to flee at even the sight or sniff.

Whilst hot smoking involves almost no forethought, cold smoking is a little more involved. First, you've got to make a cold smoker and you need plenty of time for the smoking process.

Here, your smoking medium matters a lot. If you only have wood chips or larger pieces of wood, an excuse the internet has eliminated, you will need to use a two-chamber smoking device with a linking tunnel. The most common way to achieve this at home is to build a 'trash can smoker' – a simple device created from a lidded barbeque and a metal bin. A Rough hole is cut in the side of each, and a piece of ducting is used to connect the two. A fire is lit in the barbeque, the smoke travels out of a hole in the lid and down the tube, cooling as it goes. This smoke fills the bin, which is modified to hold racks or hooks and has a small hole cut in the top as a chimney.

That's all well and good, and you can YouTube how to build one of those if you enjoy using drills and angle grinders and trips to Screwfix. But I think there is a more accessible way of cold smoking, available to everyone who wants to. All you need is a cardboard box and a sieve, pretty much, but you will need to use smoking dust (sawdust) rather than wood chips.

Note

Cold smoking is a long process and it is not realistic to supervise it. Therefore, you should probably do this outdoors on a stone surface, in case the cardboard box catches fire. I've never heard of this happening, but better to be safe than sorry. I've got to say this.

Basic cold smoking method

You will need:
a large, sturdy cardboard box
  (mine is about 80 x 50 x
  25cm/32 x 20 x 10 inches)
parcel tape
knife/skewer
a large metal sieve (with a
  flexible mesh)
a large shallow metal bowl or
  foil (to catch any falling ash)
candle or blowtorch
a pole to hang your meat from
  (such as the cardboard inner of
  a long foil roll, wooden
  dowling or, like me, some pipe;
  make sure it is sturdy enough
  to hang your meat from)
S-hooks
smoking dust (sawdust)

Stand your cardboard box up on its end, like a wardrobe, with only the two biggest flaps open. Seal any cracks or holes with tape, and seal the other side if it has been opened. You could tape two boxes together if yours isn't big enough.

Stab a knife or skewer through the sides of your box near the bottom, working your way around to make lots of holes. This is for the air that will fuel your fire. Make another hole, at least 3–4cm (1¼–1½ inches) in diameter, in the top of the box for an outlet. You can stick a toilet roll tube through the top to make it look like a chimney, if you want. This will aid in the draw and help keep the sawdust burning.

Make a hole on either side of your cardboard box near the roof to slide your pole through. The holes should be slightly smaller than the diameter of your pole. Push your pole through each side.

Make your smoke generator out of your sieve. First, push the middle of the sieve mesh upwards creating a doughnut-shaped trench all the way around. Pack your sawdust into this as tightly as you can, leaving a small gap on the handle-side of your sieve. This will prevent the sawdust burning from both ends and you will get a longer burn time.

Hook the sieve over the metal bowl, so that it is suspended, or line the bottom of the box with foil and poke the sieve's hooks through the side of your box.

Pierce your hooks through your prepared ingredients, and hang them up on your pole.

Light the candle under one end of the tract of sawdust, so that the wood begins to smoulder and smoke. Once the wood is going, remove the candle. Alternatively, use a blowtorch to get it going.

Close the 'doors' to your smoker and tape them shut. You should see a gentle, consistent plume of smoke through the chimney. This should last 4–6 hours at least, as the gentle burn makes its way around the sieve. For most cold smokes, I would empty and replenish the sieve once all the sawdust has been used up and repeat the smoking process once or twice more for an intense smoke flavour.

If you see the smoke stop prematurely, open the doors to check what's happening. If the fire has gone out, it could mean that it wasn't lit properly or that it became starved of air. Try making more air holes or make them bigger. If it has burned around the entire circle of sawdust very quickly, replenish the sawdust and tape over some of your holes to slow down air flow.

Smoke-your-own Shetland salmon

A rather predictable recipe, yes, but essential. I don't think there's an eatery in the isles that doesn't serve smoked salmon and cream cheese in a bagel, despite the immediate availability of much superior bannocks. Most of the farmed Scottish salmon you get in UK supermarkets is from Shetland, so you can produce this dish fairly authentically.

This is a simple recipe that is a great introduction to smoking. It's one of the easiest to do and one of the easiest to get right. And importantly, almost everyone will have eaten smoked salmon, so you'll know what to compare it to.

The key here is not to over-cure the fish – I've made and eaten many homegrown examples where the chef has left the fish way too long on the salt, or squeezed all the moisture out of it. Or seemingly forgotten to add the sugar, which both cures and adds much-needed sweetness to this rich fish.

Balanced with a slice of lemon and a little rye sourdough? Oh my, I've come over all funny.

side of farmed Shetland salmon, skin on
200g (1½ cups) good sea salt
300g (1½ cups) caster (superfine) sugar

For the smoke:
oak sawdust or smoke dust (you can use any wood, but oak's flavour is most recognisable)

string or a hook to hang the fish up

You can also follow this recipe for any unskinned round fish. Smaller fillets of oily fish, like mackerel or trout, will need significantly less time in the cure. Between 8–12 hours is ideal. You can slice some off to taste and find out; it should only dry mildly during the smoke.

Start by preparing your side of salmon. Run your hand down the flesh side to make sure there are no pin bones. If there are, pluck them out with tweezers. Tie some string around the tail-edge of your salmon and pull it tight, knotting to secure. Tie a loop a few inches down the string and cut off the excess. (This is so you can hang your salmon up, or you can just stick an S-hook straight through the flesh just before hanging.) Put the salmon back into the bag it came in or a large, clean carrier bag (you might need to fold the fish).

Pour all the salt and sugar into the bag and rub this into the flesh and the skin of your salmon, completely coating it. When you're happy it's smothered, place the salmon, skin-side up, so that the pink flesh is in direct contact with the salt and sugar. If the salmon is folded over, make sure there's plenty of salt/sugar next to the flesh.

Refrigerate for 12–18 hours. Overnight is best, however long that takes you. To check the seasoning level, cut off a tiny piece of fish, wash it and taste it. If it tastes good, stop. It's easy to over cure. Remove the salmon from the bag when you're happy with the taste and shake off any excess salt/sugar mixture (but don't brush it off or wash it).

Continued on page 126

Hang your salmon up to dry. If there's a cold wind, do it outside. If there's not, hang it indoors in a cool place with some kind of tray below to catch the drips. You want a sticky skin to form on the outside of the salmon, to which the smoke will adhere. Leave it for at least 2 hours to dry. Keep pets entertained to keep them sane.

Once dry, hang the fish in your smoker. Depending on the size of your box, you might need to slice your side of salmon in two so that it fits in without getting too close to the burning sawdust.

Light your smoker (see the basic cold smoking method on page 121). If your sawdust is fresh, dry it out a little by zapping it in the microwave for up to a minute beforehand.

Smoke your fish for 8 hours, or until your desired flavour is reached. The greatest thing is that you can just slice off a sliver and taste it to check how done it is.

Home-smoked salmon can be stored in the fridge for a few days but any longer than that and you should freeze it to be safe. A mild cure and delicate smoke means that this doesn't keep for long.

Whisky-smoked halibut

Halibut is an awesome fish and not readily available in Shetland. There's some impressive wild angling done off the coast by uber-men in their expensive or rented boats – indeed, the largest wild halibut in recent times was caught off Shetland – but otherwise the majority of this stuff seems to come farmed from elsewhere in Scotland or from Norway.

The first time I experienced whisky-smoked halibut was, typically, from a posh deli in the city. They had started stocking the products of a wee smokehouse out in the Campsies, the hills just north of Glasgow, and had sold out of all but one of the halibut as word had spread, despite its extortionate price tag.

Yes, it's an expensive fish. But this fish is your cold smoker's showcase. It is extremely meaty, which is accentuated during curing. Then, because its flavour is so subtle (read: bland) it takes on the flavours of your smoke more than most. This means you need to be careful not to have an acrid, over-smoked fish, as this will dominate. And you can try other flavours to infuse into your smoke – this recipe uses whisky.

Don't use a peated whisky. If we wanted peat, we'd smoke with peat. Try something mild and fruity; a lowland single malt or a branded blend. If you can get hold of some fired whisky barrel staves from which to make your sawdust, all the better. Don't tarnish this with anything like dill or fennel or any of that ilk. Pepper is fine.

2 large halibut steaks, skinless approx. 200g (7oz) each
200g (1 cup) caster (superfine) sugar
100g (¾ cup) good sea salt
freshly ground black pepper (optional)

For the smoke:
1½ tbsp whisky per smoke
enough oak smoking dust (or untreated oak sawdust) to fill your sieve 3–4 times

Makes plenty for a starter platter, with some left over for freezing

First, cure the fish. Tip roughly half the sugar and salt into a large freezer bag. Lay the bag on its side and spread the granules out. Place the two halibut steaks inside, flat, next to each other, so that all the white flesh on the bottom is touching the grains. Add the rest of your sugar and salt, and rub into the exposed white flesh on the top.

Seal the bag and place it in the fridge. Leave it to cure, unweighted, for approximately 24 hours. You want this fish not overly bereft of moisture. Turn the fish once or twice during this time.

After curing, remove the fish from the now very wet, very fishy bag and wrap it in kitchen paper. Leave it to completely dry out while you set up your cold smoker.

It's best to start with completely dry smoking dust – if you have a microwave, place your dust in a bowl and microwave for 30 seconds or so before adding your shot of whisky and mixing together.

Continued overleaf

Hang your dry pieces of fish from the pole (see basic cold smoking method on page 121).

Pack your sieve with the sawdust and light it (see basic cold smoking method on page 121). It will burn quicker than usual (because of the whisky) and you will need to replace it 2–3 times to get a full smoke out of it. Seal your smoker and aim for an overall smoking time of at least 10 hours.

Once smoked, I freeze my halibut in (fresh) freezer bags and defrost overnight before eating. Or you can eat it straight away. Remove the fish from the bone and the skin, and slice into slivers approximately 0.5cm (⅕ inch) thick.

Needs no accompaniment; bask in its glory.

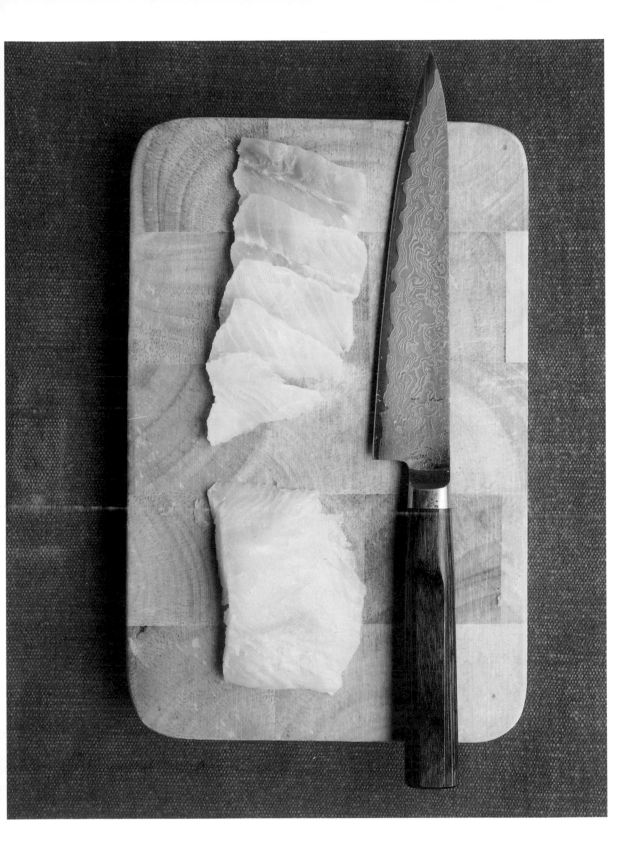

Golden syrup bacon

The vegan-crushing, cancer-causing, culture-creating behemoth. Cured pork belly: bacon.

We used to have a croft which we sold to an ex-neighbour, Ben, who has kicked out the sheep and has started rearing pigs. His ultra-free-range, heather-fed monstrosities of pigs are very tasty, and especially the extra-thick slices of mega-bacon they produce.

Dad's recipe for mutton bacon (Macon) is on page 142, which you can, of course, cold smoke. But this is the unadulterated pork stuff, included because I've never yet had a forum in which to share this wonderful thing. In fact, this recipe alone is worth going to the effort of building a cardboard smoker for. If you disassemble (and recycle) it after following this recipe, you'll have got your time and effort's worth. Make a big batch and freeze the majority.

Do streaky, regardless of your current preference. The belly is cheap and very easy to work with, as soon as you've got the skin off. For the purposes of this recipe, and for the rest of your life, there is only smoked bacon.

Bacon, as purchased in the shops, isn't simply cured in salt and/or sugar. It has added nitrates. These compounds act as a further preservative, specifically helping against spore-forming *clostridia* species (good old botulism again). They give bacon that luminous pink colour; without nitrates, usually found in the form of curing salt, your bacon will look like a dense, pinkish raw pork, plus whatever you put in the curing mixture. If you opt to make your bacon without curing salt, that's fine. It won't affect the taste. But you should freeze it as soon as possible, as I cannot guarantee its keeping abilities.

500g (roughly 1lb) pork belly, roughly square-shaped
150g (scant ½ cup) Lyle's Golden Syrup (other brands apparently available)
200g (1½ cups) good sea salt or curing salt

For the smoke:
beech sawdust or smoking dust, or similar (I like the mild flavour of beech)
dry peat, crumbled (optional)

Remove the skin from the pork belly (from which you can make amazing crackling, if you like). Start at a corner, and lift up the edge of skin. Use a sharp knife to free the skin, pulling it up and back. Use gentle strokes, lifting up all the time, to gradually peel the skin off.

Now, it's time to start the cure. This is going to take about 5 days. Today, pop your pork belly in an appropriately-sized freezer bag (preferably with a zip lock) and then add your golden syrup. Seal the bag and use your hands to smoosh the syrup around, covering the belly completely. Stick the bag in the fridge for 24 hours, turning once half way through.

Now it's time to add the salt. Pop open the bag and tip in all the salt at once (it will seem like a lot). Reseal the bag and massage your pork belly again. Give it a good hard rub – you want your salty liquid to completely cover the

belly – before returning it again to the fridge. Turn the belly over every 12 hours, for 4 more days. It's as easy as that.

After this time, and preferably in the morning on a free day, open up your bag and get rid of your sugary salty liquid. Wipe your belly down lightly and stick a sharp hook through one corner. Leave it to hang in a cool place for 3–4 hours. This is for your sticky skin to form for good smoke adhesion. During this time, you can nonchalantly set up your smoker. You've even got time to go out, buy the stuff and build a cold smoker from scratch.

Hang your meat in your smoker and smoke as desired (see basic cold smoking method on page 121) – I'd go for at least two full sieves of dust, or about 8–10 hours of smoking time. It doesn't need much more than that. Although there is nothing better than smoked bacon, over-smoked bacon is fairly awful.

Bacon keeps forever in the freezer, and this is where you should store it if you make large batches. Otherwise, it will keep in the fridge for a week, unsliced. Slice just prior to cooking – as thinly as you can using the sharpest knife you have. It will still be relatively thick cut, compared to shop bought.

To cook, always fry and never grill. Use a little frying oil, such as peanut, or some sliced-off rendered bacon fat. Fry over a high heat for a couple of minutes on each side - you want to properly render the fat down and give a deep golden brown finish.

6

LAND

It's the seaweed that makes Foula mutton special. Like the island of North Ronaldsay in Orkney, here the sheep feed on kelp and tangle, and both islands' meats sing with the taste of the sea. Elsewhere, the heather and meagre grass makes the small, hardy Shetland sheep (if they're purebred, and those are the ones you want) tasty no matter which part of the islands they come from.

As we've discussed on page 54, mutton is the meat from an adult sheep. Lamb is a sheep in its first year. So there's a moment between when lamb becomes mutton – just past the point where lamb is pretty muttony but not quite there – called 'hogget' by some gentrified farmers. 'Muttony' means tastier, stronger and (if the sheep is very old) possibly a bit stringy and tough.

The thing is, both mutton and lamb are forgiving when it comes to cooking. You can roast them from frozen – slowly, not particularly carefully. You don't need to do anything but stick either in an oven, wrapped in foil, or in a peat fire. Or you can make some slits and insert cloves of garlic, festoon it with rosemary. I like to roast a leg without covering it, so that you get what amounts to crackling on its surface fat and superficial meat. Keep it in a roasting pan with a little water topped up to stop it drying out, and to provide for gravy. And skim the fat, because there will be a lot of it, despite the leanness of these small creatures. Save it for soapmaking.

Roast shoulder of Foula mutton

Shoulder of lamb or mutton is a frustrating cut, difficult to carve and to get an adequacy of decent servings from. But Richard Briggs does a rolled shoulder of lamb, hogget or mutton, which works extremely well. His recipe and mine are almost identical in terms of simplicity. And if you're cooking from frozen, all you have to do is keep the heat low and cook it for an hour or so longer, though the privilege of being able to serve it rare is removed. Keep checking until those juices run clear.

In Shetland, we like our meat to melt in the mouth and slip seamlessly off the bone. None of that bleeding rarity, that squelchy metallic bloodiness. It's just the way we roll.

2kg (4lb 6oz) shoulder or
    leg of lamb or mutton
vegetable oil, for coating
sea salt, lots for seasoning well
handful of mixed herbs,
    such as rosemary and thyme
    (optional, preferably wild)

Makes enough for 8 people,
or fewer with leftovers (see
Stovies, on page 269)

Preheat the oven to hot. Some would say as hot as you can get it, but I'd be calm: 240°C (450°F)/220°C (430°F) fan/Gas 9.

Place the meat in a large roasting tin and rub with enough oil to coat it. You don't need much; the lamb is plenty fatty. Generously scatter with sea salt, then place your herbs on top. We use wild Shetland thyme, rosemary and a few things foraged from the garden.

Quickly open the oven door and shove the lamb in. Cook for 30 minutes to frazzle the top, then turn the oven right down to 150°C (300°F)/130°C (250°F) fan/Gas 3. Pour a glass of water – don't waste your wine – into the tin and roast, depending on how you like it.

For a pink lamb, as soothmoothers might like it, roast for a further 30–60 minutes. Use a probe thermometer, poked into the deepest part of the meat: 50°C (122°F) is rare; 70°C (160°F) is well done. Somewhere in between will be fine. Once done, remove from the oven and leave to rest for 20–30 minutes, covered in foil.

For a proper roasted lamb, though, with marrow that melts and meat that falls from the bone, cook for another 3 hours. You don't even need to turn the oven any lower, for the crispy, near-burnt layer that forms over time is truly the best bit about this cooking method. Keep an eye on it – if it's looking too black, you can cover with foil or turn the oven down. Skim the fat as you go, or all at the end.

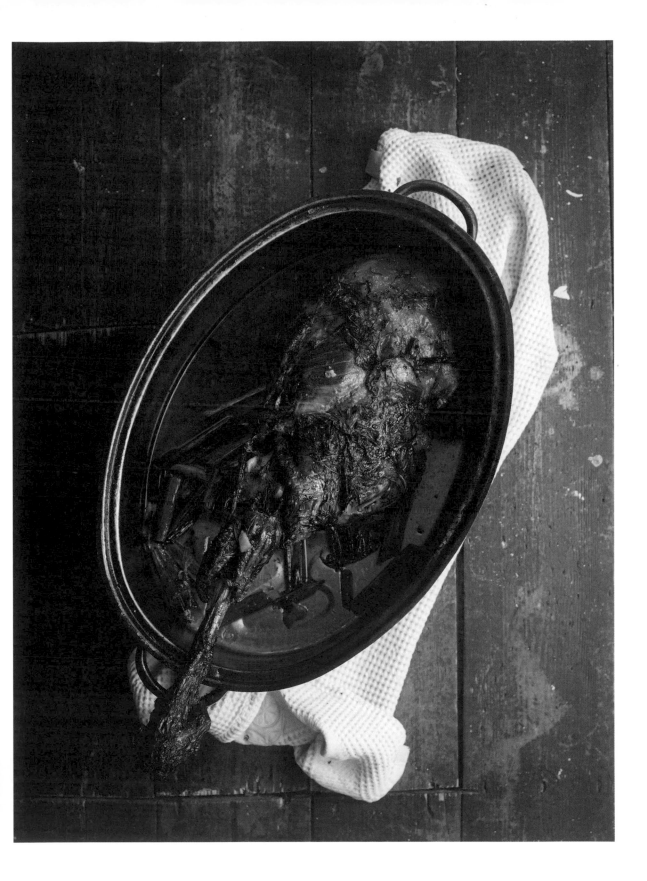

Mutton pie

Neither of us is in the habit of making mutton pies, being of West of Scotland genes and with a possibly fatal attraction toward the grey, semi-meaty fat/mince which you find in an industrial Scotch pie. (Which, I have to admit, I still occasionally enjoy deep-fried with chips, or inside a buttered roll with brown sauce.)

This, though, is something altogether different. It is highly unusual to find mutton pies at an Up Helly Aa in Shetland, but the campaign to make them ubiquitous starts here. After all, we have the mutton.

The recipe below uses the very easy hot water crust pastry. You can use ready-made shortcrust if you're feeling lazy. Because the filling is solid, you can raise your pies by hand by effectively wrapping your pastry around your meat filling, securing it with paper as described below. The safer alternative, though, is to bake inside a pie (or pudding) tin lined with paper.

For the filling:
600g (1lb 5oz) fatty mutton
   (or lamb) mince (at least
   20% fat)
¼ tsp ground mace
70ml (2½fl oz) water
   (or lamb stock, if you have it)
good sea salt
lots of white pepper

For the pastry:
160g (scant ¾ cup) cold water
½ tsp table salt
120g (4¼oz) lard
360g (3 cups) plain (all-purpose)
   flour

1 egg yolk, beaten, for glazing
   (or use 500g (1lb 2oz)
   ready-made shortcrust pastry

Makes 4 gargantuan pies

Preheat the oven to 200°C (400°F)/ 180°C (356°F) fan/Gas 6. Line a baking tray with baking parchment. You'll need four 7.5cm (3 inch) silicone moulds or cut four long strips of bakong parchment, about 5cm (2 inches) wide and 25cm (10 inches) long and some cook's string.

Mix all the ingredients for the filling together in a large bowl using your hands, adding plenty of salt and pepper. You can fry a wee piece up to check the seasoning. Divide your meat into four even, pie-shaped lumps on a plate, cover with plastic wrap and chill while you make the pastry. (Or, if James isn't looking, roll out the Jus-Rol.)

Weigh out your water, salt and lard into a medium pan. Set over a medium heat and bring to the boil.

Tip the flour into a large bowl, pour in the melted lard mixture and and stir everything together with a table knife. Let your pastry cool slightly, so you can handle it easily, then turn it out onto a lightly floured surface. You want to knead it gently until smooth and pliable; for a few minutes at least. It shouldn't stick, so try not to add extra flour whilst kneading.

Put about a quarter of the dough to one side. Divide what's left into four equal pieces. Eschew the rolling pin: hand-form a large circle out of each piece to around 3mm (¹⁄₁₀ inch) thick. Make four smaller circles for the lids, the same thickness, from the pastry that you set aside.

If you are using pudding tins or pie moulds, fit each large circle of pastry into a mould. Take your meat out of the fridge and place a lump in the centre of each pastry circle. Alternatively, if you are hand-forming, put each lump of meat in the centre of your flat pastry circles, and gather the pastry up around each one; you might need to stretch it. You want about 3mm (1/10 inch) excess poking up around the top edge.

Add a wee touch of salt to the beaten egg, and brush this around the edge of the pastry. Pop your lids on top and crimp your pastry together. Use your thumb and forefinger and work your way around to create a seal.

If hand-raising pies, you'll need to stop it from falling apart in the oven. Wrap your pies circumferentially with the long strips of baking parchment (wrap at least twice, if possible), and then tie firmly with string. If you don't have someone to help you, you can hold your paper in place by sticking two layers together with a little lump of excess pastry.

Carefully transfer your pies to the baking tray and cut a small slit in each top. Brush lightly with your beaten egg yolk and stick the tray in the fridge for 30 minutes. This, again, helps them hold their shape.

Bake from cold for about 40 minutes or so, or until dark brown in colour, but not burnt.

Stovies from scratch

Stovies are the best of way to use up what's left over from the stove after a roast (see Roast shoulder of Foula mutton on page 136).

Their reputation is tainted by microwaveable packets of mashed tatties with mince laced through, but stovies can be truly wonderful things. You can make them with any meat (and there even exists such a thing as vegetarian stovies, but frankly this is a blasphemy and one with which we shall not besmirch these pages. You can find a recipe on the vintage, dedicated stovies website stovies.com – I'm not kidding).

This recipe is for stovies from scratch. It includes the addition of a stock cube, of which James generally disapproves. I'm greatly in favour of stock cubes, but you can make your own or purchase the fresh stuff from your local supermarket if you so wish. But I think stock cubes make things taste better. HP Sauce is useful too, both as a direct addition and to serve. If you want to make stovies using leftovers, briefly fry with the onions and don't boil for an hour before adding the veg.

1 onion
2 tbsp suet, preferably mutton, butter or lard (if you're using leftovers, use the dripping)
680g (1lb 8oz) mutton, lamb (or another brownish meat)
450g (1lb) potatoes, ideally peeled
½ a small neep (swede), peeled
1 meat stock cube (preferably lamb but any will do) or 250ml (1 cup) stock
good sea salt
freshly ground black pepper

Makes enough to feed a family of 5

Finely chop your onion, or as finely as you can muster. Scrape into a large pan with your suet and fry gently over a low heat until golden. Add more fat if the onion starts to stick, and keep stirring. Add a pinch each of salt and pepper.

Cut your mutton into small pieces but don't mince it. Add this to the pan with the onions with more fat if it starts to stick. You want a golden crusty coating on most of the meat.

Just cover with water and heat to simmering, then pop the lid on. Barely stew on the lowest heat your hob will go for an hour, by which time your mutton should be cooked.

Chop your potato into wee cubes – exactitude inessential. The same with the neep. Pop these in and replace the lid to stew gently for another hour. If, after 30 minutes, you think it's too watery, remove the lid for the rest of cooking. Season with more salt and pepper to taste and serve hot. Reheats very well.

Macon

Although this might look just like the mutton or lamb version of bacon, it isn't. It's a melt-in-the-mouth, ultra-crispy and almost gamey delicacy that only a few people in modern-day Britain will have tried. You can forego the smoking, but this gives it clear waves of reest. Macon is definitely on the more textured, nay chewy, side of bacon. Maybe that's just my slicing, or maybe it's the toughness imbued by the howling winds during the years lived by the mutton-bearing sheep.

All I know is nothing goes better in a soft roll with a slice of sassermaet and brown sauce.

500g (1lb 2oz) mutton or lamb belly (breast)
150g (⅔ cup, packed) soft dark brown sugar
200g (1½ cups) good sea salt

Makes enough for a large family breakfast

Caress your meat. You're going to have to get used to it.

Rub half the sugar all over your meat on all sides and then place the belly in a large sealable freezer bag. If you don't have one big enough, use a clean plastic carrier bag. Stick the meat in the fridge and wait. Wait a full day.

Open up your bag – there should be a lot of liquid. Drain this off, remove the meat and now rub half the salt all over. Return it to the same bag and stick back in the fridge for another day.

Time to switch cures. Remove your meat from the fridge once more and again de-bag. This time, rinse it briefly under the tap. Now, mix the remaining sugar and salt together and rub these all over your meat. Put it in a fresh bag.

Leave to sit for 5 days, inside the fridge, turning over daily.

On day 6, rinse the macon with water. Slice off the ends and cut yourself a wee sample to fry – if it's too salty for you, soak the belly in some cold water for a few hours. I don't think it will be.

Slice your macon carefully into thin slivers. Place each on a sheet of baking parchment, layering them up between sheets to stop them sticking together. Freeze, so they will last indefinitely. They can be fried straight from frozen.

Lizzie's very slow-cooked beef cheek

I was first introduced to beef cheek at Aberdeenshire's Eat on the Green and it is one of my favourite cuts. Beef cheek is a lean, coarsely textured and tough meat, a bit like rump. It needs a lot of tenderising before it's edible. It must be melt-in-the-mouth. Nothing less will do.

At one of the Ratters' legendary Slow Food events, Lizzie (Ratter) produced this dish. You don't get much slower than this, in every sense of the word. This hits the brief – there is nothing quite like it. James would suggest that it's due to the high levels of umami flavours – the meat, the onion, the wine and the mushrooms – but what would I know about that?

2 tbsp frying oil
  (such as sunflower)
125g (1 cup) plain
  (all-purpose) flour
good sea salt
1kg (2lb 3oz) beef cheeks,
  sliced into large chunks
1 large brown onion, finely
  chopped
½ garlic bulb
4 carrots (other root veg will do)
250ml (1 generous cup)
  red wine
50g (2oz) dried mushrooms
2 beef stock cubes, or 500ml
  (generous 2 cups) rich beef
  stock
100g (3½oz) tomato purée
2 bay leaves
a small bunch of thyme

Serves 6

Place a large, heavy-based pan over a high heat. Add in the oil and leave it to warm. Stick the flour and the beef in a bowl together and season with a very generous pinch of salt. Mix them to coat the meat, then fry it in the pan, a little at a time. You want the meat golden, but turn down the heat if the flour is catching. Add more oil if necessary. Once each batch of beef is done, transfer it to a plate next to your pan to keep warm.

Add the onion, garlic and carrots to the (brown and sticky) pan and cook over a medium heat, until the onion is soft. If your flour or your onion sticks, add a little red wine and try to unstick it.

Meanwhile, put the mushrooms and beef stock cubes in a measuring jug, boil the kettle, then pour boiled water over the mushrooms to a volume of about 500ml (generous 2 cups). (Or rehydrate the mushrooms with hot beef stock, if using.)

Add the rest of the wine, the stock and the mushrooms to the pan with the vegetables and unstick any sticky bits.

Add the tomato purée and herbs, and add the meat back in, stirring to combine.

Cook, covered, for a very long time. Eight hours or so. Either leave the pan on a solid fuel cooker, adjusting the position of the pot on the top plate, or keep on a very low simmer on a gas or electric hob, or transfer everything to a big electric slow cooker. It should be just hot enough that it isn't bubbling, or only very seldom does so. It's ready when the beef is tender – properly tender.

Piglets' testicles

I admit I do not have a tremendous amount of experience with the consumption of testicles, apart from pigs' and piglets', and even that is now pretty much in the past. I am therefore extremely grateful to my son for some of the background information here. As for cooking pig and piglet balls, it's straightforward. Obtaining them may be an issue, but most decent butchers, especially those trendy organic ones that charge an arm and a leg for a shoulder, will get them for you if you ask nicely. "I'm looking for some testicles - do you have any?" usually sparks some kind of a response.

Testicles, or testes, is plural. Two testes. A testis is a singular testicle. Ideally, you're removing them from animals that are not yet randy. Bigger is not better – I've heard duck testicles are exquisite, please get in touch if you've ever eaten them. I would not recommend full-on ram's testicles, which can be the size of melons depending on the breed of sheep. Lamb testicles are shellfish-textured and have the pungent taste of offal. Piglet testicles, though, are mildly porky, as you'd expect, and quite delicious. Halving them is important – they are coated with a very strong layer of connective tissue which must be broken.

4 piglet testes
1 tbsp plain (all-purpose) flour, for coating
good sea salt
1 egg
panko or breadcrumbs from stale bread, for coating
500ml (generous 2 cups) oil, for deep-frying

Serves 2–4 as a starter or snack, depending on the size of the testicles

Halve each testicle with a sharp knife, even if they're very small. (When we removed them from our piglets they were about the size of grapes.) Trim off any stringy appendages.

Mix the flour and a little salt in a shallow dish. Beat the egg in another dish and place the panko or breadcrumbs in a third dish.

Cover and toss the meat in the flour, then dip into the egg, let drip and then coat with your breadcrumbs. Set aside on a plate.

Heat the oil in a large, heavy-bottomed pan over a medium heat. Test if it's hot enough by frying a little bit of clumped together breadcrumbs. Fry the meat until golden on all sides, and soft and succulent in the middle. Enjoy.

Of hares and rabbits

It's too late for me to ask Harry Tuckey, then owner, about how the Burrastow House hare was cooked in the early 1980s. Back then I'd never eaten game, apart from two pheasants: one that my dad ran over outside Glasgow, hung in the cellar until it was rancid with maggots and tasted like very bad medicine indeed; and one at my sister's graduation meal, which was absolutely full of that slippery, teeth breaking, highly toxic lead shot. So the Burrastow hare was a revelation: an epiphany almost, in its pungent delicacy, its lovely, umami-ish earthiness.

Later on in my Shetland residence, encouraged by friends and fellow crofter Drew (slightly more experienced than me; he went on to become chair of the Crofters' Commission), I took up shooting. (You can read more about Drew, Vivienne and their wonderful food on page 154). I shot both hare and rabbit, learning to cook both. One is much less fiddly than the other.

I've sold my guns now and given up my licence. Last year I even got rid of my remaining two air rifles, after the Scottish Government legislation on needing to have a certificate for them kicked in. To be honest, I don't like shooting live creatures, even if I am going to eat them. And I was absolutely outraged to hear about a local landowner's son (Shetland still has a few lairdy types, some of whom retain shooting rights over land they've leased to local crofters) who last year shot 70 – seventy – snipe just a few miles from where I sit and type. Legally, but still. The snipe is one my favourite birds, with its twilight spring drumming noise, a strange electronic whirr it makes in flight by rubbing its legs together. I'd make him eat every single bird he shot raw, at a single sitting.

I love the way Shetland hares turn white in the winter. Could you shoot a white hare? As for rabbits, well... That would be an ecumenical matter. I did consider getting a crossbow and wiping out some of our horrible rabbit population, which all but makes lettuce production impossible in our garden. But the law says you can't. Only blasting with a shotgun or (usually winging them) with an air rifle is permissible.

Roast hare

You want a young hare, and usually just the back legs and saddle will be roasted. There's not a huge amount of eating on one – at a pinch, two people will get a feed, but a glutton like me will want one to himself. And I did, at Burrastow. You can shoot, skin and joint your own hare – YouTube has videos showing how – or go to the butcher (might be worth phoning first). Supermarkets don't sell hare. I don't think.

1 saddle and hindquarters of a young hare (approximately 500g/1lb 2oz)
frying oil, such as peanut or rapeseed
4 juniper berries
1 tsp black peppercorns
1 carrot, sliced
1 onion, sliced
2 sticks of celery, sliced
good sea salt
freshly ground black pepper
250ml (1 generous cup) red wine

Serves 2, with trimmings

Preheat the oven to 180°C (350°F)/ 160°C (320°F) fan/Gas 4.

Put a good glug of oil into a roasting tin and place it on the hob over a low heat. Lightly crush the juniper berries and peppercorns using a pestle and mortar, just so as to break their outer skin. Add these, the carrot, onion and celery to the pan and fry until the vegetables have started to soften, stirring occasionally. This can take as long as 15 minutes.

Rub the hare joints with more oil and add to the tin, on top of the vegetables. Season with salt and pepper. Add the wine.

Transfer the tin to the oven and roast for 25 minutes, then check the meat. Do this the old-fashioned way: pierce the saddle to see if it is still bloody. If it is, and you're not some sort of modernist daft cheffy Hannibal Lecter-freak (thanks, Dad), put it back in the oven for 5–10 more minutes at the same temperature. If it's cooked (see below!) reduce the oven heat to 100–150°C (200–300°F)/80–130°C (176–260°F) fan/Gas ½ and leave for another ten minutes.

Remove the tin from the oven and leave the hare to rest under foil for 5–10 minutes before carving and serving on the vegetables. Pink meat is permissible; Texas Chainsaw Massacre is not.

I'm going to sneak this in, in the hope that Dad just skims over it... The middle of your hare should be no more than medium–rare. Anything more is insanity. Use a thermometer probe, and go for 52–55°C (125–130°F) at the centre. This is proper rare. Leave it to rest for a good 20 minutes and you'll have treated this delicate animal with the care it deserves. Texas Chainsaw Massacre, my arse. J.

Margaret B. Stout's stewed rabbit

I cannot recall finding the table consumption of Burrastow hare at all fiddly, but the bones are small, and you can stew a hare in the normal, everyday sort of way before deboning. When making a rabbit pie, where the bones are even smaller and more irritating, stewing is essential. Besides, rabbit lacks the gamey pungency that makes roasted hare so appetising.

This is a very simple and traditional Shetland recipe for rabbit stew. It comes from the great Margaret B. Stout's *Cookery For Northern Wives*. Here I present it in its original, unedited entirety:

One rabbit. Three onions. Two tablespoonfuls of fat. Three tablespoonfuls of flour. One pint of water. Pepper and salt.

Skin, wash and joint the rabbit. Dip in seasoned flour and fry a golden brown on both sides. Cut the onions in slices and fry also. Remove from pan, add remainder of flour, mix with dripping, add hot water or stock. Bring to boil and season. Return meat and onions to pan and simmer gently for one and a half to two hours. Dish neatly and pour gravy around.

Now, there are a few comments to be made. First, notice how 'stock' suddenly appears as an option in the 'method', without being mentioned in 'ingredients'. There's the variable cooking time. One and a half to two hours, indeed. This will depend on how old or large the rabbit was, how tough, basically. It could be longer than two hours, to be honest, but such things are not allowed by early twentieth century local publication standards, let alone national modern ones. Then there's that 'dish neatly'. Now, you could just leave the meat on the bone, but better by far (particularly if youngsters with bunny fixations are involved) to get your hands greasy and skliff off all the meat.

If you like, you can do as James's Granny used to and complete the process by turning it into a rabbit pie. She added bacon to the stewing stage (fried in pancetta-sized chunks) which brought a bit of zest to the whole business.

The rabbits of Shetland are plague-like, and although I am no longer armed, they are easily picked off by going for a 'run' in the car of an evening. As I once did to Granny Audrey's cat on my motorbike. By accident, I hasten to add. I tried to dispose of the cat's body quickly in the sea, and when I returned to the house, breathless and guilty, the phone rang. It was Audrey. "Have you seen my cat?" she asked. "Err...no. Have you lost him?" "Well, it's just I was watching you down at the beach, Tom, and you seemed to be throwing something into the water."

Her rabbit pie was delicious.

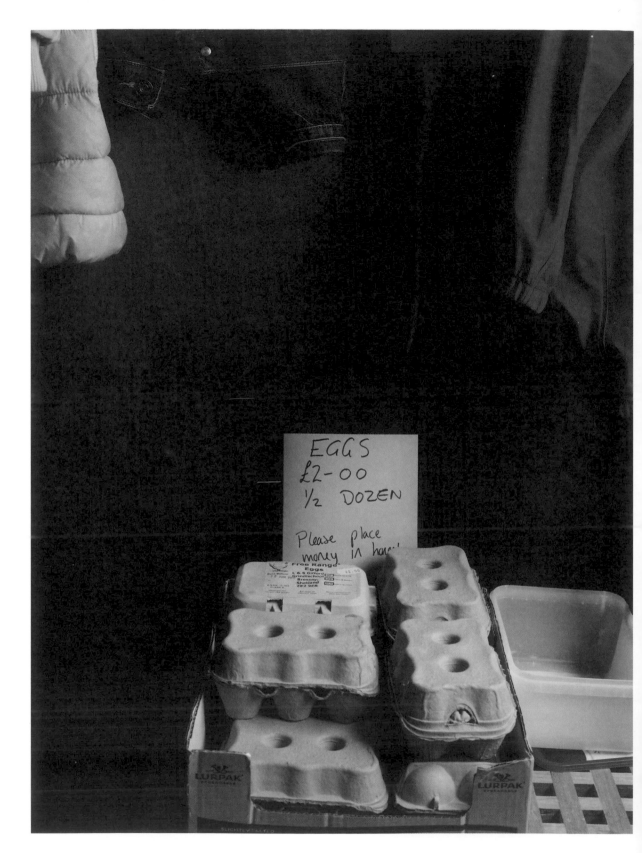

Craft chicken

I've never been a vegetarian. In fact, even the idea that some people don't eat meat was somewhat of a preposterous one when I was growing up. I thought they must be mentally unhinged. Everyone I knew was omnivorous and delighted in it. Growing up, the miniscule number who didn't eat meat were stereotypes of the antisocial, know-it-all hippies who fully deserved their ostracism.

But give me a caged hen now and I can't help but feel a sense of sadness. I do not like the process that has led this wet bald bird to sit upside down in a plastic packet in front of me, inevitably dripping in Campylobacter and Salmonella.

The emotion of catching, wringing the neck, hanging, plucking and drawing a bird of your own or your friends might be equally conflicting, but it is ultimately fulfilling. It feels natural, sustainable. Despite making me a murderous bastard, it feels like the right thing to do because it is, and has been for as long as all life has existed.

Either bird, though, needs treated with a bit of respect, and I do not think that we do treat chicken with respect. We try and copy the Delias and Jamies in order to make the perfect roast, but we end up getting in the way of the flavour that this bird has been helplessly slaughtered for.

My roast chicken is simple. In fact, it is the simplest chicken recipe that you'll find – there are only two ingredients. As such, try not to scrimp on the chicken. Make it one that hasn't travelled far, that has been dealt to you by an independent retailer and that has led a happy life until its untimely demise. Pay good money for it.

Don't waste anything – the dripping that will come off the chicken is extremely good for all kinds of savoury cooking, especially roast potatoes and roasted root vegetables. Keep it in the fridge – it will last forever. As for the carcass, make some stock. (Or is it called bone broth nowadays..?) See page 247.

Preheat your oven to 180°C (350°F)/160°C (320°F) fan/Gas 4. Find a roasting tin and take the grill out of your grill pan. Stick it in the roasting pan; it doesn't matter if it doesn't fit properly.

Unwrap your chicken onto the grill and untie the legs if necessary. Use a salt shaker to cover the skin in a thin coating of salt. Then, turn it upside down – in actual fact, this is the right way up; you want the breasts on the bottom. Spread the wings and legs apart, tucking them around the sides of the grill to keep them spread wide. Cover this side in a thin layer of salt.

Continued overleaf

1 large, best-quality free range chicken, 1.8–2kg (about 4lb)
table salt

Serve with:
Roasting vegetables of your choice – I like potatoes, sweet potatoes, celeriac and carrots. Green of your choice – cabbage or kale or some sort of broccoli. White wine, dry sherry or vermouth, to make a jus.

Serves 6

Roast the chicken in the oven for 50 minutes. Make sure there is nothing else in the oven during this time. Do not baste, ever. Do not add vegetables to the pan.

After 50 minutes, it should be starting to turn a nice golden brown. Now you can turn it over and bake it the conventional way, breast side up, for another 30–40 minutes. Cooking a chicken breast side down makes it much less liable to dry out and therefore the cooking time is much more forgiving.

During this second half, you can put any vegetables you plan on roasting into the oven, but don't add them to the chicken tin. Use separate roasting dishes, and don't add any oil or any salt to them. Don't worry, they won't stick.

After 40 minutes, your chicken will be done, unless there's something really wrong with your oven. A probe thermometer will confirm the deepest bit is over 70°C (160°F) and the juices will run clear. Take the chicken out and set it on a warm plate, cover it in foil or baking parchment and leave it to rest.

Remove the grill from the chickeny roasting tin. Pour off the juices into a measuring jug – you'll notice the vast majority of this is fat – and let it settle for a few minutes whilst you remove your slightly dry looking vegetables from the oven. Transfer a few tablespoons of chicken fat onto the vegetables and use an implement to turn them, so they're coated in fat. Return to the oven to finish off.

Pour off the rest of the fat into a jar or bowl and keep in the fridge for later use. I'd use a bit more of it now, though, to fry up the greens. Heat it in a pan and add your torn greens, adding a little water if you feel them dry out and start to char around the edges. This will create steam to cook the veg quickly.

Pour the minimal juice that is left into your roasting tin. You can add some white wine, dry sherry or vermouth and place this over your hob to deglaze and make an extremely simple delicious jus. (I like to serve it like this, but if I'm making a salad with the chicken I'll make a chicken dressing: add a little wine vinegar and good dollop of grainy mustard and stir in a little extra chicken fat.)

Carving

Blunt dissection is much cleaner and more accurate than sharp. Carving your chicken should never be a sharp knife occasion; it should only ever be done with a butter knife.

Start by lifting off your very crispy skin, and fight over it.

Draw a line with your knife down the middle of the chicken, then peel each breast off the breastbone. Keep the knife stuck onto the bone, and your breast should peel away in a single lump.

Stick your knife in each knee joint between the drumstick and thigh to peel off; I tend to get rid of the bones at this point, including the sharp fibula that is often hidden in the drumstick, as well as the cartilaginous pieces at the top.

Next, stick your knife in each hip to lever them off, again removing the bones if you wish. There should be some meat left underneath the wishbone and around the parson's nose that will also come off easily. Save the wishbone for making a wish, obviously. Remove each entire wing as one piece.

Turn the chicken over and you should find, not just a doubling of the amount of crispy skin that you normally have, but a whole load more easily obtainable and not-soggy meat. Remove all the muscles that overlie the ribs – these are the back and proximal wings and many of the thigh attachments. This is a lot of meat that often goes wasted.

Serve, artfully arranged, if possible, and let everyone know how much trouble it was for you.

Crofting

Tom

I've been based in Shetland since 1987. I was a journalist then and essentially that's what I've remained. Susan is a doctor; a GP. But both of us, at various points in our lives have dreamed of being crofters. We've dreamed of a self-sufficient life.

Inspirational was that bible of 'Good Life' dreamers: John Seymour's *The Complete Book of Self-Sufficiency*, published in 1976. Alas, it is no longer in print, though it has spawned many imitations, such as Dick and James Strawbridge's *Practical Self-Sufficiency*. John Seymour's *New Self-Sufficient Gardener* is still being published and you can see how it might appeal to a modern generation of would-be Toms and Barbaras as it is devoid of the blood-spattered pig-slaughtering and chicken-strangling of the original '70s tome.

Susan and I would try, for a year or two, to live by Seymour's rules. After four years on the Scottish mainland together, we moved to Shetland, jobless, with two children and another on the way, but debt-free (that didn't last long) and in possession of an ancient cottage. Indeed, one of the oldest houses in Shetland on maps from the fifteenth century. It had no toilet or bathroom. Just a single cold water tap. It did have electricity, though, so we installed a Swedish biological composting toilet. This was supposed to take our various faecal and urinary doings and produce sterile peat for growing tomatoes in. It had a fan, a chimney and blades which automatically churned a mixture of shit, pee and peat, before heating it up and funneling the dried remainder to a tray for removal. It broke. And it kept on breaking. Largely due to the children filling it with toys (Action Men, Barbies, large quantities of Duplo and Lego). If you've never bailed out a blocked and broken composting loo, salvaging the bairns' Batmen as you go, I do not recommend it.

Social workers paid an informal visit after my son Magnus luridly described our absence of plumbing to one of his teachers. We decided, on gentle suggestions from the authorities (and offers of grants) to take out a mortgage and go back to work, extending the house, putting in a bathroom and a septic tank. (You see what James had to go through growing up.)

By this time, we had pigs, including Derek the Randy Boar. Hens. Ducks. Later we had sheep and were narrowly and discreetly dissuaded from getting a cow (just a small, Shetland black cow; like the sheep and ponies, native kye tend to be little, or peerie in local dialect).

But we were both working full time by then and therein lies the conundrum of crofting, which has a very specific, legal meaning in Scotland. A croft is a smallholding, usually but not always rented, its status safeguarded by a number of laws dating back to the fallout from the Highland Clearances in the nineteenth century, when landlords essentially got rid of the smallholdings on their land, and all the people, to make way for industrial sheep farming.

As a crofter you have both 'in by' land – yours to control and usually surrounding your house – and a share in the common grazings, the 'hill land' held together by the local crofting community

We bred, castrated, killed (you were allowed to kill back in the 1990s, for your immediate family's consumption) and butchered, much of that knowledge being fuelled by Seymour's book and from instruction by our friends Drew and Vivienne.

I will never forget the first slaughtering I took part in. It was a cow. The sheer size of the beast was intimidating, and it took around ten of us to deal with it. The smell of cordite from a double-barrelled shotgun blast to the head; its toreador crumbling to its knees; and the swift slitting of its throat, with the blood being gathered in a bucket for making black pudding. The steaming innards, sifted for liver, kidneys, heart. The hanging and then the waiting for the mysterious 'Kenny the Butcher' to come and cut the beast up. Nowadays, there is a superbly run slaughterhouse with in-house butcher in Lerwick. There is no longer any need to get quite so hands-on. Killing a pig was different, in that you essentially had to depilate the pig's skin rather than remove the outer skin entirely, as with a cow. This meant loads of hot water and shaving. Somehow, this was far more unpleasant than with sheep, which were relatively easy to deal with. You made an incision, inserted your hand, breaking the fibrous connections between the carcass and its outer skin (with fleece attached), working your way around the whole body while it was still warm, as if you were somehow trying to wear the sheep like some kind of giant hot glove.

On the subject of castration (and I have never begun a sentence with those words before), it was Lindsay the vet who deftly demonstrated how to do it, with an understandably squealing piglet held over our crofthouse sink. Afterwards, at her recommendation, we sliced and fried the tiny objects. They were muskily delicious, though not, as one BBC Radio 4 documentarist insisted, "a transcendental, yet unsettling experience". Just one of those once-in-a-lifetime things you're happy to enjoy once in a lifetime. See the recipe on page 144.

Eventually journalism, broadcasting and medicine, not to mention rearing three active and busy children, saw us rationalise our life away from crofting, although vegetable gardening remains a passion of Susan's. (I grow potatoes and cut the grass.) One grim winter prompted the final decision. We lost half our flock of sheep to heavy snow – Drew and Vivienne helped us to dig them out, some dead, some alive. It was one of the most dispiriting days I've ever spent. The croft was sold. Now it's a commercial, organic pig farm.

Drew and Vivienne are what I like to think of as super-crofters. As well as their herd of cattle, they keep sheep, hens and ducks. They run a model operation which supplies them with all the meat and many of the vegetables they and their family need in a year. They are passionate about 'slow' local

food, and every Christmas they host a 'slow food day' where guests come from far and near bearing examples of just such food and drink to share. It's usually between Christmas and New Year and is one of the foys I look forward to most.

Our family tends to contribute a measly offering by comparison. James makes bread to go with Susan's pots of winter vegetable soup (bringing bannocks would spark discussion, nay controversy or disparagement). Martha makes some very, very good chocolate brownies that she stole from James, who stole them from someone else, probably.

One year, after much discussion, Drew and his daughter Lizzie decided to have a go at making 'macon', or mutton bacon. It is a mildly reestit piece of rolled mutton left for a few weeks, kept in the fridge and thinly sliced for frying. It was just about quite (verging towards very) good. However, perfection on preserving can be difficult to achieve, and it became clear that the brine and smoke hadn't penetrated quite to the centre of the meat. After a while, the aroma was definitely telling us to stop eating. But the idea of mutton-bacon is still a good one – see my own attempt on page 142.

As for our current state of self-sufficiency? Well, when it comes to rhubarb and tatties, we're good. Our freezer receives its annual bounty of a quarter cow and several lambs. We fish and one or two creel fishermen supply us with crabs and lobsters, mostly out of the generosity of their hearts.

But our crofting days are over.

7

EARTH AND THRIFT

James: Earth

Growing things in Shetland can be a struggle. The sun is low and often hides, it never gets particularly warm; even in bright light there's a fierce spray of salt from the sea. This is what gives Shetland its barren beauty. Heather prevails.

Any visitor will notice the lack of trees, although a few small 'woods' have been planted in the recent past. It isn't, as tourists and schoolchildren are dutifully told, because the Vikings arrived and sliced them all down for use in boat building and repairing. It's because conditions are not ideal.

But it must be said, Shetland never really gets that cold in the winter either. The summer provides endless daylight. There are a few sheltered voes and valleys with astounding microclimates of their own, that seem to bathe in sun when it's gone elsewhere and are well out of the prevailing wind.

My mother is the gardener in the family, though Dad likes to act like he is. He might aid in the growing of a few potatoes and put his back into digging them up when the house is empty, but otherwise he obeys conservative custom. I would like to claim I am an expert horticulturalist, but alas I am not. I judge vegetables by flavour and by the distance they've travelled to get to my plate. Handily, Mum's veg wins on all accounts.

The obvious things do well: carrots, neeps (swedes for the English, turnips for the northern Scots) and tatties of many colours. Frosty winter vegetables: sprouts, cabbages, cauliflowers and endless, endless kale. We pretended to like it before it was cool.

Rhubarb is almost impossible to kill – and in fact our hundred-plus-year-old patch was recently entirely dug up and re-buried upside down for some building works. It came back the following year, bigger than ever. And in a similar vein, many Shetland gardens are covered in a very peppery rocket. It grows huge, is delicious and commands quite the price down south. But getting rid of it is a chore – try it in the pesto on page 171.

For stuff that grows outside in temperate England, Shetlanders need a polytunnel. Or a 'polycrub', which is an extra-sturdy Shetland version made of re-purposed salmon farms. A standard polytunnel has its downsides, as is evidenced by an enforced break in the photography for this book during which we were required to go help re-skin a polytunnel over in a particularly sheltered part of the mainland. Think of their plastic skin as a large kite, or sail.

In ours, we have had some unusual things. Raspberries and strawberries grow well. Next to them, you'll find a bay tree, and an apple tree. In fact, as you might expect, the apple tree is growing through the roof. But it is producing apples, which cannot be said for any placed outside. Pumpkins, squashes and courgettes grow well.

For more exotic things – tomatoes, chillies or citrus fruits – a heated conservatory is preferred. Standalone glasshouses do exist but imagine what happens when one of those takes off…

I don't care much about flowers, but I hear they do grow.

The curious case of the tomatoes

Tomatoes? We have them. This year, we've had a glut of green ones. To be precise, Susan did. Susan, James's mother, is the planter and cultivator in this house, and proud possessor of a porch. She calls it a porch, but it's actually a conservatory. She designed it for social purposes, but inevitably it was swamped by her beloved plants.

It was the site of the great tomato disaster: flourishing plants in an unusually sunny summer; a crazily warm July, with Shetland suffering more sunlight than Cornwall. Native Shetlanders wandered around topless and be-shorted, while tourists cautiously removed one of their seven layers of Gore-Tex.

In the Great Porch of Constant Watering, a jungle had erupted. Fruit was sprouting green on the vines, prolific, some orange, some red...

But we had to leave. For ten days the house was in the hands of a medical student who systematically over and under-watered (forgot and then belatedly remembered), so that by the time we returned the tomato plants were desiccated then swamped, dying or dead, and the fruit was trapped between luridly unripe and heading-for-squishy.

Waste not, want not. Susan consigned the plants to the dumper and removed the fruit. There were kilograms of all colours, all sizes. Something had to be done. Something tasty, something useful, something to consume and something to keep. I started with gazpacho. Cold soup, or a kind of Shetland blasphemy. But then, under glass, in an unseasonably warm summer, so are tomatoes.

Shetland indoor gazpacho

Gazpacho originates in Andalucia, Spain and is celebratory fodder in the purest sense. It was labouring food, consumed by workers in the vineyards and olive plantations. Traditionally, it was made up of leftover bread, water and olive oil all pounded together in a bowl. Whatever vegetables were to hand and spare – ripe, unripe – were mixed in. And that was that. Something delicious to enliven and enlighten the working day, to bring people together.

This gazpacho went down well at a lunchtime gathering of a few friends. It was consumed by a certain soup connoisseur, a man of considerable rock'n'roll distinction whom I sometimes think moved to Shetland because of the availability of soup, just as folk sometimes up sticks for Guatemala because cannabis is legal there.

I will call him Alvis, as that is not his name. Alvis was not expecting, of a summer weekday, to be offered chilled garlic, pepper and tomato liquid with an ice cube. He's more accustomed to lentil and vegetable broths in which his spoon leaves a large divot with every scoop. And I provide this recipe with his blessing, though he commented on the little slivers of tomato skin, which frankly didn't bother me, as I have a filtration beard to catch such detritus. I've modified the recipe, to include the fiddly business of peeling the tomatoes. Which is annoying, but easy, really.

Place the bread in a bowl with enough water to soak, but not drown them.

Pop some water in a pan to come to the boil and half fill a large bowl with cold water and some ice cubes. Drop the tomatoes into the boiling water. After 30 seconds, remove them using a slotted spoon, or when the skin begins to wrinkle, and put them into your prepared icy bowl. Howk them out onto a chopping board, and the skin will fall off in a belatedly satisfying manner.

Roughly chop the peeled tomatoes and the cucumber, and scrape into a large food processor with the celery, peppers, onions and garlic. Add the bread. Add a good glug of olive oil and the lemon juice, then the paprika, salt, pepper, cayenne pepper and a pinch of sugar. Whizz, and keep whizzing (adding water if necessary or ice cubes if it's really hot and you're serving this immediately) until you're happy with the consistency.

You can leave the soup in the fridge overnight and it will taste better, as these things do. Cover with plastic wrap so stray aromas don't get in there.

Stir before serving and top with olive oil, fresh mint and chopped onions.

5 slices stale white bread, crusts intact

a whole heap of tomatoes in various conditions – maybe 1kg (2lb 3oz)

1 small cucumber (optional – it has to be fresh and firm, or don't bother)

1 stick of celery, roughly chopped

1 green pepper, deseeded, roughly chopped

1 good-sized red onion, trimmed, roughly chopped

2 garlic cloves, peeled, roughly chopped

some good extra virgin olive oil

juice of a fresh lemon

1 tsp sweet smoked paprika

good sea salt

freshly ground black pepper

1 tsp cayenne pepper

a little caster (superfine) sugar, to taste

Serve with:
olive oil, some fresh mint and a little chopped onion

Makes 4 big bowls

Eshaness lentil soup

You can complicate this recipe at your peril. Keep it simple.

Leek, onions, stock cubes, or James's actual stock from boiling up intestines and things like eyes and larynxes. My favourite stock comes from a big lump of unsmoked gammon, but this takes rather a long time. It does give you the fortunate side-effect of broken gammon to both mix into the soup and to serve in your buttered bannocks on the side. This doesn't count as a complication.

Whatever meat or stock base you use, the key is red lentils, not soaked, but washed. For Shetland soup purposes, they should be cooked until they've almost dissolved.

Some people add potatoes, and even neep. What fools.

For optional homemade stock:
1 small (300–400g/10½–14oz) gammon joint, unsmoked for approx 1.5 litres (6 cups) stock

3 ham stock cubes/pots plus 1.5 litres (3 pints) water
1 large onion
1 leek
a large knob of salted butter
2 large carrots
250g (1¼ cups) red lentils
freshly ground black pepper

Makes enough for 6. Scales up well – multiply recipe by 100 for Up Helly Aa night (see page 251).

If you're making your own stock, place your joint in a large pan and cover with water. Bring to a simmer and turn right down so it barely bubbles, but still does. Stick the lid on. You've got three hours of waiting now. Alternatively, dissolve your stock cubes in boiling water from the kettle.

Chop your onion and leek finely, and place in a large pan with the butter. Soften over a low–medium heat. If it starts to stick, opt for the triad of non-sticking: stir quickly, turn the heat down and add more butter. If that fails, use a little water with further rapid stirring. Under no circumstances taint it with whatever you are drinking.

Scrub the carrot of any muck, and then grate it into the soup. If this doesn't agree with you, you can chop into a quarter lengthways first, then chop. Add to the pan and begin to brown.

Place the lentils in a colander and run through several times with cold water. You want the water to run clear. Add to the pan with the veg, and stir to combine everything. Quickly follow this by adding your hot stock.

Stir and pop the lid on. Simmer over a low heat until the lentils are breaking down; this should take 20–30 minutes. Taste, and dose with pepper for mild spice. You can serve immediately, but this soup tastes best reheated, after forgetting about it for a couple of days 'without refrigeration' on the stovetop. (Don't tell environmental health.)

Rational non-magic mushroom soup

I get very nervous about fungi. One only needs to look at the case of experienced forager Nicholas Evans (the Horse Whisperer), as he poisoned himself and several members of his family by misidentifying, cooking and eating webcaps. They survived, but seemingly only just.

Psilocybin mushrooms, all joking and tall stories about goggle-eyed sheep aside, are not to be messed around with, and I speak from personal experience. Also having seen a Shetland Folk Festival performance from a fiddler who had consumed a lot of dried magic mushrooms an hour beforehand, I do not recommend them on artistic grounds. Or any psychedelics, in fact. I cite the horror that is the entire recorded output of The Grateful Dead.

Common mushrooms are common in Shetland in September and the lack of trees make the varieties available in the wild very limited. Fly agaric there is, if you fancy being a berserker and dying. I don't. You can take that Viking thing too far.

Here's some safe, non-hallucinogenic soup. The reason for the minimal stock is to let the mushrooms sing.

1 small onion
100g (4oz) butter, unsalted or salted, or good olive oil
good sea salt
freshly ground black pepper
400g (14oz) wild field mushrooms or a mixture of chestnut and dried wild mushrooms, cleaned and roughly chopped, plus another handful left whole
600ml (2½ cups) water
300ml (1¼ cups) chicken stock, or hot water with 1 stock cube added

To garnish:
a handful of wild mushrooms

Makes enough for 4 starter-sized portions

Start by chopping your onion with disregard, then add to a large pan with half the butter or oil. Soften over a low–medium heat, adding a pinch of salt; don't let it burn or crisp. This should take a good number of minutes.

Add your mushrooms and continue to fry. You want the black, bitter juices characteristic of overripe field mushrooms to seep out and help keep everything free. Keep cooking for another 5–10 minutes.

Add the water and the stock, then simmer for 20 minutes or so with the lid on, over a medium heat.

Blend using a stick blender – you only want to do this roughly, as you want a few chunks for texture. Absolutely do not add cream.

To finish, place the remaining butter in a shallow pan and melt over a low heat. Chop your reserved mushrooms into chunks and fry slowly until soft, but still a bit chewy. Stir these into your blended soup and serve.

Shetland black chips

These islands give their name to many indigenous things: Shetland ponies, Shetland sheepdogs, Shetland sheep, cows, geese and ducks, Shetland wool, Shetland fiddle and, most ubiquitous, Shetland black tatties.

People seem to get quite excited about 'blacks', as they're known – this is a variety of potato with a very dark purple skin and a yellowy flesh with a faint rim of purple that sits about a centimetre or two in from the skin edge.

It is a fluffy potato and well-suited to roasting and chips. Although it does have a great, heritage-potato sort of flavour, I used to find them disappointing. The colour doesn't remain through cooking – it seeps out, making everything else purple but the potatoes themselves. Their fluffy flesh seemed to border on the mushy. Then I found out that many of the potatoes I'd eaten weren't true Shetland blacks, but a similar variety that makes up the majority sold down south. Recognise the imposters by their shiny purple skin and smooth oval shape – true Shetland tatties are properly black, round and knobbly, with a yellower and somewhat more structural flesh.

The colour still seeps out, and so the chips aren't black. But they're very good. Epic, in fact. Better than any chip you've ever had or any chip you'll have again if you cook them as I describe here with absolute specificity. The thick skin's crinkled crispiness; the crevices of the exoskeleton of sweet crackling. The vinegar reminiscent of chip shop chips and the sting of the sharp salt as you crunch.

Note: don't attempt this recipe unless you have an accurate probe thermometer. Alternatively, use a fryer.

2–3 Shetland black tatties
1kg (2lb 3oz) beef dripping
malt vinegar
good sea salt

Makes enough for 2 people, to go with a silent pint

Wash your tatties. Leave the skins on, but chop off any particularly nasty bits and cone out any eyes that you cannot fully clean. Chop them into very chunky chips – the minimum width should be 1.5cm ($^5/_8$ inch).

Place them carefully in a large pan and cover with cold water. Bring to the boil over a high heat and then turn the heat down to a simmer. Simmer for 5 minutes.

Carefully pour the black water away, either through the lid or using a colander. Save it for flavouring a vegetable stock, if you like. Be very gentle with them. Do not shake your tatties like you would to fluff up a par-boiled roast potato – you'll have a mushy, skin-filled mess.

Carefully place your steaming, boiled chips onto some kitchen paper. Leave a little gap between each. Let them sit there for another 5–10 minutes. (You don't need to leave them longer or chill them as many might regard in a traditional 'triple-cooked'; this is just if you're frying to order later on.)

Heat your beef dripping in a pan over a low–medium heat to melt. Bring to 160°C (325°F), before carefully lowering your chips into the hot fat. Cook for 3–4 minutes, or until they've gone a kind-of-beige colour without any golden brown crispiness. Remove using a slotted spoon and place on a new piece of kitchen paper to dry as your fat heats back up.

After the fat hits 160°C (325°F) again, return your chips and fry until properly crisp. The flesh will go a reddish brown and that's what you want. The skin will shrivel and bits of other chip may stick to it. Remove from the fat when at this stage and, again, let any excess fat drip onto some fresh kitchen paper.

Serve with malt vinegar and sprinkle with sea salt that has been crushed between your fingers and no more.

Tatties with tarragon and peppery rocket pesto

The best (non-chip) potatoes I've had in recent years weren't blacks. They were the ones we ate when we went across to our friends James and Magnie's house for the purposes of this book, to have a look at their garden. We hadn't expected them to provide any kind of sustenance, but a homely, almost nutty smell of boiling potatoes was coming from the kitchen as we arrived, swiftly followed by two excited Labradors.

These potatoes were early Red Dukes of York– each no bigger than a plum. Traditionally roasting tatties, these had been boiled thoroughly, so the skins were starting to fall off, and had been left to drain well before being returned to the pan with a hefty chunk of butter and plenty of salt.

They were heaven on their own, but Magnie pulled out a second summer trick – a pesto made by one of his neighbours using his own rocket and tarragon. I wanted to punch him it was so good, so I swiftly stole the recipe and proclaimed I would use it here.

at least 500g (1lb) small
  roasting potatoes
75g (2½oz) unsalted butter
lots of good sea salt

For the pesto:
50g (2oz) fresh tarragon
100g (3½oz) very peppery
  rocket
250ml (1 cup) extra virgin olive
  oil
100g (⅔ cup) blanched or
  roasted hazelnuts
1 clove of garlic
1–2 tsp honey, preferably
  heather
good sea salt
freshly ground black pepper

The pesto doesn't take very long, so if you're doing both, start with the tatties. Don't peel them, just scrub any nasty looking pieces off and cut out any eyes. Stick them in a large pan with cold water to cover. Place this over a high heat and bring to the boil. Turn this down, and simmer for about 20 minutes, or until a fork passes easily through the middle of one.

Drain the tatties through a colander, and let them continue to drain for at least 5–10 minutes while you make the pesto.

In a food processor, add the tarragon, rocket, oil, hazelnuts, garlic, a teaspoon of the honey and a pinch of salt and pepper. Blitz well – it will initially go smooth, but it will then start to lighten. Taste it, and see how you like it. If it needs sweetness, add more honey, and season appropriately before blitzing again.

Return your drained tatties to your dry pan and add the butter and plenty of salt. Gently mix to melt the butter and season all the tatties. Serve with the pesto alongside.

Singing carrots

The temptation when deriving and writing recipes is to keep adding and adding ingredients. It's a shortcut to originality. It can be dressed up as gastronomy or flavour-pairing or ingredient supremacy.

Very few recipes are designed to make a single ingredient sing – I don't know why, for I very rarely cook entire dishes from recipe books or even online. I handpick elements I like the sound of. Like many of you when reading through a method, I might spot an interesting way of cooking broccoli, and try it alongside my own (superior) way of making chicken.

If you are blessed with carrots you feel are truly excellent, I'd prepare them one of three ways: first, raw, carefully cubed with a good knife. Pop the sharp-edged chunks into your mouth and roll them around using your tongue, before crunching and releasing all their flavour potential in a bite.

Or, use direct heat and minimal oil to sear your hard carrots in a pan. Keep going and going until you've got a crisp, near-burnt outside with a firm centre. If you've got fire, then use that instead.

And finally, there's this way. This is how you make your carrots sing. It's a tweaked version of a very classic glazed carrots dish. The original French versions might require an entire block of butter, or more, paired with half the butter's weight again of sugar; I've tried these and I think they are too sweet and too swamped in grease.

200–300g (7–10½oz) heritage or homegrown carrots
125g (4oz) unsalted or salted butter
25g (1oz) caster (superfine) sugar
200g (7fl oz) water
good sea salt

Makes enough of a side dish for 4–6 people

Prepare your carrots. Or rather, leave them alone. Scrub them to remove any dirt and trim most of the stalks. No peeling. If they are chunky (over 2cm [¾ inch] in diameter), slice them lengthways.

Place the carrots in a heavy-bottomed pan large enough to fit them lying flat in one layer. Add your butter, sugar, water and salt, and place over a medium–high heat.

Melt the butter and coat the carrots in the ever-more-amalgamated juices. Once they are fiercely spitting, turn the heat down to a brisk simmer. Cook away for 20 minutes or so, turning the carrots occasionally to stop them catching.

Once the water has almost entirely evaporated, baste the carrots and turn them. As soon as they start turning a little caramelised, stop and set aside. Serve.

Tom

Ross the builder, from the northernmost island of Unst, once told me that, until he was 14, he thought bananas were black, because in the scattered shops of that most isolated of rural outposts, fruit was never fresh. Nothing was fresh except what you caught, killed or made for yourself.

I remember Rosa Steppanova, now the doyenne of Shetland gardeners, lamenting that when she first arrived in Shetland from Germany in the 1970s, the only place you could get olive oil was at the chemist's, where it was sold for dissolving ear wax. And Peter Hetherington of *The Guardian*, a frequent visitor for journalistic reasons and a lover of traditional Shetland fiddle music, telling me he could never move to the isles as his wife would object to the lack of sun-dried tomatoes.

James: Thrift

Sometimes those who are as self-indulgent as me forget what eating is about – staying alive. Although I do make a living by promoting the consumption of things that merely augment life, I also make a living from dealing with the consequences of hedonism. You make gallstones and my friends and I will remove your gallbladder. It's a rather sweet deal, don't you think?

I think we face a near insurmountable task. Obesity is endemic. Everyone's getting fatter and my generation is going to die young, from the complications of weight-loss surgery amongst other things. Everyone's looking for something to blame – it used to be saturated fat and now it's sugar. In reality, it's neither. It still boils down to a decision to consume more than is necessary.

We need to change this. The occasional pig-out is, of course, heartily encouraged by me but portions do not need to be the size that they often are. Our instinct, when faced with a mountain of ingredients, is to provide a feast by default. It is to be hospitable. But say we turn that on its head and we view over-providing as wasteful, environmentally unfriendly and showy, maybe we're in a better place overall? I wouldn't like people to worry either way, but I think it's something to aim for.

Preserving food might be the answer. It gives you a respect for its value, and its potential. It unlocks new flavours and textures. It lets you use up vegetables and fruit that would otherwise go to waste. It should be done routinely and by everyone, not because we need to do it to avoid scurvy in the winter months, but because it's fun, tasty and keeps things local.

If you were paid your annual salary in a lump sum, you'd have to show restraint and cunning in order to make it last. Imagine that each ingredient is paid in once a year – that you do not have access to Peruvian asparagus or Kenyan Tenderstem™ broccoli all year round. You'd need to be inventive to make what is grown or killed locally last until it came around again.

This is the basis for traditional Shetland food, and for much of the modern Nordic cookery craze that has swept the world.

Pickled beetroot (and a basic pickling liquor)

In order to get people pickling, it's best to start simple. When I was very young, I loved pickled beetroot more than anything. Baxter's baby beets – I could and would easily polish off an entire jar in a single sitting. I had constantly purple pee.

I don't know what age it was that I realised you could actually get beetroot that hadn't been pickled, but it was late. I think this ruined the relationship somewhat, along with cheap supermarket imitations that my father insisted on buying. Now, pickled beetroot has returned triumphantly to my life. Thanks to Lidl. One day, their entire stock of the fresh stuff was a bit fluffy and marked down, and I cleared them out. I consolidated my half-full Mason jars and I was ready.

This pickling liquor requires three ingredients – salt, sugar and vinegar. In pickling, only the last is actually involved in the preservation of the vegetable; the others are for flavour. Preserving using excessive salt is different and called brining. Using sugar, it's… jamming? I'm not really sure. Chutney(ing) is preserving with healthy quantities of both vinegar and sugar.

You've got to be careful when crafting a 'new' recipe for a pickling liquor; is it going to have the required potency to stop bugs growing? Specifically, the bug *Clostridium botulinum*, or botulism. With these recipes, the answer is a strong 'yes'. These are strong, strong pickles – feel free to dilute them at your own risk.

The preserves you have to be really careful with are oil-preserved vegetables, such as garlic. The oil might stop bugs growing on the outside, but inside the core can rot and spores like botulism can take hold once the oxygen has been used up. Vinegar, salt and sugar all penetrate through thanks to the wonders of osmosis. Oil does not. (See page 182.)

1kg (2lb 3oz) fresh beetroot, skin on
2 bay leaves
1 tbsp black peppercorns
150g (¾ cup) soft light brown sugar
1 heaped tsp good sea salt
400ml (1¾ cups) white wine vinegar
400ml (1¾ cups) distilled malt vinegar

Makes 2 large jars

Stick your oven on at 200°C (400°F)/180°C (350°F) fan/Gas 6. Slice the stalks off the beetroot and place them, whole, in a roasting tin. Cover the bottom of the tin with 0.5cm (⅕ inch) of water, then roast in the oven for at least an hour. You want them soft.

Whilst they're cooking, sanitise your jars (see page 189).

When the beetroot is done, remove from the oven and leave to cool slightly while you make the pickling vinegar. Place the bay leaves, peppercorns, sugar, salt and vinegars into a large pan and bring them to a simmer over a medium heat. Keep simmering.

Peel the beetroot with your (purple) hands – the skins should come off
very easily. Chop into quarters if necessary, and then fit the chunks into
your sanitised jars.

Pour over the pickling vinegar right to the top of each jar, so the beetroot is
completely covered. Try to evenly distribute the bay leaves if using smaller
jars. Seal tightly and leave to cool.

Once at room temperature, if completely sealed, there's no need to keep
in the fridge. The beetroot will be ready to eat within a couple of days.
Once opened, keep chilled.

Pickled rhubarb

This recipe was a revelation, and has further supported my hypothesis that rhubarb is the best fruit. Not only is it ridiculously easy to grow (read: hard to kill), it can be incorporated into pretty much every baked food. Unlike apples, it makes awesome jam (see page 188), chutney and now pickles.

I've seen many people lightly poach their rhubarb first, and if you want a soft final product, fine. But this rhubarb, after a few days, ends up crunchy, almost the texture of a raw carrot. Yes, you still have the tart and tangy flavours, exacerbated by the vinegar and moderated by the sweetness, but never has any method of preparing this humble fruit brought out so much rhubarb flavour. It's intense.

Mackerel is a perfect pairing (see page 86), but it will go well with any strong fish. It also cuts through the richness of fatty meats like lamb, duck and especially pork. An idea might be to combine leftover roast pork, crackling and thinly chopped up pickled rhubarb in a sandwich. Mmmmm.

5–6 thin stalks of rhubarb – early rhubarb works especially well
2.5cm (1 inch) fresh root ginger (optional)
500ml (2 cups) white wine vinegar
1kg (2lb 3oz) caster (superfine) sugar
5 cloves
optional spices, no more than a ½ tsp – nutmeg, juniper, cinnamon and cardamom all go well here

Makes 2 large jars

Sanitise your jars (see page 189).

Peel the ginger, if using, and chop it into wee chunks. Pop these in a large pan and add the vinegar, sugar, cloves and any optional spices you might want to try. Mix it up, and place over a medium–high heat.

As the pickling liquid heats up, chop your rhubarb. To maintain as much crunch as possible, try to leave it longer lengthways and choose slimmer stalks. It won't be stringy or tendon-like; it will snap cleanly once pickled.

Wash the rhubarb chunks, drain thoroughly, then pack them tightly inside your sanitised jars. They'll shrink when they're pickled, so they'll be easier to get out. If you prefer a softer pickled rhubarb, add the rhubarb to your pickling liquid in the pan two minutes before jarring.

Once your hot, sweet vinegar has reached a simmer and all the sugar has dissolved, pour it over the rhubarb in the jars. Make sure your ginger and spices are evenly distributed.

Seal your lids and wipe the outside of the jars with a damp cloth (this is much easier to do while they're hot). Set aside and leave to cool.

The pickles will be ready to eat after a couple of days or so, when the rhubarb has shrunk and the liquor is obviously pink. I don't know how long they'll keep – a very long time, probably.

Pickled cucumber

There are many ways to pickle a cucumber.

I'm including this recipe not because wild cucumbers are native to the windy heathery fields of Shetland, but because of the varying techniques that can be used to preserve this horrible, bland vegetable into something that jumps with flavour and makes so many others sing. And it's so easy to grow, even in Shetland.

The pickling method here is the way I prefer because it gives me something both very salty and that heavy dill and acetic smack of white wine vinegar that I cannot resist.

These are what are colloquially called gherkins. Gherkins are, in fact, a variety of cucumber and one that pickles particularly well. They're often sold as 'snack cucumbers' in UK supermarkets. Cornichons are simply small gherkins. Both tend to be pickled in vinegar, with salt, dill and onions added. This the easiest and most reliable way to have pickles to hand and that is why I like it.

Another way is to make kosher pickles, or brined pickles. Rather than preserving gherkins in a heavily salted liquor, they are placed in a mild brine – about 1 tsp salt for every 100ml (scant ½ cup) water. There is no cooking or boiling, for that could disrupt the ubiquitous bacteria that coat the cucumber and the added dill. These cucumbers are left to ferment in their mild brine, which keeps actual critters and a few nasty bacteria at bay, in vats, barrels or jars. You might see the brine fizz as yeasts join the lactobacillus bacteria and the liquor becomes sour.

I'd avoid this with shop-bought cucumbers as the processes and packing involved with modern supermarkets mean that you could be buying something that has very few bacteria, and therefore you're at risk of culturing the wrong bacteria, which could cause serious harm. If you really are insistent, you can buy cultures of lactobacillus online, which you can add to your brine. And if you grow your own cucumbers that are exposed to the elements, then by all means give it a go.

Pickle anything using this recipe. Red onions, radishes, asparagus, cauliflower, carrots – these are just the veg I've tried. Augment with virtually any spice or flavouring – especially fresh chilli. All vegetables can be pickled raw, but if you prefer them softer then you can poach them for a couple of minutes in the pickling liquor first.

1kg (2lb 3oz) small cucumbers
5 or 6 large shallots
a large bunch of dill

For the liquor:
400ml (1¾ cups) malt vinegar
400ml (1¾ cups) white wine
    vinegar
200ml (generous ¾ cup) water
200g (scant 1 cup) granulated
    or caster (superfine) sugar
30g (1oz) good sea salt

Makes 3–4 large (450g/1lb) jars

Sanitise your jars (see page 189).

Place all the pickling liquor ingredients into a large pan and bring to a simmer over a medium heat. Stir until the sugar and salt dissolve, then remove from the heat and let cool slightly as you prepare the cucumbers.

Wash and dry your cucumbers, then slice into quarters or halves lengthways so you can fit as many as possible into your jars. If they are longer than your jars are tall, chop 'em. Slice your shallots lengthways into long, thin slices.

Arrange as many cucumbers into each jar as possible, cramming them in if necessary. Then shove the shallots in all the gaps. Tear off masses of dill and place this on top. You want the jars full.

Pour over the recently-boiled, still-warm pickling liquor, so that it comes right to the top of each jar. Tiny air bubbles are fine, but you should fill the jars so the liquid spills out when you tighten the lids. Tighten. Leave, chilled or unchilled, to infuse. They'll be ready to eat in 5 days.

Probably-not-toxic tomato chutney

In the conservatory, tomatoes appeared (see page 162). Tomatoes of many colours, from yellow through green to red. Hard, soft and squishy tomatoes. For reasons best known to my wife, we had a case of distilled malt vinegar she had bought on a whim when a nearby local shop was closing down eight years previously. And James, having been in residence for a whirlwind few days, had bought in a large quantity of sugar, brown and white, caster and granulated, which he'd never used. Being the kind of person who never throws anything away, I had plenty of empty Bonne Maman raspberry conserve jars (the only jam worth buying). And some so-called Mason jars, which I always regard with suspicion. So it seemed as if I was prepared... But not quite. I'd made plenty of jam in the past, from our plague fields of rhubarb, but I had worries about what they call 'canning' in the USA. What about botulism?

I was brought up with a terror of botulism, as I think were many youngsters in Scotland of my generation. In a manner of speaking, it was fed to us from an early age (see opposite).

Botulism is a potentially fatal illness that can be contracted by eating spoiled food or food that hasn't been properly cooked or otherwise preserved (see page 57). It leads to tiredness, paralysis, muscle failure and death, although these days it's treatable and only five to ten per cent of those who get it die (James: that's still a lot, and many of the rest will not live a well life). It's caused by the potent toxin named botulinum, the most acutely lethal toxin known, which is produced when the bacterium *Clostridium botulinum* becomes exposed to the absence of oxygen. Like in a can, bottle or jar. See where I'm going with this?

Botulism spores are ubiquitous and, these days, it is worryingly common among injecting drug addicts who can be less than careful with cleanliness of equipment. Oh, and under the trade name Botox, the very same toxin is used commercially in cosmetic surgery. In tiny quantities, obviously. Just as you can paralyse your muscles until you're dead, you can freeze them damn wrinkles.

Whatever. You do not want it in your chutney. Thankfully, I am assured that with chutneys, pickles and jams, mostly, you're on safe ground. *Clostridium botulinum*, like all nasties, doesn't like high sugar or acidic environments. And my chutney is high in both.

I'm usually a bit cavalier with amounts in recipes, but here the temptation is always to add too much water. If you do, the chutney will be too thin, or need boiling down. Hold your nerve and stir.

Oh, and here's a thing - in an emergency, a jar of this chutney can provide the base for an effective, if slightly eccentric, curry sauce. Fry up your chicken or meat, and chuck in the chutney. Simmer and serve, diluting with fresh or tinned tomatoes as necessary.

1kg (2lb 3oz) chopped green and red tomatoes (or whatever you have)

1kg (2lb 3oz) cooking apples, peeled and chopped

500g (1lb 2oz) onions, chopped

250g (2 cups) sultanas or raisins

500g (2½ cups) light soft brown sugar

500ml (2 cups) malt vinegar

500ml (2 cups) white wine vinegar

5cm (2 inch) fresh root ginger, peeled

1 tsp mustard powder

1 tsp garam masala

1 tsp turmeric

2 level tsp good sea salt

2 tsp chilli powder

Makes many jars – have at least 10 x 450g (1lb) jars to hand

Sanitise your jars (see page 189).

Find a really big pan. Put the tomatoes, apples, onions, sultanas, sugar and vinegars inside it. Place over a medium heat and cook for about 45 minutes, stirring regularly, until everything's nicely soft. Stirring is important – burnt chutney is the worst. You can never get that flavour out of a pan.

Add the spices while stirring calmly but sternly – there is no need to toast them first – and cook for a further 10–15 minutes, monitoring for stickiness. It can be tricky to tell how thick or thin the ultimate chutney will be until it cools. Use your appreciation of The Force or attempt the 'cold plate test' – spoon a little chutney onto a fridge-cold plate and check what its consistency is.

When you have the consistency you want, carefully spoon the mixture into the clean, hot jars. Seal, i.e. put the lids on. (You can use those wee cellophane discs if you like but I hate them for personal reasons involving accidentally eating one when a child.)

Many say you should leave chutney for a week before eating, but I've used this chutney immediately and it was lovely. It will improve, though, and it will last for months in the fridge. You should not, all being well, get botulism.

A warning from history

On 14 August 1922, around 35 people were staying at the Loch Maree Hotel, West Highlands. Most of the guests were there for the sea-trout fishing, which was legendarily good (as it was in Shetland at the time) and were extremely well-heeled or semi-aristocratic. Those who weren't fishing were out for hikes and hillwalking. It's thought that a group of 13 went off for the day with packed lunches, generally thought to be delicious. Within three days, eight of them were dead.

Food poisoning was suspected, but the symptoms, which included double vision and paralysis, were new to local doctors. There were suspicions of a mass murder attempt, especially given the prominence and wealth of some of the guests. It took Ross and Cromarty's chief medical officer's reading of a German medical magazine to bring botulism into the frame. The sandwich of one of the deceased ghillies was tested – it was positive.

Some accounts blame a commercial duck pâté provided by the luxury goods firm of Laxenby's. Other say the pâté was made at the hotel and preserved in jars by staff. Either way, I doubt the pâté was worth it.

Bloody Magnie

In celebration of using up a tomato glut, you should always keep some back. You could make a Bloody Mary, or a Magnie (after Magnus, Shetland's favourite saint). This former Earl of Orkney was joint ruler in the twelfth century, along with his cousin Haakon. Until, out of pragmatic political necessity, gentle Magnus was murdered at Haakon's behest by being axed on the island of Egilsay. Not by Haakon, who had turned up to this supposed peace conference with an unaccompanied Magnus with eight warships, but by his cook. As ever, the cook gets made to do the dirty work.

Haakon turned out to be an excellent, fair ruler and Magnus became a saint with one of the most beautiful religious structures in Europe being built in Kirkwall, Orkney for him. It is called St Magnus Cathedral. It is my favourite building, anywhere.

As it happens, Susan won a bottle of Blackwoods Shetland vodka in a raffle, and I used that. Not the whole bottle, just enough for a substantial snifter. It's a lovely bottle with an etched-in Viking ship which – get this – has sails that turn red when the bottle is 'sufficiently chilled'. Classy.

250g (9oz) overripe tomatoes
juice of 1 lime
2 tsp fresh grated horseradish
  (optional, but good)
a wee pinch each of good sea
  salt and freshly ground black
  pepper
100ml (scant ½ cup) dry sherry,
  such as Manzanilla
100ml (scant ½ cup) vodka
Tabasco
Worcestershire sauce
lime or lemon slices, to serve

Makes enough for 4

Put your tomatoes in a blender. Blend until blended, then pass the paste through a sieve into a jug.

Add the lime juice, horseradish, seasoning, sherry and vodka. Mix.

Add a few dashes each of Tabasco and Lea & Perrins (the original Worcestershire sauce) so idiots who claim to not like them aren't tempted to forego their greatness.

Serve in glasses filled with ice cubes and slices of lime or lemon. Add extra L&P and Tabasco to taste. Repeat until perfection or nirvana is achieved.

SauerKale

Even before kale was a thing, before it was discovered by thin and privileged teenagers who worship its magical properties, I hated it. It was my vegetable growing up that I refused to eat, which annoyed my mother because it thrives in the mild Shetland winter.

I couldn't help but be overcome with just a smidge of schadenfreude at reports that many kale evangelists have ended up with thyroid problems, due to its iodine content and the relatively massive doses that its juices and smoothies contain. Then the unthinkable happened – I started liking it. It's great lightly stir-fried with butter or oil and garlic, or bacon, or another nice fatty thing. Its minerality actually gives it something distinct from other bland greens.

But still, the best thing you can do with kale is let it rot.

Sauerkraut is awesome, but try it with kale and you get a deep, dark and ultra pungent burst of umami, that can be added to pretty much anything to make it better. It doesn't have the same versatility of the German cabbage version – it's too strong for that – but it really adds something to cooked meat, works amazingly with a burnt butter over white fish, and I think it makes the world's best pizza topping, followed closely by anchovies and capers.

Bear in mind that in spontaneous fermentation lots of things can interfere with it. If a fly gets in, for instance, it could infect the whole lot and make it nasty. If you simply have the wrong bugs, it will be bad. Go by taste – if it doesn't taste right, spit it out. Get rid of it and try again.

The first time you make this, I'd think about using a culture of lactobacillus from an online retailer. They're very simple to use (and re-use) and it drastically cuts down your risk of making someone you love unwell.

1kg (2lb 3oz) organic kale, freshly picked if possible (organic is essential)
25g (1oz) good sea salt
freshly ground black pepper (I hate peppercorns in my sauerkraut)
sachet of lactobacillus, or a few probiotic lactobacillus tablets

Find a large pan or bowl that will fit all your kale inside and wash it thoroughly. Rinse it with boiling water from the kettle, so that all of it is heated to very hot indeed. Wash your hands well.

Use a clean knife and chopping board to shred the kale very finely – you want long and thin strips, if possible.

Chuck all your kale back into the pan or bowl and sprinkle all the salt over the top. Use your hands to mix everything together, really rubbing the salt into the leaves. Once you can bear no more, stop. Go away, and

Continued overleaf

come back a few minutes later, washing your hands before you stick them in again. Try again, keeping massaging until you've got a soggy mass of kale in a very salty brine.

Now, you need to cover the kale with plastic wrap or foil – not the pot, but the surface of the kale itself. This should be loose, not tight.

Find an object that is nearly the same diameter as your pan or bowl, such as a plate, and sit this on top of your kale. Weigh it down using heavy things like jam jars or a whole stack of more plates.

Cover your pan or bowl with more plastic wrap or foil and leave it at room temperature. It will begin to fizz and ferment. It will be ready to eat after a week or so, but you can easily leave it for up to a month. Taste it every few days, checking for the level of sourness you want. If you notice mould, remove it. If mould keeps coming back, it's probably not salvageable, so get rid of the lot and start again. A little light scum is fine, but you should still remove it.

Always replace the plastic wrap/foil and weights after checking to keep any nasties out. When you like the flavour, scoop out the kale into sanitised jars (see page 189) and store in the fridge.

Rhubarb, ginger and whisky jam

I think this is the only recipe I've stolen off my father for this book. I notice he's stolen a few from me.

Rhubarb jam is my favourite jam. Apart from Bonne Maman; nothing is quite as good as Bonne Maman. This does come close, though. And it is surprisingly easy to get right, so long as you follow certain rules. These rules are all about pectin.

Pectin is made up of lots of simple sugars joined together. It gives many plants and fruits structural integrity, and when fruits are boiled it acts as a gelling agent to set our jams and jellies. Pectin is found particularly in citrus peel, allowing marmalade to set like a solid jelly and why you'll find lemon zest in many a jam recipe.

Whilst you can make a jam-like substance using only rhubarb and sugar, you will find that you have to use so much sugar to make it spreadable or you're left with a compote. And it still won't quite set completely.

Rhubarb has a very low pectin content. It isn't alone – apricots, blueberries, cherries, peaches and strawberries all contain similarly low levels, and you can follow this recipe for each of them too. You can make a 'natural' jam by adding the rind of any citrus fruit, but I prefer to add extra pectin. Usually, the easiest way of getting hold of pectin is to buy jam sugar, specifically designed for jam-making.

The magic ratio of any jam is 1:1, fruit:sugar. I'm going for a little less sugar here, because I like my rhubarb jam with a tang, and the pectin will ensure that it sets. The whisky may seem like a strange addition – it was originally added purely to keep the tops of the jam from going mouldy. Thanks to our awesome jam-making and the careful sanitisation of our jars, there's no need for it from that point of view. But I grew fond of it growing up – those first few spreads imbued with Jura or The Macallan or some other bland malt from the back of the cupboard.

Oh, and don't go overboard on the ginger. It's always so disappointing when that's all you can taste. It should be a hint, nothing more.

Sanitise your jars (see opposite).

Chop the leaves and the white roots off of your rhubarb, then chop it into 2.5cm (1 inch) long chunks. This is when you should weigh it – you want 1kg (2lb 3oz) chopped rhubarb. Place in your jam pan or large pan and add the sugar with a few tablespoons of water to help get it going.

enough rhubarb for
  1kg (2lb 3oz) when chopped
900g (4½ cups) jam sugar
1cm (½ inch) fresh root ginger
approx. 1 tbsp (half-measure)
  whisky per jar

Makes 2–3 large jars of jam
Half-full jars are fine

Finely grate the ginger into the pan – it will seem like a minuscule amount but this is what you want.

Pop your pan over a low heat, and stir regularly. You want to slowly bring it to a simmer, with slowly being the key word. And simmer; not a boil. Jam is sticky and dangerous.

Gently bubble for 15 minutes, stirring regularly. Your lumps of rhubarb should start to break up; it would be nice if a few of them kept their shape.

Once you have a big pan of gloop, carefully spoon or pour into your sanitised jars. Thanks to the pectin, there should be no need to check whether it is set. Wiggle the jars back and forth to flatten the mix, and wipe the edges. Pour a half-measure (one tablespoon) whisky onto the jam in each jar, then seal with the lid whilst still piping hot. (As it's bad luck to pour a half-measure, you'd better drink the other half each time.)

This jam is ready to spread as soon as it's cold. As for how long it lasts: I've had jars that are many years old and I am still alive.

Sanitising jars

All jam jars, Mason jars or even Tupperware, no matter their material, should be thoroughly cleaned and sanitised before using. I never say 'sterilised', because that would be an untruth. Unless you're pressure-cooking your jars prior to use, they aren't sterile. Sanitising is pretty close, and adequate for everything except home canning.

Method 1: thoroughly wash the jars and lids in hot soapy water to remove any debris. Rinse, then put them in a clean dishwasher (on their own) with no dishwasher tablets or liquid, on the hottest cycle.

Method 2: thoroughly wash the jars and lids in hot soapy water to remove any debris. Rinse, then put them into a large pan and boil them in water (with nothing added) for 10 minutes.

Method 3: thoroughly wash the jars and lids in hot soapy water. Rinse, then spread them out on a clean baking tray and place in a cold oven. Turn the oven to 150°C (300°F)/130°C (266°F) fan/Gas 2 and heat the jars for around 15 minutes. Try to time it so they're ready when your preserve is ready to pot.

8

SUNDAY TEAS

One fortunate side effect of attaining a fleeting fame is the opportunity to talk about food in public. Usually, I'm lucky enough for this to occur in a forum that encourages critical thinking and challenges one's own beliefs. Of all these times, being asked to open the Shetland Food Festival in 2017 was the greatest honour.

Introduced and beckoned onto the stage, I was chatting with some pace about how great Shetland food was in some way or another, prancing through a mental list I'd tallied of wee things unique to our society. The seafood, Up Helly Aa, reest, bannocks and all the other things that there's a chapter on in this book. Then I mentioned the Sunday Teas.

The atmosphere changed. There was a collective intake of breath and a sudden tension. Though each community is fiercely loyal to the summertime Sunday Teas held at its own hall, a few were reputed to be of higher standing than the rest. It's as if I'd moved onto the subject of Scottish Independence, or Brexit. I could only offend and divide.

I could not resist suggesting that the Ollaberry Teas were the best on the isles. There was one lone supporter, who cheered. The hundreds of others stayed silent and frowned or stared at their feet in impolite disagreement. This is how I finished my speech to open the festival.

I've not been invited back.

What are Sunday Teas?

The concept is difficult to explain to those who have never experienced it. Shetland is perhaps the only place in the country where a regular, community-regimented afternoon tea still exists, and that is what Sunday Teas are. But really, all you need to know is that they're bizarre, brilliant events and they should form a part of every community everywhere because they make the world a better place.

It starts with the paper. The *Shetland Times* is published every Friday. Its circulation might have dropped a little since the internet, but it still penetrates nearly 100 per cent of households. Near the back of the paper, you'll find the local announcements. Every engagement and graduation still goes in there. And then the Sunday Teas.

In every wee place in Shetland that's not quite a village or a town, there's a community hall, built by the oil and run by a local committee. Each hall, just a few times each summer, hosts a Sunday Tea. This is a must-attend event: for a few hours in the afternoon a community comes together. It's said that some people aren't seen but for on election day and at the Sunday Teas.

The women run the teas. They don't scorn the men, and indeed I have contributed many a muffin to the Hillswick Teas, but for some reason men, except for a few progressives, don't seem to be that involved. The 'wifes' bake and prepare sandwiches and polish the hall. Vast pots of tea and lethally strong instant coffee are left bubbling on the gas to keep hot.

Locals turn up in waves to drink tea and eat as much as they can. They pay a tiny amount, all of which goes towards a chosen charity or good cause or the hall itself. Paper plates are stacked at one end of trestle tables lined with every savoury and sweet snack you can think of – the only informal rule is that you must be able to pick up your teas and place them onto your plate. Open sandwiches, closed sandwiches, Scotch eggs, all variety of bannock and scone are laid out on trays, then further down the table, or onto the next one, lies the main event: the fancies. These should also be easy to handle, but bowls might be found if someone brings an apple pie and custard. None of this food is bought in – the fancies are a source of individual pride and sometimes sweated over for days. There is always stuff left over to take home.

The women who organise these days are local living legends spanning three or four generations and they are held in the highest regard by those who know them. If you insult a place's Sunday Teas, you insult that entire society. By saying the unsayable in public and declaring Ollaberry the greatest, I insulted every other group of exalted wives, selflessly baking bannocks to bring their community together.

The best Sunday Teas

My reasons for picking out a favourite are several-fold: meringues of unrivalled quality and size; the particularly well-stewed and gargantuan aluminium pots of tea that I like to think have never been cleaned; the variety of the savouries; the choice of jams; the buttered and unbuttered

Scotch pancakes; bannocks with saat beef; the compulsory, booze-heavy raffle. I'm coming over funny.

But each and all have their quirks and highlights, and either none or all could be said to be the perfect Teas. Like Orwell's essay on the perfect pub that doesn't exist, The Moon Under Water, one could attempt to merge the best aspects of each, but to try to perfect it would miss the point. To refine would detract from each Teas' unique way of spreading glee. And I've tried most of them, including several one-off Teas that maybe occur once a year, if that.

Each stands out. The Teas at Lunna House, the historic wartime base of the Shetland Bus, the secret link between Allied intelligence and the resistance and clandestine networks of Nazi-occupied Norway. Owned and run as a B&B by the Erwood family, who are not of Shetland descent, these Teas are not ordinary. It is like being invited into a family home and being stuffed on the best scones with imported and truly clotted cream. The best brownies. Baked tatties piled with chilli. Unorthodox, but it works.

The highest number of Sunday Teas I've attended in a single day is three, and this was as your dutiful servant for the purposes of this book. The first was a one-off Teas. It was in Walls, on the west side, to commemorate the launch of a newly built Sixareen – a traditional wooden fishing boat. We drove down to catch a glimpse of the graceful boat from the pier, and saw they were taking visitors out. And whilst you waited for your turn, tea and fancies were served.

The Walls Boating Club hosted and it was an all-you-can-eat affair following an entry fee that wouldn't get you a slice of dense vegan cake at your city hipster coffee shop. Put in this situation, I'm not a man of terribly good self-control. The bannocks and saat beef were exceptional. The caramel shortcake was like crack. I swiftly over-ate, despite a plan to return north for our local Teas.

En route, and following a de-satiating sail in a wooden boat, we set off for home. But it would have been wrong not to stop when we saw a hand-scrawled sign for an event at the Aith Hall: SUNDAY TEAS AND CAR BOOT SALE. Combined. The bric-a-brac on offer was so-so, but the magnificence of the fancies was so impressive that, despite having stuffed myself 45 minutes earlier, I piled up another plate and finished it. I even came close to admitting Ollaberry had been beaten. You had a choice of bannock – they had the wares of about five different people on display at any one time – a mixture of girdle and oven varieties. For your appreciation.

After this, we persisted. The local Teas. Another two quid paid; another plate was filled. My sister had been baking. It might not have had the widest selection, the lightest meringues, or been the busiest, but it was home. Every face was familiar. The hall is the same one that hosted every school play from the age of 5. I'd been to every life event in this local hall, from birthday parties and weddings to wakes, folk festivals and, of course, Up Helly Aa. To sit in this warm wood-lined room, surrounded by friends with a full belly and limitless cake is a privilege I am glad to have had.

Fancies (buttered shortbread; jam and coconut slice; fairy cakes)

For the shortbread base:
300g (2 cups) plain (all-purpose)
   flour
200g (7oz) salted butter
100g (½ cup) caster (superfine)
   sugar

For the cake mix:
200g (7oz) salted butter
200g (1 cup) caster (superfine)
   sugar
4 medium eggs
½ tsp vanilla extract
100g (scant 1 cup) ground
   almonds
100g (1 cup) plain (all-purpose)
   flour
2 tsp baking powder

For finishing the coconut slice:
a jar of good raspberry jam,
   such as Bonne Maman
200g (⅔ cup) desiccated
   coconut

For (too much) icing:
300g (3 cups) icing
   (confectioners') sugar
150g (5½oz) unsalted butter,
   softened

Makes 32 shortbread rounds,
16 jam and coconut slices and
12 fairy cakes

Preheat your oven to 180°C (350°F)/160°C (325°F) fan/Gas 4. Line a 20cm (8 inch) square brownie tin and a baking tray with baking parchment. There's no need to grease; I just tend to shove some torn-off parchment straight into the tin – no cutting necessary. You'll also need a 12-hole bun or cupcake tin with cases.

Start by making your shortbread mix. If you've got a food processor, you can just chuck all the ingredients in and pulse until it comes together into smooth dough-like lumps. Alternatively, use a wooden spoon to rub your butter into the sugar. This is a bit like when making a cake, but you want them just-combined and no more. The sugar and the butter should be mixed, but not light and fluffy. Add the flour and use your hands to mix it all together until combined into a similarly doughy situation.

Wrap the shortbread dough in plastic wrap and chill in the fridge for a minimum of 5 minutes and a maximum of two days.

Cut your lump of dough in two and place one half on a floured surface, add more flour on top and roll out gently until it is about 3mm (¹⁄₁₀ inch) thick and will fit in your square tin. Carefully transfer into the lined tin and cut around so that the shortbread lines the bottom. Prick your base all over with a fork and put in the oven to bake for 15 minutes.

While the shortbread bakes, take the dough trimmings and add them to the remaining half of dough. Stick this on your floured surface, sprinkle with flour and roll out to the same thickness or slightly thicker. Use a round cutter to cut out lots of 3–4cm (1½ inch) rounds of shortbread. Arrange these on your lined baking tray, leaving a good few millimetres between each. Prick each one with a fork and stick these in the oven for 10–12 minutes. You can check your first tray at this point – if the shortbread is blushing golden at the edges, it's done. Remove from the oven.

Leave your tin of shortbread to cool and make your cake mix. Melt your butter in the microwave (or oven) in a heatproof bowl. You don't want it really hot – lumpily half melted is fine. Add the sugar, eggs and vanilla to the butter and mix vigorously with a wooden spoon until you have a smooth paste. Don't worry if it curdles (but it shouldn't).

Continued overleaf

Next, add the almonds, flour and baking powder and mix together gently, until you've got a smooth cake mix. As soon as it is smooth, stop mixing. (Don't forget to check on the shortbread circles – remove from the oven when done and leave to cool.)

Spoon a few tablespoons of jam onto your still-warm shortbread square and spread to the edges. You want a thin layer. Gently pour about half of your cake mix on top, carefully spreading to the edges to cover the jam. Put this in the oven and bake for 15–20 minutes, or until golden brown and bouncy when pressed.

Spoon the remaining cake mixture into the cases in your cupcake tin (you should have enough for 12 at least). Place these in the oven and bake for about 15 minutes, until bouncy and golden brown. If in doubt, leave for a few minutes longer.

When done, leave everything to cool in or on its tin or tray.

Before serving, spread the square cake/shortbread with another layer of jam, then sprinkle with desiccated coconut. When completely cool, slice into 9 or 16 portions, depending on your frugality. I like to cut the edges off and keep them for myself, anyway.

Make the icing for the fairy cakes: mix the butter gently with your icing sugar with a wooden spoon, then use an electric whisk to beat on a high speed until it is snow-white. Hollow out a hole from the top of the cool cakes, scoop some icing in, and add your little hat of cake back on top. Finish with a dusting of icing sugar.

Simply butter the shortbread circles with good salted butter.

Sassermaet Scotch eggs

Sassermaet (or 'saucermeat') is as much a Shetland national dish as reestit mutton or bannocks. But this one we don't do much shouting about because it's as much a source of shame as a source of pride. It's the Shetland version of the Scottish lorne or square sausage. It's usually packaged in bags from the butchers or the slaughterhouse, rolled into balls and fried. You could fry every meal for a week with the fat that seeps out into the pan.

It's beef mince, finely ground with a proper fat content – over 25%, certainly. It's generously seasoned and spiced using any mixture of black pepper, white pepper, clove, mace, allspice, cinnamon and ground ginger, with an emphasis on the peppers. The exact combination is very much up to the butchers involved, but there's always a lot of spice.

While it is wonderful fried – and its subsequent fat provides a depth of flavour to everything else you later cook – it comes into its own in Scotch eggs. A deeply personal favourite of mine, I think there is no better snack in the world for accompanying a pint of pale ale. Crisp breadcrumbs, tender sausage with a barely cooked egg yolk in a handheld, portable package: what's not to love?

Here, always use medium eggs – the yolks tend to be insignificantly smaller than those in large eggs, so you get a better yolk:white:sausage ratio overall.

7 medium eggs
500g (1lb 2oz) sassermaet (or unadulterated beef sausages mixed with a pinch each of black pepper, white pepper, clove, mace, allspice, cinnamon and ground ginger)
plain (all-purpose) flour, for dusting
at least 200g (2½ cups) stale bread or breadcrumbs
sunflower or peanut oil, for frying
good sea salt

Serve with:
a pint

Makes 6 Scotch eggs

First you need to hard(ish) boil your eggs. Place a large pan of water onto a high heat to bring to the boil. Use more water than you think you need – you want it to lose as little temperature as possible when you lower your eggs in. Once boiling, add six of your eggs (keeping one for the bread-crumbing), as quickly as possible after one another, and start a timer. Set it for 6 minutes (almost runny) or 7 minutes (pretty nearly set). Once it goes off, use the lid of the pan to hold the eggs in while you pour out all the hot water, then run cold water inside on full blast to cool the eggs.

Give each egg a wee tap on the side of the pan to crack its shell, then pop them back into the water. This lets the water seep in between the cooked white and the shell and makes them easy to peel. After at least 5 minutes of soaking, peel off the shells.

Meanwhile, you can roughly split your sassermaet into six equal lumps. Tear off a sheet of plastic wrap and lay it onto a clean work surface. Place a lump of the sassermaet on the plastic wrap and smoosh it out with the heel of your hand so it is flat and less than 1cm (½ inch) thick.

Continued overleaf

Place a hard-boiled egg on top of your flat sassermaet and then use the plastic wrap to wrap the egg up. You'll get a sense of whether you need to go flatter with the meat – it should easily surround the egg forming a sealed ball. Smooth out the seams, set aside and repeat with the rest.

Next, prepare three plates: one covered with a pile of flour, one with your remaining egg beaten with a little salt and one with your breadcrumbs. Take each meat-covered egg and roll it in the flour to coat. Dust off any excess, then dunk it in the egg, rolling to cover. Let any excess drain off, then pop it in the breadcrumbs. Once well coated, set aside and repeat with the rest. If you want to eat these freshly fried (recommended), you can chill in the fridge at this stage for up to a day.

Use a deep fat fryer if you have one. If you want to use a pan on the hob, only do so if you are experienced and you have an accurate thermometer. (I am not responsible for burns, fires, et cetera.) Heat your oil to 160°C (325°F). Fry your eggs for a good 10 minutes or so, until a deep golden brown – their cooked-ness should be in no doubt. Drain on kitchen paper and serve warm or cold. Store in the fridge if not serving hot.

Eat with a pint.

Salt water biscuits

In baking today, there's an obsession with the 'different'. It's all *Bake Off*'s fault. We're encouraged to add unnecessary extras in some silly effort to make the classics unique to us. I'll admit guilt. While *Bake Off* would be boring if everyone made the same sort of vanilla shortbread, I guarantee a well-made vanilla shortbread tastes better than every single one of the 'signature' versions we were forced to pull out of our arses.

The purpose of this biscuit is to open the door for the food that sits on top of it. Whilst it might be tasty on its own if you're hungry or seriously lacking in sodium or chloride, its real job is to provide a disc for elevating cured or smoked things into your mouth. These biscuits often appear at Teas spread with butter only, or with cheese or saat beef.

150g (1¼ cups) plain (all-purpose) flour
a few pinches of good sea salt
½ tsp baking powder
50g (1¾oz) salted butter, cold
50g (1¾oz) cold water

Makes loads – at least 30 biscuits

First, preheat your oven to 180°C (350°F)/160°C (325°F) fan/Gas 4. Line a baking tray with a sheet of baking parchment. This doesn't need to be greased. If you have two trays, line two, or you'll need to bake in batches.

Weigh your flour into a large bowl. Add a pinch of salt and the baking powder and stir to combine. Add the butter and rub it in using your fingers like you do with pastry: the final result should be breadcrumby.

Weigh your cold water exactly and add this to the bowl. Mix using a wooden spoon and then use one hand to bring together into a dough. Cover the bowl in plastic wrap and stick it in the fridge for at least 15 minutes.

Flour a clean work surface and sit your dough on top. Add more flour and gently roll the dough, keeping it moving all the time. You want to roll it as thin as you can; no more than 1–2mm (thinner than $1/10$ inch). Cut out into circles using a cutter or squares using a knife. Carefully transfer the delicate pieces to the lined tray(s), prick each with a fork (or you'll have little balloons), and sprinkle with salt.

If possible, leave to rest for another 10 minutes, but you can bake straight away. Bake for 10 minutes – they should still be very pale and will crisp up as they cool. They're best eaten fresh, but will keep forever, I think.

Pictured opposite with oatcakes (page 233), smoked salmon (page 124) and whisky-smoked halibut (page 127).

Hufsie

A hufsie. I have no idea of its true etymology, though people tell me the cake itself comes from Whalsay, an island about half an hour's ferry ride off the east coast of the Mainland. Whalsay is an odd and wonderful place, as my father has alluded to in other chapters. It has many fishermen, an excellent golf course and the world's best charity shop. Most interesting is how difficult it is, even for seasoned Shetlanders, to understand what people from Whalsay are saying.

I'm already in trouble for writing that, so I'll go on. There's even a phrase that Shetlanders use to poke fun at folk from Whalsay, and to practise the accent. It's "a cup a toi un a chawffa tyake", said quickly, over and over. Can you guess what it means? Whalsay people don't find it very funny. But it is.

Hufsie, I guess, is how Whalsay people say 'boiled fruit loaf'. Each is as individual as the person who makes it, though they can roughly be divided into those with cherries and those without cherries. And yes, I mean glacé cherries. Just, don't.

At any Teas, you'll find slices with copious butter, and that's key. This and all recipes for hufsie are deliberately just a little dry   this stops the fruit from sinking and gives a great rise towards the centre with a magnificent crust and tear. So, don't serve it without some good butter and do consider serving it warm. In fact, a wee loaf of this just out the oven is difficult to put down if you start tearing pieces off.

Continued overleaf

300g (1½ cups) mixed fruit
(currants and sultanas are
best; mixed peel is fine)
225g (1 cup) water
200g (1¼ cups) soft light
brown sugar
150g (5½oz) butter
½ tsp mixed spice
225g (2 cups) self-raising flour
1 tsp baking powder
1 egg
50g (¾ cup) flaked almonds
(optional)

Makes two 450g (1lb) loaves

You can make one massive 900g (2lb) loaf, in which case preheat the oven to 180°C (350°F)/160°C (325°F) fan/Gas 4 and bake for 20 minutes, then turn the heat down to 160°C (325°F)/140°C (275°F) fan/Gas 2 and bake for another 40 minutes.

Preheat your oven to 190°C (375°F)/170°C (340°F) fan/Gas 5. Line your loaf tins with torn-off sheets of baking parchment, or proper paper tin-liners if you have them.

Place your fruit, water, sugar, butter and spice into a large pan. Place over a medium heat, stirring gently all the time. Once the butter has melted and the mix starts simmering (don't burn yersel') turn the hob off and leave the gloopy mixture to cool.

After about 10 minutes (when you should be able to touch the sides of the pan) add your flour and baking powder. Mix these in quickly using a wooden spoon. As it comes together, add in your egg and all but a few of the flaked almonds. Keep mixing until you have a lumpy, stiff cake mix.

Scrape the mix into your prepared tins and sprinkle the remaining flaked almonds on top. Bake in your hot oven for 20 minutes, then turn the oven down to 160°C (325°F)/140°C (274°F) fan/Gas 2 for a further 10–15 minutes. Do not open the oven any sooner than half an hour after sticking them in or you risk sinkage.

When checking for doneness, it's essential to stick a skewer or knife in, as bounciness is not sensitive in all cakes. A bit of dried fruit on the skewer is fine, but raw cake mix means more cooking. Once done, leave your loaf to cool in the tin. If possible serve warm; spread heavily with good butter if serving cold.

Granny's drop scones with butter (or butter and jam)

My Gran was an incomer so she was not one of the women who baked for the Teas, but she taught me to bake and I baked for the Teas.

I have purported to publish this recipe before, but that was a lie. What I gave was my best approximation of a pancake I last had more than 15 years ago, because I really had nothing to go on. It was a process of reverse engineering a distant, nostalgia-tainted memory and, of course, I never got it spot on.

Then, as I flicked through Gran's old Stork book (see page 215), this sheet of paper fell out, separate from the rest. It turns out, the world's best drop scone is made with a sensational amount of baking powder and a very complicated way of measuring milk. This is the world's best drop scone recipe, to me.

• •

DROP SCONES OR SCOTCH PANCAKES

Mrs Audrey Bowie
Ronasview
HEYLOR
Shetland

Have ready a hot girdle or strong frying pan placed over a moderate heat. Place a clean cloth on the table near the cooking stove to cover the scones when cooked

8ozs self raising flour
3 level teaspoons
*   baking powder*
Pinch of salt

Or
8ozs plain flour
3 heaped teaspoons baking powder
Pinch of salt
Or
1oz castor sugar
Stir into flour mixture
1 egg, ¼ pint and
5 tablespoons milk
Mix together

Pour the egg and milk gradually into the flour, stirring all the time with a wooden spoon and beating until the mixture is smooth

Drop a rounded dessert sp of batter onto heated girdle - careful here as it may take one or two to get it right!!! Keep them well apart. Cook approx 2 mins until g. Br, covered with bubbles on top. Then turn to cook other side. Cooked...

• •

Continued overleaf

For those who'd like to try this but have only progressive scales, here are some metric conversions:

225g self-raising flour
3 level tsp baking powder
a pinch of salt

OR

225g plain (all-purpose) flour
3 heaped tsp baking powder
a pinch of salt
25g caster (superfine) sugar
1 egg
200ml milk

I don't know what the next word was meant to be – I don't know Gran's way of telling whether they're cooked. I only know never to touch them or move them except to flip them or remove them. Anything else would gain you a slap.

My only final suggestion, for completeness, would be to cook for another minute or so before letting them finish off under the insulated warmth of the prepared clean cloth or tea towel. Serve cool, with butter, or butter and jam, spread on the smooth side.

9

BAKE

It's a conversation I have had so many times that I've become slick at rattling off an answer. Never quite the same, but a variation on a theme. It always starts the same way. It happens to me often because of the frequency at which I change jobs and have to work and make small talk with new people I've never been introduced to.

"How'd you get into baking?"

Like I can't help but break down a recipe or a dish into its component parts and see how it was assembled, I can't help but break down this story. And how I tell it.

Audrey Bowie

My maternal grandmother is not from Shetland, and nor are her recipes. She was a teacher in her earlier days, but I knew her only in the later years of her retirement. For a good chunk of my childhood, she was everything.

We lived in our little old house on the side of a hill near the end of a single track road. Gran lived a minute or two's walk away, our closest neighbour. She lived in a Norwegian 'kit house', designed for one with a spare single room. It had, and indeed has, three windows in the living room that overlook the sea and Shetland's tallest hill and the wilds behind. There's another window in the kitchen, just above the countertop. The other window over the sink looks at our house.

During my primary school years, I'd get the school bus to drop me off at Gran's house instead of our own. I'd stay there until there was a phone call to come home for tea. I had several juvenile motivations. First, and foremost, chocolate. And Jaffa Cakes. I was not a skinny child. I knew the secret places she kept the spares, and she knew that I knew, but we never said anything. She always kept them stocked.

And then there was tea. I would maintain that making tea at Gran's house is where I developed my sense of service and the unwavering requirement for praise that has rather defined my life since. It has certainly guided my professional choices. I became obsessed with making the right tea for the right person. Sugar, milk level, brew time. Trying to second-guess and improve people's choices – Gran always demanded half-and-half milk and tea, no sugar. I never obliged, and I think she was always happy. The most I ever went was one third:two thirds and even that felt wrong.

With my tea and my entire packet of Jaffa Cakes, my bar of Dairy Milk covertly consumed, I'd settle in on the other sofa from Gran next to the cat. Sometimes we'd play Scrabble and Dominoes. And sometimes we'd bake.

This baking has striking similarities to my training as a surgeon. My gran was a truly great baker, and only recently have I realised how good she was. She treated baking as a fun thing for me to do, but also as an apprenticeship. I have memories of only being allowed to watch and lick the bowl. As soon as I was big enough, I was allowed to hold the electric mixer, but I was never allowed to make the decision about when to stop mixing. I remember still, vividly, the first time that Gran allowed me to fold in the flour when making a Victoria sponge. I had to stand on the top step of the stool so I couldn't have been more than six or seven. She made me stop and start again every time I tried until I did it right, like the surgeon who would cut out every knot I tied until she was happy.

Little by little, Gran would drip-feed me skills that would serve me the rest of my life. And although I was able to go away and make the recipes that she made, whenever we baked together they were better. She might let me do every step, but she was always in complete control. She might let me add the water to the pastry, but she'd tell me when to stop.

Stork Margarine Cookery Service: *The Art of Home Cooking*

In Gran's later years, her health deteriorated. I came to see how she was beginning to doit ('become confused') as the years went on. She was more reliant on her carers, frequently lost at Scrabble and there were ever more bars of chocolate in the top shelf of the fridge door. She was increasingly frail, relying more heavily on her stick and then her zimmer frame.

She underwent a gradual decline that saw her unable to care for herself, so she came to live with us. She moved in and took the only bedroom on the ground floor of the house, next to the bathroom.

She did not bake. I often wonder if she could have, if given the chance. I like to imagine so.

Gran died when I was at school. I remember borrowing a black tie for the funeral and my piano teacher playing Debussy on the electric keyboard in the church. I remember the pallbearers' faces and the slam of the blunt wooden coffin onto the pedestal. And for the first time I remember being unable to control my emotions and that that was OK. After the funeral, we gathered back at our house for bannocks and lentil soup. The comfort and warmth of simple food; the presence of many smartly dressed people who didn't know what to say. It was odd. The dogs wandered, confused. I don't remember anything else.

We divided up or donated Gran's remaining possessions. I vied for no money, but only some battered and rusted baking tins and one possession above all else: one book, a Stork-branded recipe book, beaten up. Scribbled on. Filled with folded pieces of paper covered in that diligent handwriting, not yet tainted with the wobble of age.

I kept this book, *The Art of Home Cooking*, in the family home, and I never looked at it. It was important to have, but its content didn't matter. What mattered was that we had it. I left it there, sitting beside all the hardback cookbooks I or my sister had bought since. I don't think I ever even folded out one of the pieces of paper.

But now I have it. It's mine. In the process of writing this book, I have opened it up and looked at it for the first time. I have read every brown page and I wept and I laughed at the little quirks. I'm presenting a few select pages here, and I'd be honoured if you would bake something from them, written by her hand. I know she'd be proud.

The perfect cake

Gran's Victoria Sponge – the all-capitalised capitulation of cake cravings

Everyone who's had a gran or a mum or an aunt make *that* cake, associates them with that cake and that cake with some awareness of heaven. This cake isn't quite as Gran would make it, but a homage. Gran was brought up in wartime and post-war Britain, where butter was short and expensive. Advertisements for Stork's perfect rise with minimal effort inspired a generation of busy home-bakers.

Stork baking margarine is fairly scorned by the baking community now, but it holds a special place in my heart. It has a certain saltiness, and an artificial butteriness – achieved through a yeast-derived flavour compound called diacetyl – that reminds me of my childhood. Plus, Stork does indeed make huge and stable cakes, thanks to the emulsification properties of its vegetable-derived re-hydrogenated fats.

This is a recipe that tries to re-create some of the fluffiness of Gran's cake, with similarly minimal fuss, but with a greater depth of flavour. It's a recreation in her memory – aiming for both nostalgia and moreishness. To achieve that, I use butter, and vanilla extract as opposed to the synthetic essence she used. And I measure in grams, like all reasonable people nowadays.

150g (5½oz) salted butter
150g (¾ cup) caster (superfine) sugar
a dash of vanilla extract
3 medium eggs
150g (1 cup) self-raising flour
½ tsp baking powder
full fat (whole) milk, to loosen

½ jar of seedless raspberry jam
more caster (superfine) sugar, to sprinkle on top

Makes one 18cm (7 inch) cake, for 6 people

Preheat your oven to 180°C (350°F)/160°C (325°F) fan/Gas 4. Find two 18cm (7 inch) cake tins. (These are your standard 'small cake' size – the more engrained with burnt cake and covered in bashes the better.) Grease these using some torn-off paper from the packet of your butter, making sure to get right down into the corners.

Draw around the base of one of your tins onto some baking parchment. Fold this paper in half and use scissors to cut out two circles. These should be pressed into the base of each tin and you should then grease the parchment too.

Measure out your butter into a heatproof bowl – preferably a glass one scratched to the point of opacity. Stick it in your microwave (or oven) and buzz until about half of the block looks melted, no more. Take the bowl out and measure in your sugar, vanilla and eggs.

Continued overleaf

Sit your bowl on a folded kitchen towel – this stops the loud clanging noise from the mixer. Whisk on high speed using a handheld electric 2-beater mixer. You need to do this for A Very Long Time. You want your mixture to become almost-white and meringue-like.

Sieve in your flour (or dump it in, but Granny didn't) and your baking powder, and fold these in gently using a large metal spoon. Don't overmix. When the mixture is nearly smooth, add some milk, a dash at a time, mixing in after each addition. You want to loosen the mixture until it falls from the spoon in a swift wave.

Pour your mixture into the prepared tins as evenly as you can, and smooth flat. If it's the correct consistency, though, you should be able to flatten the mix just by shaking the tins back and forth. Transfer the cakes to the oven and bake for about 20 minutes, until golden brown and bouncy.

Remove from the oven and let cool in the tins for 10 minutes, or until just cool enough to handle. Run a butter knife around the edge of the tins to free the sides, and then tip them onto a wire cooling rack. Leave to cool, peeling off the baking parchement.

Only once cool should the jam be applied. Place one cake, upside-down, on a serving plate, then spread this with the jam and place your other cake on top. Dust with caster (superfine) sugar and serve.

Jaffa cakes

Genoise sponge, fruit jelly, quick tempered chocolate

"Why make what you can buy?" Two reasons. The first is because it's an interesting technical exercise for those masochists amongst us, and the second is that these are truly excellent. They are also very easy indeed.

They are actually not unlike the ones you can get in the orange and blue cardboard box, but they are better. Light, fatless Genoise sponge, a floral orange jelly and good, solid dark chocolate. One of the few specialist silicone moulds I own is for making perfect jaffa cakes – that's how much I love them – but you can make them in any old bun or wee cupcake tins. You can see that they are clearly cakes and not biscuits.

The key to this recipe is getting the balance right between nostalgia, flavour and texture. The jaffa cake works because of the balance between sponge, jelly and chocolate. The industrial version is heavy on the jelly because it is cheap and its moistness counteracts a relatively dry sponge. If you check out the chocolate, it's wafer-thin.

I like to counteract the extra bitterness of the dark chocolate used here by coating the underside of the sponge in icing sugar; that way, the first thing that hits your tongue is intense sweet, followed by light sponge and a bitter chocolate orange finish. Sublime.

These can be foodied-up by switching the varieties of chocolate, by adding a tablespoon of beurre noisette (burnt butter) to the cake mix, or by changing the variety of orange you use to make your jelly. The ultimate in floral flavour comes by substituting an orange for a couple of bergamots.

For the cakes:
2 medium eggs
50g (¼ cup) caster (superfine) sugar
50g (⅓ cup) plain (all-purpose) flour
½ tsp baking powder (optional, but Gran would have added it)
butter, for greasing

For the jelly:
2 sheets of leaf gelatine
6 eating oranges
25g (1oz) caster (superfine) sugar

good marmalade – whichever you like
100g (3½oz) good dark chocolate, roughly 70% cocoa solids

Makes 16 sizeable jaffa cakes

First, make the jelly. Get started by taking the leaf gelatine and placing it in a bowl with cold water – this will soften it. Line a baking tin or dish with plastic wrap.

Finely grate the zest of two of your oranges and set this aside.

Juice all six oranges and pour this juice into a small pan with the sugar. Place over a medium heat until the sugar has dissolved and the juice is hot to touch. It should not boil or simmer. Once it is hot, add the zest and gelatine and stir until the gelatine has dissolved. If it does not dissolve, return the pan to the heat until it does, stirring gently all the time.

Pour the jelly into your plastic wrap-lined 'mould' and leave it to cool. Pop it in the fridge as soon as possible, or the freezer if you're in a rush. Keep it flat and check it regularly. It should set firm in a few hours.

Continued overleaf

Make the sponge. Start by preheating your oven to 180°C (350°F)/160°C (325°F) fan/Gas 4. Grease 20 holes in two 12-hole cupcake trays with a little butter, to be safe (or have your silicone moulds to hand).

Break your eggs into a mixing bowl and add the sugar. Whisk on high using an electric whisk until the mixture almost resembles meringue – it should at least increase in size by six times, if not more, and be thick and creamy. This might take more than 5 minutes. Do not attempt to do it by hand.

Sieve in your flour and your baking powder, if using. (This guarantees you a significant rise and very light cakes.) Use a large metal spoon to gently fold this into your egg mixture. Try not to knock out any of the air you've spent ages creating, but the mixture should be smooth.

Spoon the cake mixture into your tins or moulds, making sure they are no more than one-third to half full. Bake in the oven for 7–10 minutes only – you want them on the pale side to maintain softness, and you don't have the oven set very hot so they shouldn't dome. Remove from the oven and leave your cakes to cool, then remove them from the tins.

Remove your jelly from the fridge and, if set, you can cut out circles using a biscuit cutter or the top of a shot glass. Make sure the circles are smaller than the tops of your cakes.

Slice off any domes that have risen on the top of your jaffa cakes, then spread on a very thin layer of marmalade (minus any shreds). Stick your jelly circles onto the sponges.

Melt four-fifths of your chocolate – I use a microwave, but you could use a heatproof bowl suspended over a pan of barely simmering water. Whichever way, do it very gently. Finely chop the remaining chocolate. When most of the chocolate has melted, remove it from the heat and add in the rest. Stir until it's melted.

Holding by the sides, dip your jaffa cakes upside down into the melted chocolate. Let any excess chocolate drain back in and then place each cake on a wire rack, the right way up, to set. After a few minutes, when the chocolate is half set, use a fork to make a criss-cross pattern on the top of your cakes.

These will keep for a day or two only, but they won't last that long.

The apple pie

Shortcrust pastry, stewed fruit

Whilst I always enjoyed the Victoria sponge, in this recipe lies my true apprenticeship. I remember being confused when people said to me that making pastry was hard. I had made it since my early years in primary school and I didn't think it was as hard as making a cake, and lots of people seemed to be able to do that pretty well. I didn't get that pastry was seen as this tricky thing – I just did it the way that Gran did it and it worked out.

The ingredients changed, mind you – sometimes it would be Stork, sometimes butter, sometimes a mixture of the two, and sometimes either of them with lard. The pastry was always good, though. Whichever fat we used, it was mixed with plain flour and cold water, and nothing else.

Gran didn't know why her pastry was so good – she just knew how to make it so. This is why I think that tradition should be preserved rather than scorned: if we look back at the ways things were done in days gone by – methods that have since fallen from favour – we can learn about how to do things better than the way we do them now.

You can replace apple with rhubarb in this recipe, though you'll need significantly more sugar. A little ground ginger also works wonders.

200g (1¾ cups) plain (all-purpose) flour
100g (3½oz) unsalted butter, cold
water, ice-cold
4–5 large Bramley apples
juice of ½ a lemon
caster (superfine) sugar, to taste
1 egg, beaten, or some milk, for washing
a little butter to grease

Makes a large apple pie for 6–8 people

First, make the pastry. Weigh your flour into a large bowl and then weigh out your butter separately. Cut it into little chunks before adding it to the flour. Use your fingertips to gently rub the butter into the flour – I start with a flat palm pointing upwards and lift some floury buttery mixture onto my fingers. I then sweep my thumbs across my fingers, crushing the two ingredients together. Keep going until you've got a mixture that looks like breadcrumbs. Shake the bowl back and forth to bring any lumps of butter to the top and rub these in too.

Add the water, a teaspoon at a time, using the blade of a table knife to mix the pastry crumbs with the liquid. Keep adding and mixing until the pastry starts to come together. Do not add more than 10 teaspoons of water for these quantities – if it doesn't look like it will come together, it will. Bring it together with your fingers and press together gently. Once you've got a lump that looks like a dough, flatten it lightly, wrap it in plastic wrap and stick it in the fridge. Leave it for 15 minutes or for up to a couple of days.

When you're ready to make your pie, preheat your oven to 190°C (375°F)/170°C (340°F)/Gas 5 and grease a 25cm (10 inch) glass or metal pie dish, getting into all the corners.

Continued overleaf

Prepare the apples. First, peel them. Peel them with such skill as to remove the entire skin in one piece, then chop off any bruises. Chop them in half and then half again, and remove the cores, before chopping into sizeable chunks – maybe into 3 or 4 again. Place these in a separate bowl with the lemon juice as you go. (This stops them going brown.)

Place the chunks of apple into a pan with 4–5 tablespoons of caster sugar. Place over a medium heat and stir regularly; I was rarely allowed to do this bit. Not because I would make a hash of it or burn myself on the flame, but because I couldn't resist sticking a searing metal spoon of boiling sugary apples into my mouth. Repeatedly. Bramley apples break down with cooking into a mush – and this is what you want to happen. Don't worry that quite a lot of water will come out. It will jellify. Once your pan is mostly mush with a few lumps, remove from the heat. Taste, carefully, and add more sugar to taste.

Remove your pastry from the fridge and unwrap. Divide into two lumps – one third and two thirds. Flour a work surface and place the larger lump of pastry on top. Flour the pastry and then flour your rolling pin. Roll out into a large disc, just bigger than your pie dish so you've got some to hang over the edge. Keep the pastry moving all the time, adding more flour and flipping it over if it's trying to stick.

Roll the pastry around your rolling pin, then unroll it into your dish. Push it down into the corners and fill any holes with bits torn off the edge. Roll your second lump of pastry out carefully – this bit will be on show. It should be clearly bigger than your dish.

Fill your lined dish with the apples and spread them out. Before placing your second disc of pastry on top, brush the egg wash around the edge of the pastry in the dish, as if it was a glue. Then, furl the remaining pastry disc around your rolling pin, and unfurl it over the filling. Pinch all around the edge to stick the two discs of pastry together, creating a seal.

Use a butter knife to cut the excess pastry away and then use it to make a couple of holes in the top of the pie to let steam out and prevent a soggy bottom. Brush the top with your egg wash to create a shine after baking – I remember doing this with my finger when I couldn't find the brush.

Pop the pie in the oven and bake for 30–40 minutes, until the pastry is golden brown. Serve hot or cold, saving some for breakfast the next day.

The lemon meringue

Shortcrust pastry, set lemon curd, meringue

This was the recipe of Gran's that I learned last. It was the hardest, and I held it with some esteem. In fact, even by the time Gran no longer had the capacity to bake, I still couldn't make it right. I had to ask Auntie Janie to show me how it was done.

My Gran and my Auntie Jane (my Mum's sister) both used the same recipe for lemon meringue pie. A simple, traditional recipe. It teaches you a load of what you need to know to be a good baker – how to make pastry, how to blind bake, the methods of thickening fillings and sauces, and how to control the crispiness of your meringue.

I had lost Gran's Lemon Meringue Pie recipe for years, but found it in the most obvious place: Gran's Stork book. Although simple, well-honed, old fashioned or whatever else you want to call it, this still makes a damn fine dessert. Buttery, crumbly pastry, zingy filling and sweet, soft meringue; it is the perfect combination of textures and flavours. Here we go, minus the Stork.

Part 1: Blind bake the pastry

For the pastry:
150g (1¼ cups) plain (all-purpose) flour
75g (2½oz) unsalted butter, cold
water, ice cold

For the filling:
2 lemons
2 large egg yolks
40g (¼ cup) caster (superfine) sugar
25g (1oz) cornflour (cornstarch)
170ml (¾ cup) water
25g (1oz) butter

For the topping:
2 large egg whites
80g (½ cup) caster (superfine) sugar

Makes enough for a 23–25cm (9–10 inch) pie to serve 8

First, make the pastry. Weigh your flour into a large bowl and then weigh out your butter separately. Cut it into little chunks before adding it to the flour. Use your fingertips to gently rub the butter into the flour – I start with a flat palm pointing upwards and lift some floury buttery mixture onto my fingers. I then sweep my thumbs across my fingers, crushing the two ingredients together. Keep going until you've got a mixture that looks like breadcrumbs. Shake the bowl back and forth to bring any lumps of butter to the top and rub these in too.

Add cold water, a teaspoon at a time. After each one, use the blade of a table knife to mix the pastry crumbs into the liquid. Keep adding and mixing until the pastry starts to come together. Do not add more than 6 teaspoons of water for these quantities – if it doesn't look like it will come together, it will. Mix it gently until it does.

Once your pastry is made, press it into a flat lump. Wrap in plastic wrap and stick it in the fridge for 15 minutes – you can leave it for up to a couple of days if it's airtight.

Preheat your oven to 180°C (350°F)/160°C (325°F) fan/Gas 4 whilst your pastry is resting. Butter a 23–25cm (9–10 inch) loose-bottomed tart or flan

Continued overleaf

tin, making sure your soft butter gets into all the crevices. Sprinkle flour onto a clean and dry work surface, ready for the pastry.

Unwrap your rested pastry onto your surface, flour the top and flour your rolling pin, then roll out the lump into a large flat disc, just larger than your tin. Move the pastry all the time, and sprinkle it with flour and turn it over if it sticks. Roll this up around your rolling pin and unfurl it over your tin. Press it gently down into the corners and trim around the edges, leaving about 1cm (½ inch) overhanging around the edge – the pastry will shrink as it bakes.

Prick all over the base of your tart with a fork and pop the tin in the fridge for another – 10 minutes (again, you could leave it longer, and you could delay pre-heating your oven).

Take some baking parchment and scrunch it up tight. Spread it out again and lay it in your pastry case. Fill with enough baking beans (or spare copper coins) to cover the base of the case and bake for 15 minutes. Remove from the oven, lift out the paper and baking beans and patch any holes that have appeared with leftover pastry. Bake for a further 20 minutes, until the base is a light golden colour.

Remove and set aside, keeping the pastry in the tin. Trim the edges while it is still in the tin using a sharp or serrated knife. How you like your meringue will dictate what you now do with your oven temperature: for a pale, crunchy meringue top, turn the oven down to 120°C (250°F)/100°C (210°F) fan/Gas 1; for a darker, smooth top, turn it up to 200°C (400°F)/180°C (350°F) fan/Gas 6.

Part 2: The filling

As the pastry case nears the end of its time in the oven, you can start to make the lemon curd. First, finely grate the rind from your lemons into a bowl and then add their juice.

Cleanly separate your eggs. Place the yolks in a small pan with the sugar and cornflour. Reserve the whites for the meringue. Whisk these together until smooth, then add the water and butter, and set your pan over a medium heat. Gently stir with a wooden spoon as it heats.

Once it starts to simmer, it will suddenly become very thick and gloopy. Keep cooking and stir vigorously when it gets to this point; you want to cook away some of that floury flavour. After a minute or so of being thick, remove from the heat and whisk in your lemon juice and zest.

Pour your filling into your prepared case – smooth out if necessary – and set aside.

Part 3: The topping

Now you can make the meringue.

In a large bowl, whisk your reserved egg whites using an electric mixer. Whisk on high for a long time – until they are very light indeed – then add your sugar, a teaspoon at a time, until it is all incorporated. Using this small measure forces you to add it slowly.

Scoop your meringue on top of the pie and smooth it so that it reaches the pastry all the way around.

Place in the oven and bake until how you like it (see temperature guide opposite) for a soft meringue, bake for 10–15 minutes, or until a dark golden brown, in the hot oven; for a light, brittle meringue, bake for an hour in the cool oven.

Isolationist sourdough

I've hardly written a recipe for bread since my first book, published over four years ago now. I've not written a recipe for sourdough since. I felt it was done – that bread deserved the respect of that entire book and to try and compress a way of life into a recipe was foolhardy. I still think it is, but I also think this is important to include here.

When winter is tough in Shetland and the boats are cancelled, bread is one of the first things on the list of stuff to panic about. This is something that has always confused me – bread disappears from the shelves, but flour remains.

Every time I head home, I make bread. And every time, I make a new sourdough starter from scratch. It's just one of the things I do. It's nice to have a hungry family to appreciate the efforts, and the sheer time to give proper care and attention to my loaves. This means that I have debauched access to better bread than virtually any money can buy, in one of the most isolated places in the country.

I think I have the process so down, now, that you don't need to know the theory. If you want to you can still, and should still, pick up a book about it. But if all you want is awesome bread, no questions asked? Read on.

Ingredients and the equipment you'll need:

1.5kg (3lb 5oz) any wholemeal, stoneground flour, preferably organic: rye, wheat, spelt or beremeal
1.5kg (3lb 5oz) strong white flour
table salt
water

large Tupperware or Mason jar
large mixing bowl
wooden spoon
accurate scales
lidded cast-iron pot, Dutch oven or baking tray
2 tea towels
plastic wrap
sharp knife or razor blade

Day 1

Clean a Tupperware box or a large Mason jar very thoroughly with soapy water and then rinse well. This is going to contain your sourdough starter.

Into this, weigh out 200g (1¼ cups) of your wholemeal flour. Run some cold water into a jug and top up with warm water until the water in the jug is tepid. Tepid does not mean warm – it should not feel warm to touch. But it should not feel cold either. Colder than lukewarm.

Add 200g (¾ cup) of the tepid water to the flour in your container and mix with vigour using a wooden spoon. Pop the lid on and leave it for a day somewhere that's at a good room temperature, preferably 20–22°C (68–72°F).

Day 2

Open the lid and mix up your starter thoroughly using your wooden spoon. You might notice some bubbles already starting to show their face. Once mixed, cover again and leave for another day.

Day 3

Your starter should be picking up now, so get some fresh flour in there. Don't worry if it still doesn't look like much. Add in 100g (⅞ cup) of your wholemeal flour and 100g (scant ½ cup) of your tepid water, and mix again. Tomorrow, you'll have lift off, hopefully.

Day 4, AM

If your starter is ready to use, you'll notice a lot of bubbling and activity in the 12 hours after feeding it the day before, as well as a sweet, alcoholic aroma. The starter is now filled with enough yeast to rise a loaf of bread. Pour 250g (generous cup) tepid water into a large bowl. (This recipe is scalable – for two loaves, just double all these quantities.)

Add 200g (1¼ cups) of your sourdough starter and stir together with your water until you've got a very loose gloop that's largely mixed. On top of this, weigh 400g (3 cups) strong white flour and 10g (¼oz) salt (or 1½ teaspoons, to be safe). Use your fingertips to mix the salt into the flour, then your wooden spoon to mix everything together into a sloppy dough.

Cover your bowl with a wet tea towel, or some plastic wrap, and leave it for half an hour. After this time, take the bowl to your sink. Leave the tap running just a dribble and use it to wet your hands. Use a single wet hand – the moisture stops your fingers sticking – to fold the edges of the dough over and into the middle. You should feel it becoming stretchy. Repeat this for about 30 seconds.

Re-cover your bowl and repeat this stretching and folding every 30 minutes or so, three more times. Timings aren't that important, as long as the stretching is done. After the fourth stretching session – 1.5 hours in – cover the bowl and leave it this time for 2 full hours, somewhere not too cool. Avoid draughty windows.

Day 4, PM

Flour a work surface with some of the wholemeal flour. Rub some more flour into a tea towel, and place this, floury side up, into a separate large bowl and sprinkle it with more flour.

Turn your dough out onto your floured surface. Move it around to make sure it's not sticking and add more flour as necessary. Using lightly floured hands, press the dough out slightly flatter. Next, you want to roll up your dough as if rolling up a Swiss roll, or a Persian rug. Do this really tightly.

Turn the rolled dough 90 degrees and roll it up again. This time it will be harder – it will feel tight and try to spring back – this is good. (Don't let it.) You'll now have a square-ish piece of dough with a seam on the top and a smooth surface on the bottom. You want to keep this smooth surface on the bottom and sit the dough in your prepared tea-towel-in-a-bowl.

Leave your dough to rest in your homemade proving basket for another couple of hours. After this time, if you don't have time to bake it that day, you can stick it in the fridge to rest overnight. If you are baking straight away, about half an hour before you want to bake, stick your cast-iron pot (if using) with the lid on into the oven. Preheat to 220°C (425°F)/200°C (400°F) fan/Gas 8.

Don your oven gloves, remove the pot from the oven and take off the lid. Taking great care not to burn yourself, turn your dough out into the pot, so the tea-towel side is on top. Gently peel the tea towel off the dough, leaving a floured surface. Score the dough in a cross shape with a sharp knife or razor blade. Replace the lid and put the pot back in the oven to bake for 20 minutes with the lid on.

After this time, remove the lid and bake for another 20–30 minutes, or until the loaf is golden brown and very crusty looking. Turn it out onto a wire rack to cool but wait for it to mostly cool before slicing. If you don't have a heavy pot or Dutch oven, you can use a baking tray instead – just turn out the dough onto the tray, score and bake for 40–50 minutes.

Oatcakes

Ah ha! I couldn't get through this book without providing my own recipe for this Shetland staple. I was tempted not to, mind you, considering their omnipresence and their almost clichéd ubiquity in the Shetland food scene, second only to bannocks.

Oatcakes have great variability, both in Shetland and around Scotland. You've got the shape – round, square or farl (roughly triangular). You've got the texture – rough or smooth. And, er, that's it.

Obviously, there are subtleties to which I will not allude here, but you can and will discover for yourself once you begin your oatcake journey. Oatcakes are the only legitimate use for oatmeal (which is not flaked porridge oats). When you find yourself with a kilogram bag of the stuff, these are pretty much the only thing worth making.

I tend to agree with the Shetlandic consensus that oatcakes should be rough and crumbly, to the degree that they lose any idea of shape. When you try to move them from one place to another, they should crumble between your fingers. (The only place you need move them to is your mouth.)

This is achieved through the liberal addition of pinhead oats, or steel-cut oats. This contains loads of the groat, or the wholegrain kernel stuff that oats have just as well as barley or wheat. It gives a texture almost like rough sandpaper on your tongue. There really isn't anything quite like it.

100g (3½oz) boiling water
100g (3½oz) butter, salted
225g (1¾ cups) oatmeal ('medium', if you have the choice)
100g (⅔ cup) pinhead (steel cut) oats

Makes 12 large, thick oatcakes

Preheat the oven to 170°C (340°F)/150°C (300°F)/Gas 3. Line a baking tray with baking parchment.

Boil some water in the kettle and weigh it out into a large mixing bowl. Add the butter and stir to melt them together. Tip in your oatmeal and pinhead oats and mix together to form a paste. It should be moist. Take a big tablespoonful of the paste and place it on your baking tray. Smoosh it out with the heel of your hand into a small round. Repeat with the rest of your mixture – you should get about 12 oatcakes.

Pop the tray into the oven to bake. After 25 minutes, remove from the oven and carefully turn the oatcakes over, if you can, using a palette knife or fish slice. If you can't turn them, bake them for a further 5–10 minutes. Once turned, they'll need another 10–15 minutes on the other side. Both sides should be a deep golden brown. Remove from the oven and allow to cool completely before touching or trying one; if you don't, you'll ruin them and scald yourself.

Once cool, store in an airtight container. They last forever, I think.

Martha's 'slow' brownies

For some reason, Martha is usually given the task of creating a pudding for one of Drew and Vivienne's slow food days. I say 'some reason': it's because she is a fantastic baker. (I cannot let James take all the credit.)

Martha is James's sister and another near-doctor; she was at the final of *The Great British Bake Off*, the one James baked a tragic Union Jack cake for, and Mary Berry actually asked Martha if she was going to enter. But James is the showbiz baker in this family, and in fact this is Martha's recipe as appropriated by James, and then reclaimed by Martha. I'd let either of them do it, to be honest.

This recipe uses Morello or sour cherries, either frozen or preserved. You can use fresh cherries, but they are a pain to de-stone. Do not ever use those neon-red glacé cherries. They are purest evil.

Morellos have much of the flavour of fresh cherries but are subtly sour – more reminiscent of cranberries, but with a bit of that almondy taste that synthetic cherry flavour has in abundance. You can buy them online or from most supermarkets. They will release a lot of water during baking.

250g (9oz) salted butter, chopped into chunks
250g (9oz) dark chocolate, broken into small pieces
60g (½ cup) self-raising flour
60g (½ cup) cocoa powder
150g (5½oz) dried Morello (sour) cherries
300g (1⅓ cup) caster (superfine) sugar
3 medium eggs, plus 1 extra yolk

Makes enough for at least 16 portions

Preheat your oven to 160°C (325°F)/150°C (300°F) fan/Gas 2. Line a 20cm (8 inch) square tin with baking parchment.

Zap the chopped butter and chocolate in a heatproof bowl in the microwave (or oven) for a couple of minutes, until just melted. Mix them together thoroughly with a spoon.

Weigh the flour, cocoa and cherries into a small bowl and toss around to mix. Set aside.

Whisk together the sugar, eggs and egg yolk in a large bowl.

Add the butter and chocolate mixture to the egg and sugar mixture. Hand whisk them together really quickly for 20 seconds or so – you don't want the eggs to scramble with the heat and you want to create a little air within the warm mixture.

Once whisked, add your flour, cocoa and cherry mix. Using a large spoon, gently fold everything together until the flour is just incorporated.

Scrape the mixture into your tin and bake for 45–50 minutes, depending on how squidgy or firm you like your brownies. Leave to cool completely in the tin and then cut into small squares. Never chill, or they'll go rock hard.

George Stewart's Demerara Rum tiffin

The story of tiffin can be traced back to a woman called Edith Tiffin, who came up with the basic no-cook recipe in Troon, Ayrshire, in 1900. My first home. Edith, I presume, had access to an early refrigerator or she may have used an ice-house, the half-buried stone structures lairdy folk used to store meat and the like. I know there was one at the now-vanished Fullarton House in Troon, as I used to play in it as a child. I once stole a gun and stashed it there (I was 10), but James will not allow me to tell that story.

The tiffin recipe is fairly standard from Mary to Chuck Berry but I owe Rachel McCormack a dram of Ben Nevis for the tip regarding raisins. She soaks them in whisky. I choose rum.

Then there's the chocolate: not just anything will do. Some say make it half-dark, half milk. I've experimented with half-Green & Black's white and a few bars of Bournville from the local shop. Frankly, I don't think you can beat Dairy Milk. Ubiquitous and delicious. Avoid rancid American chocolate as it is all horrible.

a handful of raisins
1 half-bottle (350ml) Stewart's Rum
110g (4oz) unsalted butter
30g (1oz) caster (superfine) sugar
2 hefty tbsp golden syrup
4 level tsp cocoa powder
225g (8oz) Waas Bakery 'Ada's Abernethy' biscuits (Rich Teas will do), broken into small pieces
125g (4½oz) milk chocolate
100g (3½oz) good dark chocolate

Makes enough for at least 16 portions

Place the raisins and the rum in a large bowl and leave to soak overnight. I'd cover with plastic wrap to stop any alcohol evaporating. You can speed this up by placing your covered bowl inside another, larger bowl that is filled with just-boiled water. This will only take a couple of hours.

Line a 20cm (8 inch) square tin with baking parchment – there's no need to grease it. I tend to tear off a rough square and press it down nonchalantly.

Measure your butter, sugar, syrup and cocoa into a medium pan. Place over a medium heat and stir frequently until melted. Add the biscuits and the plumped-up raisins and stir thoroughly, but not so rough as to destroy the delicate fruit.

Pour the mixture into your tin and press it down with the back of a spoon. Leave it to cool while you melt the chocolate.

Break all the milk chocolate and all but around 50g (1¾oz) of the dark chocolate into chunks in a heatproof bowl. Buzz in 20 second intervals, stirring gently in between. Once completely melted, add the reserved chocolate and stir until it has melted too. (You can also do this by sitting a heatproof bowl above a pan of not-quite-simmering water if you're one of those strange people without a microwave.)

Pour the melted chocolate into the tin, spread evenly over the biscuit mixture and leave to cool to room temperature. Only once cooled should you put the tin into the fridge for the tiffin to set. It will need an hour or two to be sliceable. To serve, cut into as many pieces as you feel comfortable with.

10

A YEAR OF SHETLAND CELEBRATIONS

Tom

Christmas 2012 looked, for many Shetlanders, like a grim business.

The weather of that winter hadn't just been bad, it had been apocalyptic. Hurricane-force winds for days on end. Huge seas. NorthLink, operator of the daily passenger and freight services, had suspended all sailings, and food was running short. Well, some foods.

Up in Northmavine, we had frozen cuts of sheep in our two freezers and a quarter of a cow, butchered by Davie at the abbatoir and packaged into seemingly endless bundles by Drew, Vivienne, Lizzie and me. It had been Drew and Vivienne's cow, and their habit every winter is to offer friends and acquaintances the chance to buy an eighth, a quarter or even half a cow. A quarter, given frequent entertaining and the descent of offspring and associates, lasts us the best part of a year.

When you get your portion, you get an evenly divided share of all the different cuts, wrapped and labelled in magic marker: fillet, rump, sirloin, stewing steak. Silverside, rib roast, flank, brisket, neck. Tongue, liver, kidney if you want it. Sassermaet and sausages made to Drew's recipe. We no longer keep sheep, but we have a little grassland that is used by another crofter, and so we also get a couple of sheep in exchange for the grazing.

So, in the run-up to Christmas, we had meat. We still had tatties clampit (clamped – stored in soil and straw) from the garden, and there were plenty of local potatoes, kale and cabbage for sale. There was rhubarb in the freezer, some salt fish, reestit mutton, neeps (swedes) and local carrots. We could (and did) bake bread – good grief, our son has written two books on baking – and get milk, eggs, butter and cream. Whatever happened, we could feast at Christmas. Our Yule (Jöl) would be well fed. We even had a turkey ordered, again from Vivienne. She promised we wouldn't have to wring its neck ourselves. But James did have to pluck and gut the thing. (Four years later I was still finding feathers in odd corners of the old barn.)

In the toon and its suburbs, the story wasn't quite as rosy. Folk in Lerwick have grown up there as dependent on machine food and supermarket supplies as anyone else. And Tesco does home delivery throughout the isles (the sight of that blue-and-white van arriving at a neighbour's door is capable of striking jealousy and rage into the most militant of slow-food-fuelled hearts). But for days the supermarket shelves in Lerwick had been essentially empty.

When you're properly cut off, medicines can't get through, medical transfers to Aberdeen become risky affairs involving helicopters. And accidents happen: ships sink, cars crash. People face Christmas without recourse to cranberry sauce or, for that matter, a turkey because there are not enough croft-reared birds to go round. In times past, Shetlanders made do. But in 2012, it was Tesco to the rescue:

"A retailer has airlifted supplies of food to Shetland because the usual ferries and freight boats have been disrupted by the weather. Tesco said islanders had stripped shelves bare of produce. The firm chartered the plane to help restock." (BBC News)

Saved. Suddenly there were frozen turkeys everywhere. I'd be lying were I to claim we didn't avail ourselves that year of the emergency sun-dried tomato flight. But what we, and I think many others in Shetland, particularly in the remoter areas and the outer isles, have to do is live not so much within our means, as exploiting the possibilities of our restrictions.

It is dark, darker than dark, for a good portion of the year. That's the time for lighting the fire, for visiting, for telling tall tales over a dram and bowl of tattie soup. For late dances at the local hall, for parties.

In Margaret B. Stout's day, it was very different. Margaret is one of my heroines; an inspiration and a towering presence in Shetland to this day. The line of successions flows from her championing of traditional Shetland cooking through to Charlie Simpson's out of print *In the Galley* and Marion Armitage's recent *Shetland Food and Cooking*. At Shetland Boat Week in 2017, together they demonstrated some of the classic Shetland recipes preserved by Stout, such as Stap (haddock or ling stuffed with their own mashed livers).

We thought about including many of these traditional dishes in this book, but the truth is that they are only going to be made today as pieces of nostalgia or as historical demonstrations. But the necessity of cooking and eating such things, of using everything conceivably capable of sustaining life, is rooted in Shetland culture and, for Margaret Stout, survival was at the forefront of her mind. Margaret herself said, in the difficult and 'lean' days of Shetland life, "out of the native fish, flesh, fowl and grain, generation after generation of housewives evolved such a wide variety of dishes that there was no suspicion of leanness there in the eyes of the contents folk who knew not the allurements of our imported eatables". "No suspicion of leanness…" I love that. And if you missed the hint that this food was not just for sustaining simple survival, but for enlivening and celebrating, for bringing the community and families together, then Margaret continues with yearning:

> "Certain Shetland dishes were always eaten on certain days long ago. For instance, on Beainer Sunday, the Sunday before Christmas, it was usual to hang up an ox head in the chimney to make broth with. On Christmas Day breakfast was the main meal at which all kinds of meat available, except pork, were served. Stovies formed a popular dish. Fastern's E'en, a movable feast, had to have a supper of brose and half a cow's head. On Bogl Day, about the end of March supper was served, consisting principally of cakes named 'bogles', one for each member of the family. On Lammas Sunday, milgruel was served for breakfast; next day the meadows were begun to be mown. 'Bride's Bonn' appeared at weddings."

These customs are dead and were perhaps dead when she wrote this. You can see how Margaret longed for these ritual feasts to be revived, and there is a great argument for pacing out the year with food celebrations. Today we call it being 'local and seasonal', and unless a restaurant proclaims its commitment to locality and seasonality, you face the possibility of being consigned to a forgotten past. These celebratory occasions deserve to be marked, so we've marked them.

New Year's Day (1st January) Ne'erday

First, we have to deal with a small Shetland anomaly. The old Julian calendar was replaced in Britain by the Gregorian in 1752; not so in Shetland. In many parts, the Julian was followed, cussedly, right up into the late nineteenth century. This gives you Yule (Jöl), a season of winter feasting lasting for up to a month, and Old Yule, a single celebration that takes place on 5th January. In some parts of Shetland, notably the island of Foula, this habit sticks – although in the selfish form of two Christmas Days and two New Year's Days.

Foula is indeed an interesting place. No matter what the suburbanites on Fair Isle will tell you, it is, by a long shot, the most isolated landmass in the UK. Isolated, as in really difficult to get to, and Very Far Away From Anywhere. Only about 35 real people live there. They are heavily outnumbered by ponies and sheep. All kinds of arcane ceremonies, including The Great Shag Hunt – the shooting of small cormorants, and very dodgy as far as the RSPB is concerned – are reputed to still occur there. Most of them are innocent nods to nostalgia, honest.

I've even heard Foula residents hibernate in winter. That's called Hygge now, right?

Hogmanay, or New Year's Eve, is a big deal on mainland Scotland, and the habits of black bun, mincemeat pies and first-footing have caught on to some extent in Shetland. But they're not treated with great enthusiasm.

Traditional New Year food in Scotland is steak pie or a roast ham, and nobody ever makes a steak pie from scratch (except my son out of spite). You buy one from the butcher. In industrial west-central Scotland, where my family hail from, the pie was often eked out with sausages, which I kind of still prefer. Obtaining a decent steak pie in Shetland from a local butcher is possible, but the supermarket equivalents are nearly all awful: tinfoil containers of fatty, gristly 'meat' and a brown chemical sludge.

Of course, we have access to a lump of cow, courtesy of Drew and Vivienne. There is no excuse. It is an incoming tribute to Shetland; a gift from the settlers. Oh, and I think we'll add some sausages, because these are local sausages and, anyway, I like it that way. The Great Margaret has a recipe for what she calls 'Sea Pie', which you might imagine contains seaweed and discarded flounder heads mixed with her favourite, ling liver, but in fact it's her rather basic 'brown stew' with a crust on top. Our steak and sausage pie is little more refined than that, but not much.

New Year steak and sausage pie

This is what's called in Scotland an 'ashet pie', which means you only need enough pastry for the top. There is no soggy bottom because there is no bottom. Time is the key here. The best thing is to make the contents, henceforth referred to as the stew, the day before. It will need to be slow cooked for at least three hours depending on which cut of meat you end up using, but keep cooking until it's tender. Really, really, tender. There is nothing worse than chewy meat in a steak pie. Do not add the sausages (which must be beef sausages) until the meat is approaching softness, about 45 minutes or so away from perfection. You need gravy to go with the compulsory mashed potatoes and mashed swedes accompanying this dish (remember, it was pioneered in the west of Scotland, where people rarely have teeth). And, after numerous arguments, we've come to the compromise that you should buy the ready-made puff; don't mess around. Go for the all-butter stuff. Puff pastry is a faff to make and, anyway, you're pushing the boat out by not buying a perfectly serviceable butcher's steak pie. No guilt.

75g (2½oz) lard or beef dripping, for frying
1 large onion, finely chopped
3 tbsp plain (all-purpose) flour
500g (1lb 2oz) stewing beef or beef skirt, cut into 2.5cm (1 inch) chunks
table salt
freshly ground black pepper
1–2 beef stock cubes, or 2 tbsp concentrated beef stock
a 330ml (12oz) bottle of stout or porter (one that you're not particularly fussed about drinking)
225g (8oz) beef link sausages

1 x 500g (1lb 2oz) block all-butter puff pastry
1 egg, beaten with a pinch of salt

Makes a large pie for a large family at New Year

Day 1 (Hogmanay or the day before)

Preheat your oven to 150°C (300°F)/130°C (265°F) fan/Gas 1–2. Find a large, preferably cast-iron casserole dish and pop it on the hob over a medium–high heat. Melt the lard, then add the onion to your hot pan. Reduce the heat to low–medium and gently fry the onions for 5 minutes. If they're sticking or browning too quickly, add a touch of water.

Measure your flour into a bowl and season with a good pinch each of salt and pepper. Add your beef to this, coat the pieces completely, then add to the oniony pot and fry until brown all over – another 5–10 minutes.

Crumble in your stock cubes and add the beer of your choice, stirring until the foam has dispersed. Stir in a good teaspoon or two of black pepper. Once it's up to a simmer, taste, and season with plenty of salt. It might need quite a bit. Cover with an ovenproof lid, transfer to the oven and cook for two and a half hours. Keep checking every 30 minutes or so to ensure it doesn't dry out. Add more beer or some water if necessary (remove from the oven and stir it in).

After about two hours of cooking, brown the sausages in a frying pan to your taste (I like them quite dark) then cut up each link into three pieces. Add the sausages to the stew, stirring them in, and top-up the liquid again

Continued overleaf

(you may need more beer) so that the sausage pieces are covered. Pop the lid back on and put the stew back in the oven for another 40 minutes.

Taste the meat. When it is perfectly tender, remove the stew from the oven. Let cool, then stick it in the fridge overnight. If you're making it two days ahead and you're working on the assumption that Hogmanay will be a drunken write-off, it will keep until Ne'erday (New Year's Day) if you're careful and keep it covered.

Day of serving (New Year's Day)

(Ideally, you should have one of those trendy, oblong white and blue enamel baking tins.)

Preheat your oven to 180°C (350°F)/160°C (325°F) fan/Gas 4. Spoon the cold stew mixture into medium baking dish, and set aside while you prepare the pastry.

Empty your packet of puff pastry onto a floured surface. Add more flour on top and roll the pastry out until it is about 3mm ($\frac{1}{10}$ inch) thick (surprisingly thin). You want it big enough to completely cover your tin, with spare left over to cut strips for the edge and for any intricate latticework you may want to attempt.

Carefully transfer your sheet of pastry onto your tin and lay it over the stew with excess hanging off the edges. Press around the edge, trim the excess and brush all over with the beaten egg. You can add strips or lattices of more pastry on top, if you like. Just brush it all with egg wash when you're done, and make sure you've got a few holes cut somewhere to allow steam to escape. I like to score my pie with the back of a knife to give a diamond pattern reminiscent of the butcher's pie.

Transfer to the oven for 40–45 minutes, or until the pastry is golden brown and perfect. Serve with neeps (swede for the English, turnip for the Scottish) roughly mashed with salt, butter and black pepper, and tatties (potatoes), mashed with milk/cream and butter.

Bena Sunday

We're in the New Year, now, and moving along. Celebrating Yule like crazy until we get to Up Helly Aa, the first glimmerings of the year and a great shout of anger at the darkness. This is where the festive folklore becomes a little complicated. One of the next winter festivals is Bena (prayer) Sunday, as described in a 1970 interview with Jimmy Johnson, a clerk from Reawick, Shetland:

> *"Jimmy cannot remember the exact date, but thinks it was either late February or early March, when the provender was running low. Bena Sunday was marked by a special soup made of the beef and mutton bones that had been kept. After this, the bones were dried and given to the poor, who tried to make soup from them again. It was said that a person's charity was known by the quality of their bones, that is whether or not all the strength had been boiled out of them."*

It's a lovely idea. The name of the foy sounds similar to Margaret B. Stout's Beainer Sunday, in the run up to Christmas, when hoarded provision would be prepared for one of the main feasts of the year: "an ox head was hung in the chimney to make broth". Jimmy's sounds like the last gasp as winter ran into spring, like Fastern's E'en from down on the mainland, a well-known feast in Scotland held on the last Tuesday before Lent. That would be exactly the same date as 'Fat Tuesday' or Mardi Gras, and very close to the date of Up Helly Aa, though two weeks afterwards. All share the same immersion in gluttonous consumption. Fastern's E'en is, on the face of it, the opposite of Jimmy's Sunday. Jimmy's is about deprivation and selflessness, and the other is about heedless consumption in the face of coming fasting. I'm inclined to think they're only chronologically related.

Bena Sunday bone broth

This is Jimmy's bone soup for Bena Sunday. For the coming of Lent. After the hangover from Up Helly Aa. Margaret would surely approve.

You might have heard the term 'bone broth' as popularised by the 'clean-eating' gang and their band of delusional followers. It has assumed near-mystical status on the internet as a cure for everything from warts to cancer. Which it isn't. It is still good for you, though, being full of bone.

You can make it with beef bones, leftover chicken carcasses, lamb bones or use the saved bones from a roast. Meat attached is fine and indeed better. 'Big' bones from the slaughterhouse in Shetland are free, and many butchers will save you some if you ask. I used to get them for the dogs, but the St Bernards would bury them and then remember to dig them up a year later. Which was never nice.

1 large onion
2–3kg (4½–6½lb) bones
a few root vegetables (neeps and carrots are best)
1 tbsp black peppercorns
a few dried bay leaves
100ml (½ cup) cider vinegar or white wine
5 litres (1.3 gallons) water

Makes about 4 litres of broth (this may be more than you need but you can freeze it and use it as a stock at a later date)

Peel your onion and slice it in half. Place a large stockpot on a high heat until very hot, then place your onion halves inside, flat-side down. Cook until they start to char.

While those are nearly burning, add the bones, vegetables, peppercorns and bay leaves, followed by the vinegar and water. Keep over a high heat so that it comes to the boil quickly. Once boiling, turn down to the lowest heat and simmer, with the lid on, for a long time. A really long time. I mean, 12 hours if you start this in the morning. If it's filling your house with a pleasant bony aroma, make sure the lid is on and the heat is right down. Anything you can smell is flavour lost. Skim off any scum as you go for a clear broth. I tend to boil it all day, and then leave it to cool, lid-on, overnight. Gradually.

You can strain the liquid hot or cold. I like to use a sieve, but you could go as far as using muslin. Serve hot, in a mug, or use as a replacement for stock.

For a broth of consommé-levels of clarity, you can freeze it in freezer bags and then pop the frozen lumps in a coffee filter dripper (such as a Hario V60) lined with rinsed filter paper. Leave this for 24 hours for a beautifully clear drink.

Beltane: May Day

While the church did its best to eradicate May Day superstitions in Shetland, they are intertwined with what I am interested in: what was eaten. At Beltane, huge bonfires were lit, around which people danced in a most unpresbyterian fashion. Beltane cake was served, as described in 1922's *The Golden Bough*, by Sir James George Frazer:

> *"Towards the close of the entertainment, the person who officiated as master of the feast produced a large cake baked with eggs and scalloped round the edge, called am bonnach bea-tine—i.e., the Beltane cake. It was divided into a number of pieces, and distributed in great form to the company. There was one particular piece which whoever got was called cailleach beal-tine—i.e., the Beltane carline, a term of great reproach. Upon his being known, part of the company laid hold of him and made a show of putting him into the fire; but the majority interposing, he was rescued. And in some places they laid him flat on the ground, making as if they would quarter him. Afterwards, he was pelted with egg-shells, and retained the odious appellation during the whole year. And while the feast was fresh in people's memory, they affected to speak of the cailleach beal-tine as dead."*

Am Bonnach Bea-tine, or Beltane cake

So, this is not a bannock. It is cake with eggs, a bit like a scone. Margaret B. Stout even offers some advice, but steers clear of mentioning the pagans.

220g (1¾ cups) plain (all-purpose) flour
1 tsp baking powder
a pinch of mixed spice
75g (2¾oz) butter, salted
100g (½ cup) caster (superfine) sugar
25g (1oz) mixed peel
100g (½ cup) currants
1 medium egg
3–5 tbsp milk, for loosening
2 tbsp whiskey, optional
icing (confectioners') sugar, for dusting

Makes a big bun, torn for at least 6

Preheat your oven to 190°C (375°F)/170°C (340°F) fan/Gas 5. Line a baking tray with a piece of baking parchment.

Weigh your flour, baking powder and mixed spice into a large mixing bowl. Add your butter, and rub it in like you're making shortcrust pastry – it should end up like breadcrumbs.

Add in your other dry ingredients and stir to combine. Add the egg and 3 tablespoons of milk. Mix to stiff consistency, adding more milk if it isn't coming together. For a malty finish, add a bit of whisky instead of more milk.

Turn out the dough onto a floured surface and flatten out into a large disc, at least 2.5cm (1 inch) thick, then transfer to the lined baking tray. You can attempt to scallop the edges using a knife, or bake it as is; I quite like the rough edges of the unadulterated version.

Bake for 25–30 minutes, or until the edges have turned a little golden brown and it's cracked as it has risen. Dust with plenty of icing sugar and tear pieces off to eat while still warm with nothing added.

Up Helly Aa (and embracing the darkness):
The inner Viking in us all

Darkness. It's about finding ways of fighting against it. And who fought better than the Vikings?

The identification of Shetland with the Vikings is perhaps natural, as some islanders – male islanders, for the most part – have a tendency to portray themselves as raven-winged, helmeted warrior types, roaring with bloodlust and lust. And there's no question that there's a great deal of that Scandic-DNA in the native population. Shetland is the nearest UK landmass to Scandinavia and this is the first lump of land the galley fleets would have come to after casting off from Bergen or Oslo.

Some curmudgeons point out that Shetland's proximity to Greater Scandinavia indicates that the heroic Norse warriors tended to use the somewhat rugged islands as a dumping ground for the whingers and seasick liabilities among their crews, before heading off to more profitable or interesting pastures. Orkney was fertile and full of farming potential, so those Vikings interested in a more sedentary lifestyle settled there, they say, while Shetland got the ones with yet poorer sea-legs and bad attitude. Possibly.

In fact, Shetland was part of Scandinavia, part of the Viking world, and fully incorporated into it, until those infernal Scots took it over in the fifteenth century.

The process of Britification was inexorable and by the early twentieth century led to the use of terminology such as 'North Britain' to describe Scotland, and 'Zetland' for Shetland. It was only following World War One, that great trauma of national identity, that a small group of young war veterans, all intellectual socialists and temperance enthusiasts, took an interest in the history, rituals and iconography of Viking times and applied them to Shetland. They founded or re-engineered a festival and they called it Up Helly Aa - 'The Lightening of the Year'. They took the traditional fiery elements of pagan end-of-winter celebrations, combined with the Christian festival of Candlemas, the final spurting of Jøl or Yule, and Viking-ised them in a picture-book kind of way.

Though it might seem eccentric now, there have always been fire festivals at this time of year and throughout Britain – the end of winter; the determination to hurry away the darkness and claim spring back. In Burghead, Moray, they 'burn the Clavie' and in Stonehaven, just south of Aberdeen, the fireballs are still whirled. 'Tar barrelling' – a kind of mobile processionary multi-bonfire with drunken rioting – continues throughout Scotland and England, sometimes for touristic purposes and often in rural redoubts where resentment against incomers flourishes. The implicit threat is: local light and warmth for local people; scorched Farrow & Ball front doors and empty holiday cottages for blow-ins.

As an aside, Stonehaven and Shetland share one other non-immolatory phenomenon: they possess the best and second-best chip shops in these British Isles: Frankie's in Brae, Shetland and the Bay, doon sooth. Next door is Aunty Betty's Café and ice cream emporium, also superb. Both are worth a trip on your way north or south.

Setting fire to tar barrels had for decades been a winter occurrence in Lerwick, much to the fury of local shopkeepers and police. Now we have an excuse, and Public Holiday no less, for the same. Up Helly Aa remains a night of truly riotous disorder and vengeful attacks on unpopular politicians and businesses. In the nineteenth century, prior to its inception, special constables were called in to curb trigger-happy drunks firing shotguns in the air and rolling blazing tar barrels through the streets, sometimes leaving them on the doorstep of the year's least popular resident. Today's festival is somewhat better behaved.

After World War One, there was both a romanticisation of Norseness that much precludes and predicts the Hygge-obsession of today, as well as a politicisation of this outbreak of fiery disorder: 'Vikings' were symbolic of equality, social justice and moral rectitude. This was, to say the least, historically dubious. With parades, burning torches, male-bonding and a big bonfire; "From grand old Viking centuries Up Helly Aa has come," we sang, and still sing the assembled men. But a lot of so-called 'traditional' European festivals are of comparatively recent, and sometimes commercial, origin. So, purchase your plastic helmet and wear your wooden sword; don your Thor wig and wear with pride.

There is feasting of course. Lots of feasting. Frolicking and cavorting. As the festival developed and grew, multiple 'squads' – 40, these days – of men began dressing up in themed costumes and performing little skits commenting on local and national events. Foys in private homes and then in public halls, today about a dozen, were organised, with alcohol making its appearance very discreetly. In most of Lerwick's Up Helly Aa 'Halls', there are no bars, but a room where you dump your carry-out and quietly retire to consume it with guests.

Drinking in public is frowned upon by that all-powerful group of bearded men, The Committee. The same committee which bans women from doing anything but cooking, 'hosting' halls, serving food and tea and dancing with men, many of them these days dressed, with sometimes alarming attention to details, as women. Not for nothing is the Lerwick Up Helly Aa known affectionately as 'Transvestite Tuesday'. Reassuringly, the 'country' (see below) Up Helly Aas are more progressive.

"No postponement for weather." That's an annual, defiant boast considering Up Helly Aa is held in mid-winter on the same latitude as southern Greenland. But it's true: gales, sleet and snow have never yet stopped the Up Helly Aa guizers of Lerwick from burning their Viking galley in the town's play park and then dancing into the dawn and beyond. The weather will, however, sometimes cut the parade a bit short. All those sparks and embers from flaming torches can get out of hand in a mighty gale. Expensive spectating anoraks melt, eyes over-water, hair frazzles.

And don't mention one country version of the festival, where all those flames waft merrily past a petrol station.

Up Helly Aa is more than a boozy parade for fire-raisers, though. It's a spectacle, a somewhat fantastical celebration of Shetland's history, and a demonstration of the islanders' skills, spirit and stamina. It lasts just one day (and night). But it takes several thousand people 364 days to organise. Much of the preparation is in the strictest secrecy. The biggest secret of all is what the chieftain of the costumed Vikings, the 'Guizer Jarl', will wear and which character from the Norse Sagas he'll represent.

The Jarl will have been planning (and saving up for, often via an expensive insurance policy) the longest day of his life for up to 12 years or more, before he dons his horned or raven-winged helmet, grabs his shield and embarks on 24 hours of formalised partying while wearing a dress, brandishing an axe and singing with volume and cheer.

On the evening of Up Helly Aa Day, over 800 heavily-disguised men (there is a growing lobby of local female would-be Vikings who wish full parity in the burning stakes) form in the darkened streets. They carry wooden fence-posts, topped with a fist of paraffin-soaked sacking.

At 7.30PM, a signal flare bursts over the Town Hall. The torches are lit, the band strikes up and the blazing procession begins, snaking half a mile astern of the Guizer Jarl, who stands proudly at the helm of his doomed longship, or 'galley'.

It takes half an hour for the Jarl's squad of Vikings to drag him to the burning site, through a crowd of four or five thousand spectators.

The guizers circle the ship in a slow-motion Catherine Wheel of fire. Another rocket explodes overhead. The Jarl leaves his ship, to a crescendo of cheers. A bugle call sounds, and then the torches are hurled into the galley. The biggest bonfire of the year ensues, there is singing, and then everyone disperses. The squads to prepare for visiting the halls, there to perform acts ranging from the innocent to the scatalogical before dancing, drinking, smooching and beyond (what happens at Up Helly Aa stays at Up Helly Aa); the lucky ticket-holders to watch and be danced with and to eat and to drink.

People get drunk, clearly. It's a feast, after all. There are elements of frenzy, and loss of control is part of that. There's a great Shetlandic term for drunkenness: 'falling by'. Someone who 'falls by' will be loaded into the back of the unkempt van being used for squad transportation to and from the halls, in the hope of recovery before the festival stutters to a close at about 8AM Those unlucky enough to be working that day will often see swaying, staggering figures, be-costumed in every outfit imaginable, from Teletubby to Giant Tin of Tennent's Lager, making their sorrowful way home. They gather a few hours of sleep before heading out in the evening for 'Da Hop', the dance attended by squad members and ticketed women.

And it's worth saying that there is a Mardi Gras-element of sexual mayhem associated with Up Helly Aa. Wives and partners are anchored firmly either at home or in one particular hall while their menfolk are off cavorting as Vikings or other guizers in a drink-equipped truck or bus, going from hall to hall. Free. The Jarl Squad's motto is 'we axe (ask) for whit we want'. And sometimes they do. Sometimes they get it.

Lerwick and Country Up Helly Aas

I remember my first Lerwick Up Helly Aa; a callow youth, really, dipping my toe in Shetland and Shetlandism, and in the first flush of romance with Susan, the woman who would become my wife and mother of James, Magnus and Martha.

The smell of paraffin, the burn and flicker of embers from the wind-whipped torches. The exultant thrill of something so unfamiliar, so alien. The slightly guilty realisation of how easily we're seduced by brass bands, singing, fiery brands, men marching... We're all suckers for a night rally. Is that a cross glowing on that there hill?

The silence as male hordes gathered in Gilbertson Park. The three cheers for Up Helly Aa, and then the carefully organised throwing of the torches onto the giant galley; the crackling, then roar of flames. The night was on fire.

We are all Vikings now. Or wish we were.

Susan was friendly with Muriel and Tammy, founding hosts of the 'hall' at Bells Brae School. She was therefore able to obtain the hen's-teeth-rare tickets, and it was there I was taken, some 30 years ago. First, though, we obtained that traditional stomach-lining Shetlandic sustenance of a Chinese Banquet for Two.

We arrived at the hall around 9.30pm, to encounter a milling mass of glammed-up women, a few bewildered civilian men, and squad members in a variety of ridiculous costumes. There were gonks, I remember, and trolls. A band played Scottish country dance music, with every second dance the Boston Two-Step. I was shown into the 'secret' alcohol room, and whisked past the cloakroom where, even at this early juncture in the night, a girl was having energetic sex with a man in a partially discarded orangutan outfit. It seemed natural.

I was on my own, trying to cope with this efflorescence of astonishing visual and physical data, as Susan had been whisked off to do her duty as a serving wench. All women – all with paid-for tickets – had to do one session in the kitchen and one serving sandwiches. They were not to refuse an invitation to dance.

So, Susan danced and served and washed dishes and the men were allowed to dance, though not with each other. You could find yourself woman-handled onto the floor by one of said partnerless females, not at present engaged in wench duties. I watched, occasionally stood on some poor woman's toes in a rhythmical fashion, and ate. There was food all the time.

Reestit mutton and 'Tattie' soup, that ideal accompaniment to sub-arctic heavy drinking, and the concomitant mutton, with bannocks. (See elsewhere in this book for frequent mentions and the recipes.) There is no foy without reest, no frolicking without bannocks. Sandwiches, often with straightforward roast or boiled mutton. Fancies, or cakes, and tray-bakes and tiffin galore. And stovies. Once an absolute staple in Shetland culture, but somehow less popular these days.

And tea, strong tea, made in gigantic aluminium pots with great ladles of loose Nambarrie leaf. Tea that caught in your teeth, turned them yellow, dissolved your fillings, and went exceedingly well with dark rum.

We stayed there for what seemed like days but was only hours. Skits were performed, their structure growing increasingly haphazard, any speech became less decipherable. There were some extremely convincing women who were, eventually, revealed, if reluctantly, as men. Some skits were unashamedly racist, with 'blacking up' not infrequent (and an Up Helly Aa staple until the last year or so). Local politicians were viciously defamed and there was a great deal of bellowed singing. The Jarl Squad, the only group allowed to dress as Vikings, arrived before breakfast, apparently fresh, sober, and as if they hadn't been up and at it for 24 hours. We left. It was extraordinary, wonderful. And I was glad to get to my bed.

After moving to Shetland permanently, I discovered the secret most tourists are never told: that the giant conflagration of the Lerwick Up Helly Aa, with its all-male restrictions and its arcane rules and regulations, is just one of the islands' fire festivals. In fact, there are at least nine: Nesting and Girlsta, Uyeasound, Northmavine, Norwick, Bressay and Cullivoe, with Delting and the most recently founded festival SMUHA, the South Mainland Up Helly Aa, famous, infamous or indeed legendary for having the first ever female Guizer Jarl.

But the 'country' Up Helly Aas are nearly all stalwart bastions of gender equality. There are all-female and mixed squads, female Jarl Squad members (Vikings and 'Viking princesses') and a relaxed, laid back attitude to everything from alcohol availability (bars are open in the public halls) to access – tickets are readily available to anyone. And food. I have seen mutton pies at Up Helly Aa – not the water-pastry roundel of grey amorphous sludge you get in the west of Scotland, but a proper, pungent, hot-water-crust fountainhead of juicy minced sheep meat! And lentil soup as opposed to reestit mutton, for there appear to be more vegetarians in the Shetland countryside. Not just country dance, but a variety including techno and trance, too.

Nothing could surpass that time, many years ago, when one punk-folk band, all off their faces on dried and processed magic mushrooms, were expelled from the Territorial Army Hall along with their local promoter (me) and a man – now a professor of logic and metaphysics – who had been impersonating me in order to gain access.

Up Helly Aa is about belonging, about community. The exclusionary formality of the Lerwick festival, and the welcoming ease and open-armed good fellowship of the rural ones. Though you do have to beware, as an incomer. There were the friends of mine – a couple who found themselves, a week after moving from 'Sooth', asked to take part in a squad in a local Up Helly Aa – playing extremely precise, written parts, with spoken dialogue. It quickly became apparen, from the tense silence in the hall they performed in, that they had been ruthlessly chosen to represent two very unpopular local people who were actually there in the audience.

Darkness

The various Up Helly Aas signal the coming of the sun and intensify the darkness. When the torches dim, when the galley embers burn low, you can walk back in the absolute blackness of a Shetland winter night, allow your eyes to adjust and actually enjoy the absence of light, or the flicker of the aurora. Up Helly Aa is about the lightening of the year, but one of their great pleasures is the celebration of darkness.

Shetland's dark skies are an often-ignored asset. The 'Mirrie Dancers', the Northern Lights, are a much sought-after sight for visitors, and they are best enjoyed against the cold, clear inkiness of a sky unpolluted by streetlamps. You'll have seen the photographs, nearly all deceptively taken on long exposures and utterly failing to capture the variety of the aurora's manifestations.

What's it really like? You may see only a vague greenish glow on the northern horizon. A flicker, a quiver in the air, sometimes accompanied – and only for a few people on a calm night – by an insistent hum or buzzing noise. A vast, constantly shifting array of searchlight beams cutting clear white and green, pencil thin and massively wide. Great whirling crosses of colour: red, pink and green again, somehow overwhelming and disturbing. It's as if the universe is restless. And of course, there's no predicting when they might appear – 'atmospheric conditions' and 'sunspot activity' give an indication, married with merciful clouds and utter darkness.

Connoisseurs of the night, though, go for starlight. In very isolated places, the stars can play tricks. I woke up once in a tent, very far from the nearest road, camping in the first frosts of September. Outside, I looked up and was inside Van Gogh's Starry Night, the famous painting of the view from his window in Saint-Rémy-de-Provence. The stars overhead were as big as saucers, haloed and misty, with pin-sharp centres. Apart from the mutter of the waves and nearby waterfalls, it was completely silent. Utterly still.

And the lightlessness of winter Shetland provokes parties, dances, and eventually the communal groping for coming spring that Up Helly Aa represents. But for me, best of all are the gatherings in stove-warmed houses, the telling of tales, the shivering and laughing at the mythical creatures of the past who may be lurking outside (but who cannot come in as long as the whisky or rum is flowing and the fellowship is good). And then, when you have to walk home, you find that really, they were just stories all along, and the darkness is there to be enjoyed, to provide you with a new appreciation of this extraordinary environment.

The days lengthen, the longest on their way, and the promise of the Simmer Dim, the midnight sun, sends a tingle through us all. But as spring flows into summer, many of us are already thinking and planning ahead, cutting, raising, stacking, bagging peat, preparing for the winter. For the

coming darkness. The planet spins, orbits the sun. The year turns. The various Up Helly Aa committees are meeting, even as the flowers bloom and the harvest is gathered. Galley keels are being laid down, costumes designed, axes ground. Guizer Jarls are meditating on what will happen the following year.

And for the rest of us, as the skies lower and the nights draw in, we look forward to the flash of fire, the flying sparks and defiant, flaming destruction. It's the little, out-of-season-summer Shetlanders make for themselves out of paraffin and matches, fireworks and flares, and take joy and comfort from in the midst of winter.

A few of us treasure the night: the winter darkness which we see as essential to Shetland as the white nights of summer. Even as summer comes, the hillsides bloom and the days lengthen towards infinity, let's embrace, even look forward to The Short Days, The Dark Skies. Because they don't last long.

Modern annual events

Our Beltane cake is very nice, but it is not the massive cake of yesteryear, baked over a roaring fire with a bad black bit in it symbolising death in the midst of life. That is very similar, though, to the legendary Big Bannock, baked each year in North Roe as part of Da Big Bannock, a wholly non-traditional festival invented by a few imaginative and rather bored fellows not unknown to the Morton family. Each year, a full-length satirical film is shot, lampooning local society. A theme is found – *Star Wars*, the Moghul Empire, Relativity – and a fancy-dress code is set. Main events include the Merry Tiller Grand Sprix: an off-road race of walk-behind tractors, attempted whilst being pelted with eggs, bombarded with fire hoses and made to stop for compulsory drinking of sherry. There is feasting, dancing and of course, the baking of The Biggest Bannock in the World Ever.

It is probably the most enjoyable event in Europe. I'd tell you more but obviously I'd have to kill you, or I'd be killed. In truth, it's almost impossible to explain. Think Craggy Island's FunLand from *Father Ted*, only funnier, louder and much more dangerous. For any more, you'll have to come. But you'll have to find out when and where it takes place for yourself.

What I can tell you about is the flurry of agricultural shows that happen every summer, and which kind of take the place of the midsummer Johnsmas Fairs and Foys of the past. Johnsmas – or St John the Baptist's day – was important for fishing, and indeed Shetland used to have an official, council-organised Johnsmas Foy, a 'festival of the sea'. Johnsmas was the time when fishing crews celebrated together (or nursed their wounds) and agreed to stay together for another year (or not).

James has judged the baking at the biggest of all the annual shows, the Cunningsburgh Show. At Voe and Walls and in the islands of Yell and Unst, animals – from ponies to goats, sheep to hens and dogs to kangaroos – are shown and judged. Fruit and veg is displayed and awarded prizes, as are crafts, art, photography and baking. These shows are a real outpouring of all the sweets of being; of all the good things that can be grown or made in Shetland. All the skills of its population. There are bannocks, of course. There are always bannocks.

I've made James slot in the cake that is my favourite of all his, and the one which would undoubtedly have won that year he judged the Cunningsburgh Show. The reason it is my favourite is that I can make this too. I have, and it actually works.

The critical approach to winning the Cunningsburgh Show (The best lemon drizzle cake)

When making lemon drizzles – essentially a dry madeira cake that's re-moisturised with syrup – there are a lot of places where we can go wrong and still end up with something that tastes OK. That's why a lemon drizzle is so popular, widespread. There's a category for it at every agricultural show. But if you want to win – if you want the perfect lemon drizzle cake – you should treat it with the same respect and timing you'd use to make macarons or sourdough.

Start with a good recipe. This is a good recipe. Some have way too much flour in them, so they end up a little bready – if you don't obtain the perfect seepage of syrup, bits of your cake will be tough and dry out very quickly. The acid from the yoghurt keeps the cake very soft, and having proportionally fewer eggs than a traditional Victoria sponge stops it becoming too rich.

Then, the processes. If you overmix your cake once the flour is added, you will develop the gluten in the flour: this is just like kneading a bread dough. It will actually lead to a greater rise, but towards a peak in the centre and it will make the cake tough and cloying.

Finally, the baking. If you bake your cake at a higher temperature, it might rise more initially, but it won't rise flat. It might peak in the middle, or it might rise with such vigour that it can't support its own weight and collapses in the middle when removed from the oven. If you want a really flat cake, such as one to be covered in fondant icing or stacked high in tiers, turn the oven down by 20°C (70°F) or at least a gas mark over what the recipe says. The cake will rise minimally less, but it will rise perfectly flat.

150g (5½oz) salted butter, plus extra for greasing
150g (¾ cup) caster (superfine) sugar
2 eggs
50g (1¾oz) natural yoghurt
zest of 1 unwaxed lemon
150g (1 cup) self-raising flour

For the drizzle and icing:
juice of 3 lemons, plus the zest of 1
100g (½ cup) caster (superfine) sugar
200g (2 cups) icing (confectioners') sugar

Makes a large 900g (2lb) loaf cake

First, preheat your oven to 160°C (325°F)/140°C (275°F) fan/Gas 2–3. Line a large 900g (2lb) loaf tin with a long piece of baking parchment that is as wide as the length of the tin. Place this in, and grease the remaining shorter sides with plenty of butter, getting into the corners. Or use a loaf-tin liner.

Weigh out your butter into a large mixing bowl, and then melt it in the microwave (or oven). Add your sugar, eggs, yoghurt and lemon zest and whisk everything together. The mix will very quickly go light and fluffy – less than 30 seconds of mixing will do. Don't worry if it curdles; this is common in this cake and won't be of any consequence.

Add your flour, and fold this in very slowly and carefully with a large spoon. Stop as soon as you've taken care of the lumps – the mixture should be just-smooth. Pour your mixture into your tin and place it in the oven to bake for 25–35 minutes.

Continued overleaf

Your cake is done when it bounces back when pressed. There should be no need to skewer it; if your thumb leaves any kind of depression, give it another 5 minutes. When done, leave it to cool for a few minutes while you make the drizzle.

Pour the juice of one and a half of your lemons into a small pan, add the caster sugar and stir over a low heat. Stir all the time. As soon as all the sugar has completely dissolved remove from the heat. Poke all over the top of your cake with a sharp knife or skewer and drizzle the syrup on top. The holes are so the syrup can track, infiltrating the crumb of the cake.

The final touch, if you fancy it, is the icing. Once the drizzle has been soaked up, loosen the cake from the sides of the tin and lift it out using your baking parchment. Weigh the icing sugar into a bowl, and add wee dashes of the remaining lemon juice, a teaspoon at a time, until it comes together in a gloopy slop. It should be thick enough so that it isn't going to soak into your cake, like the syrup. Pour this over your cake so that it runs down the sides, preferably when the cake is still a bit warm. Sprinkle the lemon zest on top and serve when cool.

Hairst - Autumn

And after that outpouring of sugary self-indulgence, we come to Lammas Day, or Harvest thanksgiving. Summer is slipping away. The meadows have been cut, and it's time for 'milgruel'.

I love this. there's something wonderful about the simplicity. No faff, no dancing, no drunkenness. Just, well, milgruel for breakfast. An acknowledgement of the harvest at its most utterly basic. Milgruel is simply porridge made with milk as opposed to just water. That's it. There's no need for a recipe.

In reality, porridge made with water would have been the standard Shetland breakfast. All winter and summer. Shetland families' everyday winter food would have centred on oatmeal at every meal, with fish (fresh, salted, dried, pickled) and meat (mostly reestit or preserved, sometimes fresh). Salt was omnipresent. It still is, and it is probably something to do with our quite astoundingly high blood pressure.

But milgruel, made with milk, was a luxury. It was a sign for Lammas, for hairst (autumn), of plenty and of the hard winter ahead. Today, though, I never make porridge with milk alone. Half and half milk and water, with some salt. Then cream. And brown sugar. And for very special occasions, like Lammas, perhaps a tot of rum.

Lammas and Halloween tend to run into one another on the Pagan calendar – both have that end-of-harvest thing going on. But as the darkness begins to fall on Shetland, the guizing tends to begin. The dressing up. The pretending to be someone else.

And this still happens. There are, at the last count, three fancy dress shops in Lerwick, a town of just 11,000 people. While the guizing element of Halloween is well attested in Scotland, indeed throughout the westernised world, pretending to be someone else is ingrained in the Shetland character. Hiding. Partly it's a result of life in a very small community where the familiar becomes tiresome. Partly it's to hide from the forces of darkness, strangeness and sheer invasion (Vikings, the press gang, pirates) represented by the mythical creature called a trow (troll). And partly it's to prepare people for those visitors, so that fear of the stranger is cultivated. And partly it's just a bit of a laugh.

At Halloween, there's kale casting. This occasionally vicious business involves folk in the community who have misbehaved or are unpopular (or very popular) having their chimneys blocked by kale plants, and 'trowies' throwing kale at their windows and doors. It can get out of hand and quite violent.

Kale, though, boiled, oiled, and crisped in the oven, can be very tasty. It's one of the few native sources (after tatties and neeps) of vitamin C.

Bride's Bönn

Weddings in Shetland take place all year round, and they can be huge, three-night affairs, incorporating every conceivable form of celebratory food. Bride's Bönn is a kind of caraway biscuit with variations aplenty, but they all have one thing in common: breakability.

Bride's Bönn was known as, sublimely, dreaming-bread. Before we leave you with the recipe, I think it's wise to hear what F. Marian McNeill, Orcadian folkloreist, wrote about the same phenomenon in 1929:

> *"A decorated form of shortbread is still the national bride's-cake of rural Scotland, and was formerly used as infar-cake. The breaking of infar-cake over the head of the bride, on the threshold of her new home, is a very ancient custom, having its origin in the Roman rite of confarratio, in which the eating of a consecrated cake by the contracting parties constituted marriage. (Scots law, unlike English, is based on the old Roman Law.) Portions were distributed to the young men and maidens "to dream on".*"

How lovely is that? I'd propose this as a frugal gift to take to a wedding, rather than the predictable confetti or mere money. If the next wedding is your own, try these as favours, and bring something to get the crumbs out of your hair.

75g (2/3 cup) plain (all-purpose) flour
25g (1/4 cup) cornflour (cornstarch)
60g (2oz) butter, unsalted
25g (1/4 cup) caster (superfine) sugar
1 tsp caraway seeds
1–2 tsp milk, to mix
edible wild flowers, for decorating

Preheat your oven to 180°C (350°F)/160°C (325°F) fan/Gas 4. Line a baking tray with baking parchment. There's no need to grease it.

Weigh your flours into a bowl. Add the butter and rub it in with your fingers, like making pastry. When incorporated, add the sugar and caraway seeds, stir to combine, then work a little with your fingers to bring together to form a dough. If it doesn't come together, add no more than a teaspoon or two of milk. Keep working until it forms a dough.

Wrap the dough in plastic wrap and chill in the fridge for half an hour or so. Flour a work surface, plonk the dough on top and sprinkle with more flour. Roll out the dough so that it is about 1cm (½ inch) thick, then cut into long rectangles, the size of large shortbread fingers. Prick lightly with a fork and space out on your baking tray.

Bake for 10–12 minutes, or until just the edges are starting to blush golden. They will seem soft when hot but will crisp up as they cool. Tie with ribbon and balance small wild flowers on top.

Christmas

Shetland didn't really have Christmas until Christianity came calling in the middle of the last millennium, initially in the form of strange, clifftop monastic communities from Ireland. When it took root, Christmas grew in the fertile soil of Yule or Jöl.

And now we get to the trows or trowies – a word derived from the Scandinavian Troll. Their legend is intertwined with Yule. There are all kinds of abstruse academic discussions in Shetland as to who the trowies were or who they represent – some say they were the remnants of the Pictish inhabitants of the soaring brochs: the stone-built structures that remain best preserved in Shetland.

To me, the trows signify some of the darkest fears of a small rural community. The child-stealer. The thief. The kidnapper and the husband-grabber. The dreadful monster from the sea that lurks in the dark and will destroy you and all you love. Best guard against the trows. And, if you happen to be seduced by their music and end up in their hollow mound or cave, never, ever eat their food. Or they will have you forever.

Seven days before Yule Day, legend says that trows had permission to live above ground. Various precautions were taken. Two straws were formed into a cross and laid at the entrance to the yard where the corn and hay were stored. Animal hair was pleated and pinned over the door to the byre. And a blazing peat was carried through all the outhouses.

A day later it was Helya's Nicht, another occasion for milgruel. Then came Tammasmas Nicht. No work was done after twilight on Tammasmas and breaking that rule was bound to bring bad luck:

> *The very babe unborn cries, "Oh dül, dül",* ('dül' - sorrow)
> *For the brakkin o" Tammasmas Nicht*
> *Five nichts afore Yule.*

The Sunday before Yule was Byaena's Day, and it was time for the head of an ox or cow. Substituting a sheep's head was permissible. Once the fat and meat from the head was used, the skull was thoroughly cleaned and a candle placed in the eye-socket, ready for Yule morning. This was considered both acceptable and indeed, welcome.

On Yule Eve, even the poorest family would eat meat. There was ritual washing: three pieces of red-hot peat were dropped into the water when hands or feet were washed, or the trows would paralyse them. People put on clean clothes, cleaned the house and hid away anything considered unholy. All doors were left unlocked with a lamp lit and a piece of iron near the door.

For Yule dawn, the candle in the cow's skull was lit and carried through the house and adjoining barn, where the animals were especially well fed.

There was a morning glass of spirit – sometimes home-distilled, sometimes imported rum – and breakfast was taken. Yule cakes (more scalloped bannocks) were made to resemble and symbolise the lost sun. From then, meat was key. Salted, smoked fresh mutton, beef – no dirty pork – along with salt or dried fish. Vivda (dried meat). Some even had wild ducks, captured in early December and fattened in cages. Oh, and stovies.

Once the animals were fed, Yule Day was a day of rest, although as the short day passed and night fell in the town of Lerwick, bored young men's thoughts turned to dangerous pastimes. Namely, lighting tar-filled barrels on fire. This practice morphed into the festival of Up Helly Aa (see page 251), which was once the name for the twenty-fourth night of Yule. Fire always played a part – it signified the lightening of the coming days and scared away those pesky trows.

Our Christmas

I love Christmas, and I love it for the way it brings light to the darkness. It's all about being together, at home. Has my entire extant family ever been at home together at Christmas? Not yet. But a large chunk of them regularly do trek to Shetland, amid the extreme weather, the cold, the darkness and the risk of trow attack. And there is fire and warmth from the Rayburn and the well-oiled central heating. There is good food, fine wine, and the best whisky I can afford.

We watch TV. We squabble and fight and laugh. We even go to church, for that once-a-year visit to the otherwise disused Hillswick Kirk. Candles flicker in its cavernous interior, which smells of damp. We sit and remember other Christmases, those that are lost to us. We sing hymns, badly, and listen to a sermon nobody remembers. And I think of that one magical year when we went into the Kirk in hard, blustery frost, and emerged into the calm, muffled silence of heavy snow, falling, covering our sins like forgiveness. We took off our gloves and shook hands and smiled.

Leftover stovies

More stovies because stovies are wonderful. And the reason stovies were so much a part of Yule is because they are made from leftovers. Imagine all the aspects of a roast dinner, chopped and mushed together with gravy. Astounding.

Cooked meat is an essential – if you fancy making these from scratch, see page 140.

2 large onions
2 tbsp dripping
  from your roast (lard will do)
1kg (2lb 4oz) potatoes,
  peeled and sliced
500ml (2 cups) leftover gravy or
  meat juices (or stock)
500g (1lb 2oz) leftover cooked
  meat, cut into 2–3cm
  (1 inch) chunks
good sea salt
freshly ground black pepper

Slice your onions as finely as you can be bothered. Chuck them into a large, heavy-bottomed pan with a lid, together with the dripping, and stick it on a medium heat. Fry until soft.

Slice your potatoes thinly – this can take a wee while. Layer them all over the fried onions and pour in your gravy. Add the meat, then top up with enough water or stock to cover.

Stick the lid on and bring to a boil. Then, once boiling vigorously, turn down to a low heat so that it barely simmers.

Cook for about half an hour, stirring occasionally. Check regularly and keep cooking until the potatoes start to fall apart – this is proper comfort food. Taste, and be ready to add a good bit of salt and a healthy dose of pepper for that background bit of Scottish spice.

A swift drink

George Stewart and the merchant navy heritage lends dark Guyanan rum a particular popularity in Shetland (see page 275). And there are the red McEwan's Export tins that have become known as Shetland Roses, due to their ubiquity at one time along Shetland roadside verges. But Shetlanders do drink other things.

There's tea. Tea is essential to the Shetland way of life. It should be strong, and in some houses, older people will serve it with sugar and condensed milk, a cast-off from the lack of refrigeration even seen until recently in many crofts.

And there's beer. Home brew is still very popular and is taken to extremely sophisticated lengths by some practitioners. It was as a home brewer that Sonny Priest gained the reputation which led him to set up the Valhalla Brewery in Unst, the first commercial brewery in Shetland and Britain's most northerly.

Shetland, with little barley produced locally (unlike Orkney), has never had a tradition of distilling whisky. Though there were, back in the nineteenth-century herring boom, plenty of 'sma' stills' operating at the fishing station, making hooch from any handy source of sugar and starch. Local inns – often doubling as trading stations for crofters and sailors – would import whisky in casks and do their own bottling, as was common for many years throughout Scotland.

There has always been whisky bearing a Shetland label, sold only through one backstreet cornershop in Lerwick. Brucefield Stores, which doubles as a major supplier to fishing boats and visiting yachts, offers a Duty Free section. It's owned by the shipping supply firm Zetland Bonded Services. There, Bert would sell you, as a local, a litre of Zetland North Sea whisky for £12.99. I have a bottle, or what's left after cleaning various windows with it. It's a Loch Lomond/Glen Catrine blend, grainy and hot, like many supermarket or privately labelled bottlings. Most of it apparently ends up in western Norway, and for good reason: a visiting (Norwegian) yacht skipper can buy it duty-free for £3.50 a litre.

About 15 years ago there was a plan to build an actual whisky distillery in Shetland. It would have been Britain's most northerly. Blackwood's was the company concerned. Various products carrying the Blackwood's label and heavily branded with Shetlandic blarney hit the marketplace: Jago's cream liqueur, Blackwood's gin and vodka. Spirits were high.

But somehow it never happened. The location for the planned distillery switched. Partners came in. Plans for the con that was Muckle Flugga Whisky, a blend from Scotland to be 'overwintered' in Unst, Britain's most northerly isle, were announced. And then there was a robbery. Liquidation. A new firm took over the proposed whisky plan and what stocks remained of Muckle Flugga. The gin and vodka brands were sold and are still available. Blackwood's Gin is still very good indeed. Muckle Flugga, meanwhile, is a brand now widely available and ostensibly 'matured in a cave on Unst', which I think it's fair to say is somewhat doubtful. It's not bad though.

There is not, as I write, a whisky distillery in Shetland, but there is a distillery that currently makes gin. It's in Unst, and Shetland Reel is both award-winning and has been much praised throughout the world. Their Ocean Sent seaweed-flavoured gin is impressive if you like that sort of thing, and there are various Shetland Reel blended bottlings available. Stuart Nickerson, one of the partners in Shetland Reel, which inhabits the same former-RAF base at Saxa Vord as the Valhalla Brewery, is keen to start making 'proper' whisky, but we are still waiting for the stills to go in, and anything made there will have to wait the legal minimum of three years in oak barrels before it can be called Scotch whisky. We shall see.

For me, the favourite Shetland drinks (as in drinks I will most happily consume in Shetland) are Highland Park whiskies, from Orkney. Some of the best-made Scotch whiskies on the planet. A unique taste, slightly peaty but not aggressively so. A teardrop of water is all you need with it. Magnificent, and in its basic 12-year-old form, great value for money.

Battle of Largs Scots MacCocktail

When I was a wee boy, a Peerie Lad, Largs was our perennial holiday destination. In common with hundreds of thousands of Glaswegians. I was always fascinated by the Viking connections, as made iconic by the gigantic war galley frontage of the Viking Cinema. This had been converted into the home of Wham's Dram, a horrendous cocktail of sweet South African sherry and whisky called Scotsmac, a precursor to Buckfast as a cheap electric soup for would-be alcoholics (and schoolboys with a need to get wasted cheaply).

You can still buy Scotsmac today, and it is foul. Better by far, and much more expensive is a Shetlandic variant which has been developed for extremely cold conditions and is a guaranteed cure for any ailment you could possibly suffer: from a dose of the flu to pleurisy. At least, temporarily. I call it the Battle of Largs Scots MacCocktail. (James: Catchy, Dad.) It is essentially a combination of the traditional toddy and a whisky mac. I was introduced to it by the great Dr Jonathan Wills whose training in medicine is non-existent. His doctorate is in geography, and his skills are in journalism, controversy and boatmanship. He administered a Battle of Largs to me for the first time on the eve of press day at the *Shetland Times* newspaper in 1987, when I was suffering from a combination of a hangover and a heavy cold. It worked miracles.

35ml (6 tsp) dark rum, preferably Stewart's Demerara Guyana
35ml (6 tsp) green ginger wine, preferably Crabbie's
1 infinitesimal (tiny, miniscule) portion of crushed Naga chilli, dried (or small pinch of dried chilli flakes)
2 tbsp boiling water
1 tsp honey

Makes one warm glass

Boil the kettle. Fill your heatproof glass, placed on a saucer, with boiling water. Leave for 2 minutes to stand, then empty out.

Measure the rum and ginger wine into the glass. Add the chilli, then add the honey and the two tablespoons of boiling water and stir with a teaspoon until dissolved.

Drink.

Portable alcohol – an aside

For Up Helly Aa purposes, we need to talk spirits and in Shetland that would be rum. Dark rum, and by choice Stewart's Demerara Dark Rum.

Stewart's is a traditional rum from Guyana and the company name – J&G Stewart of Leith – indicates a mainland provenance. J&G Stewart was originally a Leith grocery business founded by expatriate Shetlanders, one of whom, George Stewart, later became (after a bizarre life which included emigrating to British Columbia as a woodcarver) the author of the first major book in Shetland dialect – 'Shetland Fireside Tales'.

Stewart's rum remained in production although ownership of the brand passed from hand to hand until, several years ago, Lerwick wholesale grocery firm Hughson's bought it. By that time, and no-one can quite work out why, the vast majority of Stewart's sales were on the Islands. Stewart's, in a very real sense, had come home. Home because dark rum was a sailor's drink and the Shetland habit of sending menfolk 'deep sea' – to the Arctic whaling or the merchant marine – fuelled a taste for rum. Stewart's (sweet, dark and warming against the winter) always had that Shetland connection.

These days the hip flasks and half bottles hidden away in guizers' hand-sewn pockets (see page 255) may contain vodka, whisky or gin. In the controlled environments of the halls, buses and trucks, red tins of McEwan's Export prevail and rotgut cider or bottles of local microbrew will lurk. But the ideal nip for a freezing cold Up Helly Aa remains rum, and preferably Stewart's.

Dark Skies red hot poker fireside Aurora;
Up Helly Aa hangover mulled ale

This is one for connoisseurs of darkness.

Of a winter's night, one of my prime occupations is to sit by our solid fuel (peat-fired) stove, a cast-iron Rayburn, sipping a glass of hot porter. I know, I know: I'm living out a bit of fantasy here, or rather, a few paragraphs from a book. Namely, Sir Walter Scott's 'Rob Roy'.

Scott based this story of Bailie Nicol Jarvie, Rob Roy's cousin, on a real person, and the incident described in the book apparently happened. Bailie Nicol Jarvie, a 'colourful' Glasgow magistrate and cousin of the infamous outlaw, Rob Roy MacGregor (1671–1734), was travelling on business in the hills north of the city. He stopped at an inn at Aberfoyle where a tired and emotional Highlander took exception to his presence and, drawing his sword, challenged him to a fight. The Bailie, not a man in the habit of sword-fighting, tried to draw his weapon but found it rusted to his scabbard through lack of use. As the ferocious Highlander advanced upon him, the Bailie grabbed a poker from the fire where it had been heating before being applied to ale, and poked said poker at his attacker. It set fire to the Highlander's plaid and sent him fleeing, though he later returned to congratulate the Bailie.

The poker was being heated in order to make a flip, or mulled ale. And the best beer to heat is black stout or porter, such as from my son's brewery thing. Add a few spices, maybe an egg yolk, and some obligatory dark rum and you have food, drink, comfort and restoration. Perhaps you've been indulging too much in the pleasures of Up Helly Aa over the previous night. Or two. Or three. This is your remedy.

2 large measures of dark (Stewart's) rum
75–100g (scant ½ cup) dark brown soft sugar
2 egg yolks
¼ nutmeg, finely grated
a pinch of ground cinnamon
2 pints of dark porter or stout (locally brewed, if possible)
more grated nutmeg and cinnamon sticks, to serve

First, prepare a red hot poker. Place a cold poker in your fireplace. The peat smoke will not flavour your drink directly, but will add the appropriate ambience. If this is not practical, forego the poker and warm this cocktail in a pan on the hob.

Place the rum, sugar, egg yolks, nutmeg and cinnamon into a cocktail shaker. Add a couple of ice cubes (yes, ice cubes) and shake and shake and shake. This is to create a thick foam.

Pour the beer very carefully into a stout pot, preferably made of clay or cast iron (a jug will do). Pour in your eggy spice, mix together, then plunge the red hot poker in and stir until steaming. If no poker is available, pour everything into a pan and heat, stirring all the time, until warm. Pour messily into goblets and drink until you, too, are steaming, pleasantly. Skøl!

Willie and Nancy's tea

This is the double espresso of tea. It leaves a brown staining on your teeth and a coating in your mouth, and it sets you up for an hour or so of outdoor labour. It is the equivalent to me of Vietnamese filter coffee. A blackened kettle, never fully emptied, should always be kept warm on a peat-fired Rayburn. Always expect the door to open and a neighbour to walk in.

loose-leaf black tea, Scottish
  Blend or similar
evaporated milk
granulated sugar

Transfer your kettle from the Rayburn to a single gas ring nearby. Place your old aluminium teapot onto the Rayburn to heat and add three tablespoons of loose-leaf black tea.

When boiling, pour your water into the teapot, and stir. Place the teapot on the gas ring and boil vigorously for a minute or so.

Make a hole in either side of the top of a tin of evaporated milk with your pen-knife. Serve your tea, tin on the side, with at least two white sugars per cup.

Whipkull

I'm going to return to Margaret B. Stout for some dairy-based drinking which you may wish to try when the heating is broken and your teeth are chattering like my keyboard rattles. This is rather simple to make, and gets the job done. Her initial quantities involve a dozen eggs and a pint of rum, but I've scaled this back for the sake of responsibility.

It's quite like eggnog, but simpler and richer and altogether nicer, unlike that modern North-American drink that has only recently found its way into the Scots' consciousness. As far as I can tell, this is the original without any polluting spice.

2 egg yolks
50g (¼ cup) caster
  (superfine) sugar
150ml (⅔ cup) double
  (heavy) cream
100ml (½ cup) dark,
  sweet rum

A healthy measure for 2;
a taste for 4

Beat the egg yolks and sugar together in a bowl, until thick and creamy. (They will go very creamy indeed, James assures me.)

Do not whip the cream – add it as it is to the eggs and then add the rum. Stir gently.

Allow to stand but not to separate (you've got a few minutes). Pour into glasses and serve. Stand well back.

Blaand

I would not be surprised to find out that Shetland consumes more buttermilk per head of population than anywhere in the Britain, and that would be through bannock-making alone. We don't just use our dairy by-products in baking, though. We drink it. Or some of us do.

Most famous of the Shetland dairy drinks is blaand. Made from buttermilk, it is mildly alcoholic and acidic at first, becoming more so as time goes on. It was introduced by the Vikings and has undergone a relatively recent resurgence in the USA and mainland Scandinavia, thanks to the power of the internet. Blaand can be aged and if left to stand, for a month or more, it will eventually become a clear, yellowish colour and can be bottled. Most Shetlanders preferred to drink it fresh and still sweet; as it became more sour, it was known as 'sharp blaand'.

Although many people are using commercial yeasts and enzymes, the traditional method of making blaand was using the natural yeasts lingering about, as well as the bugs in the buttermilk. It works a bit like a sourdough starter – the acid-producing bacteria create fuel that is used by yeast, which makes alcohol and gas – and I'm sure it has similar, supernatural probiotic powers. Yakult, eat your heart out.

While you could make it this way, I prefer to avoid possible death by pathogenic bacteria. The safest way to make blaand is to make it more alcoholic by adding sugar and commercial yeast. Oh well.

2 litres (4 pints) fresh buttermilk
800g (1lb 12oz) caster (superfine) sugar
1 sachet of dried yeast (instant bread yeast will do)

Equipment:
2 large pans or bowls
muslin bag (or sieve lined with muslin)
5 litre (10 pint) demijohn or plastic water bottle, washed and rinsed with boiling water

Pour the buttermilk into a large pan or bowl. Add enough just-boiled water to the buttermilk to make it separate – you might need two kettles. It will look nasty.

Pour this through a muslin bag into your other large pan or bowl to separate the curds from the whey. (You can drain and press the curd and serve this as a cottage cheese equivalent, called kirn-milk.)

While the whey is hot, add the sugar and stir to dissolve.

Pour the whey into the demijohn or bottle. Top up with cold water, leaving a good couple of inches of clearance at the top. Add about a quarter of the sachet of bread yeast, then cover over the top with plastic wrap.

Leave the whey to stand at room temperature – you will notice it start to fizz after a day or two. It will continue to become more alcoholic and less sweet as time passes, and once the initial fermentation has subsided the liquid will start to clear. Drink it fresh, after 7 days, or leave it for longer and store in sanitised bottles (see page 189) – it will keep forever.

Suppliers

Getting hold of pure Shetland lamb or mutton is not hard, no matter where you live. Lamb from Foula is a little more tricky. The excellent Richard Briggs on the west side of the Shetland Mainland – the main island – offers a mail order service and you can order through his website at briggs-shetlandlamb.co.uk. There's a fellow on Dartmoor keeps Shetland sheep, but that kind of misses the point as far as I'm concerned. Ronnie Eunson at Uradale Farm just up from Scalloway (uradalefarm.blogspot. co.uk) specialises in organic lamb, beef and native Shetland wool, but his meat is available either at the deli counter of Scoop Wholefoods scoopwholefoods.co.uk in Lerwick, or to the rest of the world through the prestigious London butcher C. Lidgates (lidgates.com).

Sassermaet is not easily or healthily (or legally) transported by mail or courier, so for that and 'Voe flour' you'll have to come to Shetland. Irish soda bread flour, though, is a reasonable substitute for the Voe variety.

Generally, the Taste of Shetland website at www.tasteofshetland.com will point you in the direction of many other suppliers, and it has its own shop, with seasonal changes in availability. This is the only place that you can find Reestit Mutton for sale online.

Glossary

Most of the Shetland dialect terms used in this book are explained in the text; however, one or two Scots, Scandinavian and Shetlandic usages have crept in unacknowledged.

AALD: *Old*

BONXIE:
Great Skua. A large, predatory seabird, known for eating puffins and attacking, though rarely hitting, humans who wander into the nesting areas

CLABBY (OR CLABBIE) DOO:
Horse mussel

DA: *The*

DIS: *This*

DREICH:
Grey, dull depressing. Applicable to anything from weather to religion Recently topped a poll as Scotland's favourite word

DU: *You*

DU'S OR DU IS: *You are*

DUNK: *Submerge*

DY: *Yours*

FEARTIE:
A cowardly and nervous person

HAAF:
Area of deep sea used for fishing, traditionally in open boats up to 40 miles from land; known as The Far Haaf

JAMP: *Jumped*

KYE: *Cow or cattle*

MATJES: *Pickled adult herring*

MUCKLE: *Large*
See 'Peerie'

NORT: *North*

OO: *wool*

PEERIE:
Small. Often used as a humorous diminutive, and actually meaning Very Large, as in Peerie Alex (6ft 7) or indeed peerie dram (many, many large drams)

RAYBURN:
Solid fuel stove. Less wealthy person's Aga, now owned by same company. Once specified in every Shetland council house

SASSERMAET: *Saucermeat*

SASSERMAET CLATCH:
Saucermeat hash

SILD: *Young herring, often salted*

SOOTH: *South*

SPOOT: *Razor clam*

TATTIE: *Potato*

TOON, TOONIE:
Town, (Lerwick), Lerwick-dweller. Though 'toon' is also used (not in this book) as a traditional term for an area of croftland

WHELK: *winkle, except in Shetland*

"And, in the end, the love you take…"

In the end, Da Aald Rock will remain, Shetland will abide, no matter how many noisy upstart hacks arrive, more or less on the run, and stay for 30 years, or a lifetime, whichever comes first. No matter how many children grow up loving the isles and leave to become city-dwellers, doctors, brewers, bakers and greyhound-owners. And that's just James, so far.

Shetland waits for you to come and discover its many aspects. Its food, yes, but as this book (we hope) shows, what we cook and eat here is intimately bound up with how we live, with land and sea, with survival and celebration.

And there is a Shetland of the heart and mind, a way of being, of living together which remains with anyone born and raised here, anyone who has lived here for any length of time. Yes, and a way of cooking and eating. Of dealing with flesh and vegetable. Of eating to live and love.

We hope this book communicates a sense of place, people and the joy - the foy - of preparing and eating. But we hope too that it opens up the possibility of inhabiting Shetland, no matter where you are in the world.

You're always welcome.

James and Tom Morton
Hillswick, 2018

Acknowledgements

Sarah Lavelle, without whom none of this would have happened. And the family too – James, Elliott and Tilly, you are wonderful.

Susan, for everything (both of us); Fenella, for putting up with James; Martha, for knowing she's the best cook in the family (probably) and rarely mentioning it; Magnus, for keeping us on the straight and narrow, mostly.

Andy Sewell and Nat Smith, whose wild swimming caused great concern but never necessitated the coastguard being anything more than forewarned. Tim Hayward, for his astounding hospitality and ever-growing collection of kitchen utensils. Will Webb for his taste in fonts and excellent kerning.

The late Audrey Bowie; Sandy and David and their families; James and Magnie for the delicious food and great garden tour – to James especially for putting up with *Wir James* at the Peerie Shop Cafe all those years ago.

Linda – whose bannocks will never be beaten; The late Nancy and Willie Hawick; Jim Sandison; Tommy Poleson; Everyone at the Walls Sailing Club; Hillswick Hall Committee; Northmavine Up Helly Aa committee; David Brown and the 2018 Northmavine Jarl Squad; Sullom Hall; Ollaberry Hall; Hillswick Hall; Dr Jonathan Wills; St Magnus Bay Hotel - Andrea and Paul; Mike Skinner and those at James's first kitchen job at the Shetland Museum.

This book is dedicated to Lizzie Simmons (formerly Ratter). Lizzie passed away on 1st May 2018, shortly after the birth of her second child, Maisie. This is for Maisie, Archer and their father, Jay. Lizzie inspired us both. She was the daughter of local heroes Drew and Vivienne Ratter, and the sister of Emmie and Tom.

Index